BRAVE HEARTS

Extraordinary Stories of
Pride, Pain and Courage

BRAVE HEARTS

Extraordinary Stories of Pride, Pain and Courage

CYNTHIA BROWN

For information on purchasing bulk copies of this book for educational, business or sales promotional use, contact American Police Beat Publishing Group, 43 Thorndike Street, 2nd Floor, Cambridge, MA 02141. 1-800-234-0056 Ext 104.

Printed in the United States of America

First Edition

Cover Design: Karin Henderson Kid Designs. www.kiddesignsNYstudio.com

ISBN: 978-0-578-06589-2

For Ray Kelly
and the brave men and women who keep us safe

I think continually of those who were truly great. …
The names of those who in their lives fought for life
Who wore at their hearts the fire's center.
Born of the sun they traveled a short while towards the sun,
And left the vivid air signed with their honor.

—*Stephen Spender*

CONTENTS

FOREWORD

I have just had the pleasure of reading *Brave Hearts*, a book by Cynthia Brown, that stalwart and perennial friend of the nation's law enforcement officers. *Brave Hearts* is about some of the people whose lives and causes she has been depicting and defending for many years in her monthly publication, *American Police Beat*. Although this book is about New York City police officers, they represent the values and commitment of law enforcement officers everywhere.

Cynthia is certainly well equipped to write about the service police perform every day. From experiences early in her career in a Boston police station to her ongoing work as publisher of *American Police Beat*, she knows firsthand the triumphs and tragedies of our profession not just here in New York City but across the country as well.

In the pages of *Brave Hearts*, which is a sort of *Profiles in Courage* set in the police precincts of New York, the author tells the stories of fifteen officers of various ranks and specialties who repeatedly risk their lives, and in some cases their physical and mental health, to serve and protect the citizens of this city, often doing so, in that time-worn and time-honored phrase, above and beyond the call of duty. These officers are all members of a larger team who work together to save lives, drive down crime, and strengthen our communities.

Prior to becoming Police Commissioner, I had the privilege of serving alongside the men and women of the NYPD for almost thirty years in many different commands. Over the course of my career, I continually witnessed the quiet professionalism, compassion, and heroism practiced day in and day out by our law enforcement officers. That commitment, courage, and self-sacrifice have been superbly captured in the profiles of the extraordinary people you are about to meet in the pages of *Brave Hearts*.

–Ray Kelly, July 2010

PREFACE

In the late 1970s, I accepted a part-time job working on an early community project with the Boston Police Department. At that time, the relationship between the Department and the people of Boston was tense. A federal court had ruled that Boston schools were unconstitutionally segregated and ordered students bused outside their neighborhoods to correct the situation. Anger, particularly, in the white neighborhoods, resulted in near-riots and numerous incidents of violence.

My job was in a busy police station in one of the most crime-ridden areas of the city. At that time there were very few women or minorities on the force. Most of the two hundred officers assigned to the station where I worked were very outspoken about their conservative views on everything from the Vietnam War to women's rights to homosexuality. One officer told me he didn't think "girls" should have driver's licenses. It was quite a culture shock for a liberal-minded young woman who came of age in the 1960s to find herself plopped down in the middle of this strange world.

I worked there for three years, organizing and facilitating meetings between residents and the officers who patrolled the district's neighborhoods. During that time I saw firsthand the officers' constant dealings with armed assailants, drug dealers, drunks, rapists, gangs, the homeless, the mentally ill, and a whole range of garden-variety crooks. I was continually amazed at the restraint, humor, and humanity they showed as they went about their difficult task of keeping us safe.

I also witnessed extraordinary acts of human kindness and compassion. I will never forget the time I came back to the station and found an older officer sobbing—the kind where your whole body heaves. He had just returned from a call where he had found a three-month-old baby dead in a bathtub. The day of Christmas Eve the first year I worked there, I saw one officer take home a particularly violent eleven-year-old boy so he wouldn't have to spend Christmas Eve alone in a cell. The boy was black. The officer, who had six children of his own, was white. Then there was the policeman who was reading the book *Against Our Will: Men, Women, and Rape,* Susan Brownmiller's seminal history of the crime of rape, after he responded to a brutal sexual assault of an older woman near a church. When I asked him about it, he seemed a little embarrassed. He told me, "I'm just trying to figure out why it would happen. My daughter told me to read this book."

After those three years in that station, I knew I wanted to do something that would help the law enforcement profession. Several years later, when I founded *American Police Beat,* my goal was to create a publication for law enforcement officers around the country to communicate with one another about the most pressing issues affecting their personal and professional lives. Today, *American Police Beat* is the leading police magazine in the United States, with over 250,000 readers every month.

Brave Hearts is the story of fifteen men and women who have worked for the New York City Police Department. Whether they are shutting down international narcotics operations, making arrest for brutal homicides, settling marital disputes, getting illegal weapons off the streets, finding serial killers, or preventing another terrorist attack, they routinely face injury and death to serve and protect people, many of whom they don't know and will probably never meet.

The officers profiled in *Brave Hearts* work for the New York City Police Department, but their stories could come from any law enforcement agency in any community in the United States. Their personalities are as varied as their assignments. But they all share a passion for their work and a conviction that they are doing something important with their lives. Despite the constant exposure to America's dark side, they all view their work as a privilege and a job they are lucky to have. These real-life heroes are also moms and dads. They get sick, suffer moments of weakness, and don't always emerge victorious. But no matter the circumstances, they are right back to work for their next shifts, trying to do their jobs a little bit better than the day before. They are ordinary people, no different than you or me, except when it's time to risk their lives to save a stranger or get a criminal off the street. Then these individuals display qualities we rarely see.

The years have only strengthened my admiration and respect for the dangerous, stressful, and unpleasant work law enforcement officers do. I know that some people have negative perceptions of police officers. It is my hope that after reading about the extraordinary efforts these brave men and women make to protect us from evil and violence, those folks will begin to see them in a new way.

–Cynthia Brown, July 2010

Chapter One

RICH MILLER: Always Above and Beyond

*"You can send me to hell, but I'll never let
go of your hand." —Tom Waits*

When the first plane hit the World Trade Center, Rich Miller was sound asleep. He was scheduled to attend a diver rescue training exercise at noon and was using the rare free morning to get some extra rest. When his wife woke him and told him what happened, he ran into the living room just in time to see the second plane smash into the South Tower. He threw on some clothes, kissed his wife and youngest daughter Nikki goodbye, jumped in his car and drove straight to the Bronx.

When he pulled into the police station parking lot, he saw John Mc-Cullough. The two men found a pickup truck loaded up with rescue equipment and quickly headed toward the Trade Center. As they raced down the West Side Highway, the North Tower began to fall.

"Before that happened, voices were coming through pretty clear over the division radios," Rich recalled. "I could even recognize certain people. But when the North Tower fell, there was dead silence."

As they got closer and the streets became narrower, Rich remembers people jumping out of the way when they saw the pickup truck piled with equipment. "It was like the sea was parting," he said.

When a major disaster occurs in New York City with hundreds, if not thousands, of possible fatalities and injuries, every available officer assigned to the Emergency Service Unit gets his or her equipment and reports to the command post. When Miller and McCullough got down to the site, ESU commanders had already assembled several rescue teams to go into the rubble and start saving lives. By this time, the Pentagon had been hit and everyone was preparing for the worst.

Despite the catastrophe unfolding before them, ESU officers grabbed their entry tools and medical bags and rushed toward the towers. Just as the cops from Team Five entered the South Tower, the building fell and buried the six-member team. Miraculously, they dug themselves out, regrouped, and went back into rescue mode. While every other person was running away, the cops and firefighters were going back in.

As Team Five returned to the North Tower, steel girders began to fall. Then came the bodies, people who decided to leap to their deaths rather than be enveloped in fire. There was blinding dust and horrendous noise. Members of Team Five had lost all their equipment, and they could barely see. Along with a group of firefighters and other police officers, they managed to form a human chain. As soon as they were lined up, they began passing traumatized and injured people down the line, one to the next, until they were safely out.

It was only twenty-nine minutes after the first tower collapsed when the North Tower started to go. "Debris was literally raining," Richie Hartigan recalled. Richie frequently partnered with Rich Miller and was one of the officers on Team Five.

"The ground was heaving like an earthquake," Hartigan continued. "Steel was crashing down everywhere. I cannot describe how loud it was. It sounded like two freight trains coming right at you. You couldn't see your hand in front of your face. Everyone was choking on the dust. Shards of glass were everywhere."

Death was random. Who lived and who died all came down to luck. Some made it out, some didn't. The NYPD lost twenty-three officers in the World

Trade Center attacks. That included fourteen of twenty-nine Emergency Service officers who ran into the buildings but never came out. Three members of Team Five were taken to the hospital with serious injuries, including a lieutenant whose hand was almost completely severed.

Rich said everywhere you looked there were fires. "The smoke and dust were awful. We were worried about so many innocent victims and our buddies who still had not come out."

Miller and his team were instructed to go as far down into the wreckage as possible. "We hoped we would find people who were still alive," he recalled. "Three or four floors below street level we began using hydraulic entry tools to cut into the vehicles. We thought the steel around the car might have protected them, but we never found anybody."

Despite the grim situation, it took a long time before Rich and his fellow officers faced the reality that many of their colleagues were not coming out alive. "We really believed we were going to find them," he said. "We wanted them to see the American flag waving when they came out."

The Department had set up a command center at the Stuyvesant High School a couple of blocks north of the Trade Center. Rich remembered seeing a flag on the stage in the school's auditorium. That's the flag, he thought, we will fly at Ground Zero.

The following morning Rich and his team were back conducting searches in the third-floor subbasements of the collapsed towers. "At some point we decided to crawl back up to street level," he said. "We were climbing over this huge pile of debris on all fours. As we made our way up toward Buildings Four and Five, we came across this gigantic crater. That's when I saw the bronze globe that stood between the South and North Towers. It was damaged but still intact. Lying next to it was an antenna from the North Tower."

Rich turned to Richie Hartigan. "That's our flagpole," he said.

After asking Thomas Purtell, Chief of the Special Operations Division, for permission to take the flag from the Stuyvesant High School back to the site, the two officers found a pickup truck. They got as far as Church and Dey before a mass of fallen debris forced them to stop. Carrying the folded flag on his shoulder, Rich almost lost his balance walking across a steel beam trying to get back to the antenna.

Rich asked a battalion chief to help him find a ladder. Two firefighters quickly got one from their truck. With Richie Hartigan behind him, Rich climbed the ladder and attached the flag to the antenna. As the battalion chief yelled out, "Present arms," there was dead silence. Everyone stopped and saluted the flag fluttering in the gray dust and wind.

"Everyone there helped get that flag up," Rich said, "police officers, firefighters, construction workers, ironworkers, and medical personnel. Richie Hartigan and I were the ones up on the ladder, but they were all right behind us. After our flag went up, each time we came above ground, more flags were flying. The day after that, there were hundreds of flags. If our flag inspired other flags to go up and those flags inspired a nation, I am proud to have been a part of that. Our country had taken a heavy hit, but seeing all those American flags made me confident we would survive and we would rebuild."

* * *

Every officer assigned to the NYPD's Emergency Service Unit is a certified rescue diver. The training is extensive. Scuba officers learn to dive in sludge, mud, vegetation, cold water, strong currents, poor visibility, rough seas, and every kind of debris imaginable. By 2005, Rich Miller had participated in over two dozen rescues of victims who found themselves submerged somewhere in the five hundred miles of water that surrounds New York City.

On a hot and humid day in June 2005 around 3:30 in the afternoon, someone dialed 911. The caller was hysterical, and it was difficult for the operator to understand what she was saying. As best as she could determine, two boys and a girl had been fooling around on a makeshift raft on the Bronx River when it capsized. One of the kids was missing. "Every cop assigned to Emergency Service was familiar with this area of the Bronx River," Rich said. "The currents are strong and it's totally off-limits for swimming."

He was working as a chauffeur that day. The chauffeur's job goes to the most senior ESU officer on the six-person team. He or she is responsible for handing off the lines, tanks, dry suits, and other equipment and working with the commanders to coordinate the response.

"When we went over the Bruckner Bridge, we saw a spot where a crowd was gathering on the shore," Rich remembered. "We wanted to get the truck right down next to the water, but we discovered there was a cement processing facility with a heavy chain-link fence blocking our way. We decided we couldn't wait. Ben Kalinsky retrieved some bolt cutters out of the truck and cut an opening through the gate."

A paved road ran down to the water, but they were still forty feet away when they ran into several cement barriers. Rich and the other officers jumped out of the truck and ran to the water.

"When we got down there, the girl who had been on the raft with the two boys was standing waist deep in the water," Rich said. "She was screaming, 'He's out there. He's out there.' She was pointing to the place she thought she last saw him." When the officers asked her if she was sure about the location, there was no doubt in her mind. "That's where he went down," she said.

The job ahead was complicated, and the cops moved fast. When children are involved, there is always an added sense of urgency for responders. "You eyeball where you're going to work," Rich explained. "Then you mark the area for the search. The divers work in a Z pattern. Each line has to be pulled taut. It's not easy to do, but most times it is very effective.

"Once the lines are set, the divers swim out. The first one in the water goes to the farthest point on the tender. When they are all in position, they dive down to the bottom and dump some air out of their dry suits to get the right buoyancy. If they don't get it right, there will be trouble staying on the bottom.

"When the diver is ready to go, he pulls on the line twice. That signals to the person on shore he's ready to go. If the line is slack, the person on land won't get the signal, and that can get dangerous. One pull means the diver is okay. Two indicates he is ready to go. Three tugs signals he's started his search to the right. Four pulls, he's gone to the left. Five or more pulls means the diver is in trouble or for some other reason the search needs to be stopped."

Setting up the lines takes a lot of practice, especially if there is a drowning victim. Rescues in the Bronx River are particularly challenging. One experienced diver compared the bottom to a giant underwater yard sale. "It's hard to describe to someone who's never been down there," he said. "There's cars, shopping carts, tires, old engines, and all kinds of machinery. Everything is encased in globs of mud. It's easy to get caught in that stuff, so we always carry one knife, sometimes two, along with wire cutters and other tools in case we get tangled up."

"These are murky, muddy waters," Rich added. "When the sun shines on the mud, it can be blinding. We usually don't get a choice, but if you gave us one, we would much rather dive at night because the visibility is so much better. The ambient light during the evening lights up the water. There's less glare.

"Once the lines are set and we've checked to make sure they're taut, we send the divers out. The first diver, at the farthest point on the tender, descends. As long as the diver is not too buoyant, he will be able to stay on the bottom, follow the line, and methodically search the area. You need a lot of divers to do this kind of search. We were fortunate that two other ESU trucks showed up to help us."

Despite the extensive training police divers receive and the monumental efforts they make, things can and do go wrong. That day the divers had several things working against them. The witnesses were confused about where they last saw the boy. An incoming tide would eventually make some of the areas so deep that there was a good possibility divers would run out of air while they were conducting their searches. And last but not least, the crew was relatively inexperienced in the arduous task of scuba rescues.

From his vantage point on the shore, it was not long before Rich could see the divers were struggling. "I could tell their buoyancy wasn't right," he said. "They were having trouble staying down. I pulled on the line once to get their attention. When they surfaced, I waved them in. As they swam into shore, the people on the shoreline started yelling, 'No, no, no. Go back out. He went down over there.' Everyone was pointing in different directions."

When the divers got to shore, Rich told them to concentrate on what they had to do. He was playing the role of a coach, except the objective was a lot more important than winning a game. "I told them to go back out, take their time, and get their buoyancy correct."

By that time it was getting dark. They had been diving for hours, and any hope of finding the boy alive was dwindling. The divers picked up their pace, but as they methodically approached the shore, they had to deal with something else. Ten feet out from the shore there was a big drop-off, an area that had been dredged out for barges.

"At high tide it's very deep," Rich said. "You had to dive much deeper than forty feet to get to the bottom. I started to worry about the divers. Since September 11, we had an influx of new officers with less experience than I had as a rookie ESU cop. These scuba rescues require an enormous amount of practice, and I was getting worried."

If regular ESU protocols are followed, the chauffeur is not supposed to dive. But at some point, Rich felt he had no choice. Lieutenant Joe Goff was the highest-ranking officer on the scene. He agreed Rich should go in.

Rich suited up and began his search back and forth, following the Z pattern. He started out at the farthest point and angled back. The visibility was close to zero. As he felt his way along the bottom, he was careful not to tear his dry suit. He had ripped it several times in the past, and he was not eager to deal with the myriad of skin infections and diarrhea that is almost a given when coming into direct contact with the waters off the coastline of New York City.

When his tank was almost empty, Rich swam in, grabbed a full one, and went back out. Experts say divers should never go out more than twice. Anything beyond two is considered life threatening for the diver. By the time he finished his second dive, Rich was totally exhausted. They had been at it so long that the tide had come in and was now on its way out. Along with hundreds of bystanders, there were fire trucks, scores of police cars, and ESU trucks. The NYPD's Air Sea Rescue helicopters had flown in and were circling overhead. Their divers started their own pattern dives after dropping lines from a helicopter. Several boats from the Harbor Patrol idled anxiously outside the search area.

After finishing his second search, Rich swam to shore. He found a stump on the beach and sat down. "I can't understand how we missed him," he said.

Veteran ESU Officer Richie Gundacker brought Rich some water and pointed to two men sitting nearby in the sand. "The one on the left is the dad," Richie said.

Rich got up off the stump and walked over so he was in earshot. He tried to hear what the men were saying, but he only got bits and pieces. "It was terrible," he said. "I could hear the father reminiscing about his recent birthday with his son. He was asking his friend how God would let this happen." Five years later, Rich's eyes still fill with tears when he tells the story.

He was spent, but after listening to the grieving father, Rich felt he had no choice. If he couldn't save the boy's life, at least he could find his body.

As he swam out, his arms felt dead and his legs were cramping up. He found the line, tucked his head down, thrust his legs out behind him, and dove. When he got to the bottom, he let out some air and began to inch his way along the bottom.

He can't say exactly when he knew there was something terribly wrong.

It could have been seconds or maybe it was minutes. All he remembers was that at some point he found himself tangled up in some sort of plastic netting. He struggled to find the line and pulled hard on it once, but it was slack. That meant the officers on shore had no way to know he was in trouble. His only option was to cut himself free of the netting that was slowly but surely strangling him.

"I went for my knife, but it wasn't there," Rich said. "Later I realized I must have left it on shore after the second dive. That's what happens when you get tired. You start screwing up, forgetting your equipment, panicking instead of staying calm."

When he checked his tank, he discovered he only had five hundred pounds of air left. He feared the worst. "I thought, this is it. I'm not going to get out. After all the things I've survived, I couldn't believe I was going to die because I got tangled up in a construction net."

The harder he fought to break free, the worse it got. When he first got tangled, he was praying for a rescue, but now things were so bad, he was worried anyone who came out to help him would get caught up, too. "I didn't want anyone else to get hurt out there," he said.

Dragging the netting and debris, with the air in his tank getting dangerously low, Rich clawed his way along the bottom toward shore. He didn't have the energy to keep on going, but he was aware if he died, his death would occur on his youngest child Richie's second birthday. Summing up almost superhuman strength, he kept crawling through the mud and muck along the riverbed. When he could not go on any more, he pushed against the netting in the outside hope he could get into a kneeling position. As he raised his head, he broke through the surface. It was hard to remember later the exact number of people who came out to help him, but he saw Tommy Belatoni, Ben Kalinsky, and Sergeant Wilson Arambolis rushing into the water. As soon as Rich was safe on land, the sergeant called off the dives. They would resume in the morning.

The following day witnesses told the cops that when the raft flipped, the girl swam to shore. But she ended up in an area far away from where the raft went over. Late in the afternoon, NYPD divers found the body of fourteen-year-old Joseph Johnson.

* * *

Richard James Miller was born in Cold Spring, New York, in 1960, across the Hudson River from the U.S. Military Academy at West Point. The oldest of four children, Rich had three younger sisters. He was five years old when his parents divorced. His mom, Patricia, worked hard to support the family. His dad, Richard, a high-tower line worker for Consolidated Edison, died of lung cancer at age thirty-two when Rich was twelve years old. He had moved seven times by the time he was ten.

He joined the U.S. Marine Corps after graduating from high school with intentions of becoming a military police officer. He graduated at the top of his class from the U.S. Army Military Police School in Fort McClellan, Alabama. A four-year stint in the Marines was followed by two years providing security for some of the most high-profile targets in the world, including the royal family of Jordan; the son of the Shah of Iran; and Ivan Boesky, the famous Wall Street trader who went to prison in the 1980s after being convicted in an insider trading scandal.

A few months after he turned twenty-seven, Rich enrolled in the NYPD Police Academy. He was thrilled when he got his first assignment, the 44th Precinct in the South Bronx. The 4-4 was overrun with drug dealers, prostitutes, junkies, and homeless people. Every year the precinct was named one of the busiest and most dangerous in the city. His first day on patrol, he found himself out on the ledge of a thirteenth-floor balcony, where he managed to save the life of an elderly man who was trying to jump.

His partner that first year was Charlie Wassil, a childhood friend from Peekskill, New York. Like Rich, Charlie had served with the U.S. Marines, and over the years the men have stayed close friends. "As a cop, Rich is very quiet, and he is respectful of everyone," Wassil explained. "He doesn't say much, but he is very observant, and he has a great ability to figure out when something isn't right on the street."

Skilled police officers like Rich have keen instincts and powers of observation. Wassil noted that Rich always had an unusual ability to predict whether a situation would turn dangerous, and he was especially good at figuring out who had a gun.

Rich was a natural for Emergency Service, and in 1993, after the first World Trade Center bombing, he was accepted into the prestigious unit. Over his eighteen years with ESU, he has crawled out on ledges to rescue jumpers, pulled people from car wrecks and construction site disasters, delivered babies, helped homeless people find shelter, and talked violent men with in-nocent hostages into surrendering. He has executed over 2,500 high-risk war-rants, requiring him to bust through doors and put people under arrest for the most serious crimes imaginable. Almost every time, he served the warrant without ever firing a shot.

Wassil says when it comes to cops like Rich, looks can be deceiving. "He seems so mild mannered," Wassil points out, "but when things go bad, he's the one you want by your side."

Rich never complains, but he lives with constant pain. The ringing in his ears from being too close to gunfire and explosions from grenades comes and goes, but he will never be free of it completely. He's learned to live with painful headaches since the time he fractured his skull when a hydraulic tool collapsed while he was rescuing an eight-year-old boy trapped in an elevator. Another time an emotionally disturbed woman who had barricaded herself inside her apartment sliced through his hand with a saw when he tried to help her. He's broken his right hand several times and his ribs twice, once while trying to grab a jumper off a ledge of a tall building, the other time during a high-speed pursuit. On cold days, he has trouble loosening up in the morn-ing, and his right hand, which was mauled by a pit bull, aches. When people ask him if he would have chosen another career if he had known about the injuries, he tells them no. Never.

Rich has four children: a stepdaughter, two daughters, and a son. Wassil has always been impressed by what a good father Rich is. "This is a man who is totally devoted to his family. He loves his kids."

There is a lot of emotion in Rich's voice when he speaks about his chil-dren. "Marissa, my stepdaughter, was five years old when I met her," he said. "I'll always remember driving her to dancing classes three nights a week and teaching her to ride a bike and swim. She and I went together to pick out her first puppy. One of the most frightening moments of my life was when I got a call that she had been in a car accident. During those few seconds, before I knew she was okay, my heart stopped."

When his first child, Kristie, was born, Rich remembers it as the happiest day of his life. When her younger sister, Nikki, arrived eighteen months later, he was just as thrilled.

"Nikki is a lot like me. She can be very quiet at times, but she's not afraid to speak her mind, and she's quick to step up when a friend is in trouble even if it means getting in trouble herself. When she was little, she always wanted to go everywhere with me, even Home Depot. Most kids are very impressionable, but even at her young age, she has a quiet wisdom. She knows right from wrong, good from bad, and she's fierce about protecting the people she loves.

"Kristie didn't have much time to be the baby of the family, falling between her older stepsister and Nikki. She was only twelve when her mother and I went through a difficult divorce, and I have not seen as much of Kristie as I'd like. But she does well in school and is growing into a pretty, young woman who plays sports, is on her school's cheerleading team, and loves to socialize with her friends. Like any concerned father, I worry about her and say my prayers that she finds the wisdom to make the best choices for her life."

Rich's youngest child and only son was born after the attacks of September 11, 2001. "I'll always think of him as a miracle," he says. "My marriage was failing, but the experience of September 11 brought us back together. I'd hoped we might be able to work things out. Richie's birth brought me great joy after losing so many friends and working for months at Ground Zero. He's seven now and a very loving, affectionate child. We go fishing, bowling, swimming, and he loves visiting Truck Three. He has a hard time saying good-bye every other weekend, and I do as well, but he gives us plenty of hugs and kisses to hold on to until the next time."

* * *

Rich Miller had been a police officer for a little over one year when he was forced to shoot an EDP, the expression cops use to refer to an emotionally disturbed person. The call came in at two in the morning. A man with a knife was banging on doors in his apartment building. Rich, Charlie Wassil, and two other officers backing them up arrived on the scene. When they heard music coming from the sixth floor, they assumed they were dealing with a loud noise call.

"As I was coming down the stairs from the roof, Charlie was knocking on the door where we thought the music was coming from," Rich said. "The door burst open, and a man yelling in Spanish lunged at him with a knife. Charlie fell back on the floor as did Officer Joel Plass."

Quickly, Rich drew his service revolver. He yelled back at the perpetrator, "Drop the knife, drop the knife." Rich was able to force him back into the apartment, but all the while the man was yelling and swinging the knife dangerously close to Rich. "I saw Joel trying to get up off the floor. That's when the guy came back at us. He lunged at Joel, and I fired off one shot. The round hit him in the chest."

Rich's courage would be acknowledged a few months later when the Police Benevolent Association gave him their Rookie of the Year award. But he still had a rough time coping with the fact that he had taken a life, and there were very few people he felt comfortable talking to about it.

In 1989 the NYPD did offer counseling services, but most officers were reluctant to use them. "That was a bad year for me," Rich recalled. "Most of the time I felt totally alone. I had a lot of support from the cops I worked with, but that was it."

One of the lowest points came when Rich was called to testify before the grand jury. Robert Johnson had just won a bitterly contested election for Bronx district attorney, making him New York City's first black DA. The man with the knife was Hispanic, and it was one of the first cases of "suicide by cop" Johnson would deal with.

At that time the NYPD was changing its policies and procedures for dealing with emotionally disturbed people. Tasers and other nonlethal devices were not readily available, leaving few options except lethal force when a life was in danger. Rich and other officers had only seconds to respond when a perpetrator attacked with a knife.

Studies have reported that over 50 percent of officer-involved shootings are the result of people acting intentionally in a way they know will leave the officer no choice but to shoot them. But Rich was not sure the courts would see it that way. "I went into that courtroom knowing I was facing a possible indictment for manslaughter or worse," he said.

News reports on the incident were filled with inaccuracies. It was painful for Rich to read the articles in which the man with the knife was portrayed as an innocent victim and someone much older than he really was.

It took only seconds for Rich to make the decision to protect his fellow officers and himself. It took months before he was exonerated of wrongdoing by the Bronx grand jury. "In the long run I guess I was fortunate," he said. "Eventually, after months of negative press on both me and the Department, the truth came out about the character of the individual I shot and his actions that day."

"I never opened up to my wife about it," he continued. "She kept asking me if I wanted to talk, but I just couldn't do it." At the time he felt it was the right thing to do to protect his wife from the pain and anguish he was feeling.

A year later he got a call from Phil Caruso, President of the police union. Phil asked if Rich would be willing to talk to reporters about what he had gone through and how he was coping. Caruso explained that officers involved in traumas thought they should keep their emotions to themselves, be stoic, and go back to work. If Rich opened up, Caruso thought it would encourage other cops who had gone through similar experiences to think about getting help.

Rich told Caruso he was not interested. "I explained things were a mess and I didn't feel I could talk about it."

He had only fired a single shot, but his ears were still ringing and he was having trouble sleeping. He and his wife had put their plans to buy a house and start a family on hold, and he was not feeling very positive about the future. When Caruso called him a second time and asked him to reconsider, reluctantly, he agreed to grant some interviews.

Reporters from the *New York Post,* the *New York Daily News,* and the *Bergen County Record* interviewed him over the phone. *New York Newsday*, a Long Island daily, sent reporter Peg Tyre to talk to him in person.

"We met at a diner," Rich said. "Right away I felt comfortable with her. We talked for hours. For the first time in over a year, I talked about everything that happened. I told her about the guilt I had for taking a life and the anger I felt toward the criminal justice system for treating me like a criminal. The story ran a week later. It took up three full pages in the newspaper."

Talking brought tremendous relief. "The ton of bricks I was carrying around disappeared," Rich said. "I started to laugh again, and I slept better. The whole world looked different."

The response from his fellow officers was overwhelming. "I don't know how they got my phone number, but they were calling me at all hours of the day and night and thanking me for sharing my story. They told me how much it helped them personally. The cops who had been in shootings were particularly grateful."

As fall waned and the days got colder, Rich put on his winter uniform jacket for the first time since early spring. As he headed out the door, another officer asked him what had happened to his coat. He looked down and saw slice marks. He realized he had not worn the jacket since the night of the shooting and the man had cut right through it with his knife. He had not noticed it before. It was an eerie reminder of a time he was trying his best to forget.

* * *

It was a warm, muggy Saturday in August 2000 when Rich Miller's alarm went off at 5:30 in the morning. The weatherman was predicting showers for later in the day, and the gloomy weather matched Rich's mood. He had been a cop in New York City for over a decade. His current assignment was Emergency Service Truck Four in the Bronx. He had tried to switch his hours so he could be with his family, but Saturday is the hardest day of the week to change schedules, and his request was denied. His shift that day was 8 to 4. He was hoping it would be quiet so he could leave work on time and get home to his wife and kids.

It was a little after 8 in the morning when Rich and his partner, Joe Ocasio, headed out on patrol. The first call came in barely a half-hour later. An emotionally disturbed man was threatening his neighbor with a knife. A little after 10 they got another call. A gunman had taken hostages and was threatening to kill them. It took two hours for Rich and several other officers to talk the man into surrendering without hurting the hostages. He thought if things quieted down, there was still a chance he could get out by 4.

At 2:03 p.m., they got a 10-13—NYPD code for "officer in trouble." Rich remembers the dispatcher's voice. "You could tell right away it was something bad," he said. "There were a lot of people all talking at once. It was hard to understand, but we knew someone from Emergency Service had been shot."

Seconds later a sergeant from ESU headquarters was calling on the radio. He told Rich to get his rifle and go quickly to 16 Parkway Court in Brooklyn. Three people had gone to their local precinct in Sheepshead Bay and told the police a family member had assembled an arsenal of weapons and thousands of rounds of ammunition. He was threatening to kill as many New York City police officers as he could before they killed him. It was a textbook case of "suicide by cop."

Arthur Alalouf, a former Marine and corrections officer, had wanted to join the NYPD, but when he flunked the stringent psychological tests required of all new police officers, he wanted revenge. Minutes after the family's disturbing visit, Emergency Service officers, armed with heavy weapons, ballistic vests, helmets, and bunkers—the Kevlar-enforced shields that cover the top of the head to below the groin with a bulletproof glass port at eye level—were dispatched to the Alalouf home.

Bunkers positioned, firearms drawn and ready, a team of four officers led by Gregory John approached the house. Their mission was to isolate and contain Alalouf. The first order of business was to secure the doors so the suspect could not escape. Greg John and Dave Isaacson moved quickly to make sure a door on the side of the house was locked from the outside. Before they got there, shots rang out.

As Greg John dove for cover, the side door of the house moved slightly. Greg thought he saw the barrel of a shotgun protruding through the door. But as fast as it appeared, it was gone. He kept watching the windows and doorway, hoping to get a glimpse of the shooter. Seconds later another round went off, but this time it was coming from the second floor. Greg looked up and saw a terrifying sight. The shooter was standing in a window, calmly smiling down at him. The next thing he remembered was a muzzle flash just before bullets from the shotgun blast tore into his left shoulder. Wounded and bleeding, Greg pulled himself up. As he made his way around the corner of the house, he was able to fire off a few rounds from his Heckler & Koch MP5, but the man was gone. Clutching his bleeding shoulder, Greg staggered out to the street where Dave Isaacson was waiting. Dave picked Greg up in his arms and carried him to a waiting ambulance.

The quiet neighborhood was now a war zone. With red lights blinking and sirens wailing, scores of cops pulled up. Over forty ESU officers were there in their trucks along with some of the highest-ranking people in the NYPD, including the Chief of Patrol and the Chief of the Department. TV news helicopters, hoping to get footage for their broadcasts, circled overhead before they were shooed away by a Department chopper flown to the scene by Sergeant James Cohan, a pilot with the NYPD's Aviation Unit. To the bystanders, reporters, photographers, and television news crews who were arriving in droves, the scene must have looked like chaos. They probably never noticed that the police had already established a crime scene perimeter around the blocks that surrounded the Alalouf home that restricted access for everybody except the cops.

Once the police lines were up and the perimeter was secure, a team of officers quickly went door to door, evacuating terrified residents. Outside the perimeter, another team was directing traffic and keeping the narrow streets open so police cars, ESU trucks, and ambulances could pull in close if needed.

* * *

As Greg John's ambulance pulled away and the EMTs worked furiously to stabilize the wounded officer, Rich Miller and Joe Ocasio pulled up to Parkway Court. Sergeant Joe Malteso was waiting for them. Rich was one of the department's top marksmen, and Malteso knew he was going to need someone with those skills today.

The sergeant told Rich to set up an observation post on top of the nine-story building across the street. After describing the suspect, Malteso warned Rich to keep his firearm ready. Rich manned his post on the roof of the building for close to two hours before the sergeant sent another officer up to take his place. Malteso had chosen Rich along with Dave Kao, Andy Nugent, and several other key ESU officers to be on the entry team and search the house.

While every one of the four hundred officers assigned to ESU is a certified emergency medical technician, some are also paramedics and physician's assistants. Dave and Andy had advanced paramedic training. With the possibility that more cops were going to be wounded or worse, commanders knew they needed their most experienced SWAT officers to stop the gunman and be ready to provide life-saving medical treatment as well.

When there is a serious threat from an armed assailant and the police breach the door to make entry, the officer at the head of the line is always the most vulnerable. With his bunker for protection, the first one in is expected to provide cover for the other officers who follow. The pressure was palpable. Every man on the team was aware that their friend and colleague Greg John might be dying. It was on them to bring this rampage to an end.

The plan was to clear the first floor, then the second. The basement would come last. As soon as they were inside, the cops planned to pull the pins and toss their flash-bang devices. If Alalouf was still in the house, the bright light and loud noise emanating from these loud, smoky, but harmless grenades might give them seconds of valuable time.

Just seconds before they went in, Rich realized there was a flaw in the plan. If the shooter was in the basement and armed with a semiautomatic rifle, he had the firepower to shoot straight up through the floorboards and kill the entire team as they searched the first floor. Rich urged the men behind him to move fast along the hallways and not to bottle up in the doorways.

It was getting dark. Without some natural light, the search would be more difficult. As they fastened their Kevlar helmets and readied their bunkers and firearms, the team got into position. "God," Rich prayed. "Help us get through this." It was one of the few times in his twenty-two-year career he could remember asking for God's help while he was on duty.

It was a little after seven o'clock at night when the lieutenant gave the signal. The breaching team busted through the door. Five hours had passed since Greg John had been shot.

As they got ready to toss the flash-bangs, the cops were confronted with an ominous sight. In the middle of the front hall, the barrel pointed straight at them, was a shotgun. "It was just laying there in the hall," Rich recalled, "pointing at us like a welcoming party."

Once the distraction devices were thrown, a brilliant white light flashed, an ear-shattering explosion rocked the house, and the first floor filled up with dust. Body bunkers placed strategically to protect their heads and torsos, weapons in hand, the officers made their way quickly over the first floor. After a thorough search of the rooms, they went upstairs to the second floor as Rich waited and secured the hallway leading to the basement. Once the second floor was cleared, they went to the basement. Rich was the lead bunker man in the progression.

In the basement, weapons were everywhere. "There were swords, guns, all sorts of battle gear," Rich said. "Then we found the bottles of propane. We learned later he bought the propane the day before. He must have decided if he couldn't kill us with one of his rifles or swords, he'd incinerate us with the propane."

After checking all the rooms in the basement and conducting a secondary search, the officers were confident Alalouf was not in the house.

* * *

As Rich and his team moved to the backyard to get their next assignment from the commanders who had gathered there, another team of six Emergency Service officers began a methodical, house-to-house search on the next street. As they checked the homes on Avenue Y, whose backyards faced the rear of the attached row houses on Parkway Court, the officers noticed a door ajar at 523. Quickly, they formed an entry team. Officer Joe Guerra took the lead position as bunker man. Everyone checked their weapons and lined up in single file. Guerra gave the signal, pushed open the door, and yelled "Police!" before taking a few steps inside. The instant Joe was fully inside the house, a muzzle flash went off, followed instantaneously by an ear-shattering boom.

Arthur Alalouf was waiting for them.

Bullets tore into Joe Guerra's face, but even with blood streaming down his nose and cheeks, somehow he was able to keep hold of his bunker. As he took a few steps toward the gunfire, the shooter fired off another round that ripped into his upper thigh and hit his shield. The force of the round was so intense, it knocked the bunker and his gun out of his hands. With no shield and no weapon, he was now helpless in the face of the rounds that just kept coming. The last thing he remembered was getting hit in the leg. Bleeding profusely, Guerra lost consciousness and collapsed.

Jimmy McGrath was behind Guerra. In his statement to Department investigators following the incident, McGrath said he was about to enter the house when he heard an explosion. Seconds later when a muzzle flash exploded, McGrath was sure Guerra was hit. McGrath tried to get to his wounded colleague, but when he was just a few feet away, a bullet ripped into his face. Jimmy slumped to the ground, and Bill Madigan carried him out. Once Billy had carried McGrath to safety, he turned around and went back into the gunfire, hoping he could help Guerra.

Looking back, Rich said it was hard to describe the panic in the voices coming over the police radios after Guerra and McGrath were shot. "Everyone was talking at once. There were dispatchers, cops, supervisors. They were all yelling, 'Cop shot, cop down, 10-13, 10-13.' It was bad."

While Arthur Alalouf kept shooting at the injured Guerra and McGrath, Rich and Joe Ocasio were in Alalouf's backyard conferring with the commanders about their next move. When they heard the sound of gunfire, Rich was sure the shots were coming from a house down the street on Avenue Y. He looked at Joe Ocasio and said, "Come on. Let's go."

What Rich and Joe didn't know was the gunman was setting firing points and fields of fire so he would be perfectly situated to kill them as they approached.

* * *

The Sheepshead Bay neighborhood is a dense grid of attached row houses. At the time each home had a deck in the back with a small grassy area backing up against the backyard of the house on the next street. Chain-link and wooden fences separated the yards. The chain-link fences were a little over four feet. The wooden fences were double that height. Rich sprinted down the backyards, leaping over the fences he found in his path. His speed and agility were remarkable, considering he was carrying over fifty pounds of extra equipment, including a heavy ballistic vest, a Kevlar helmet, a body bunker, and two 9mm semiautomatic handguns.

He ran down the length of the backyards toward the gunfire. When he got to the end, he cleared the last fence, crashing down in the middle of a tangled mess of tomato plants. The gunman was watching Rich the entire time. When he leapt over the fence separating the two men, Alalouf released two dogs. One was a pit bull.

As Rich pushed his way through the tomato plants, he was startled to see two dogs running toward him. He had been around dogs his entire life, and for a split second he thought he should wait to see if they were going to attack. But his experience coupled with the rapidly unfolding events told him not to take any chances. In the split second it took to aim his firearm, the dogs were at his feet, snarling and snapping. Rich shot one of the dogs, and they both scurried away.

The sun was going down. A light rain was falling, and Rich realized he had lost track of Joe Ocasio. He was still clutching his bunker, keeping it positioned to protect his head and torso as he pushed his way through the plants. He looked around but he couldn't see anyone.

When Rich was running toward the source of the gunfire, he wasn't sure exactly where his opponent was positioned. He had no way to know how much ammunition the gunman had left, but from the looks of the arsenal they had found in his house and the sounds of the rounds flying through the air, Rich assumed he was still well stocked.

"All of a sudden I heard a pow!" Rich said. "I was on a deck just above the perpetrator's location. I could see the muzzle blast of the shotgun, but thank God the rounds hit the side of the house."

Rich cantered his shield up over his left shoulder. "The bunker has a bulletproof glass port at eye level," he explained, "but it narrows the field of vision, and the view is distorted. I took the risk and moved it to my side to get a better look around."

His eye caught something. At first he thought it might be an animal. But when he looked closer, he realized it was Arthur Alalouf hunkered down in a stairwell leading into the basement of the house next door. Only twenty feet separated the two men.

The gunman was positioned perfectly for his mission. Tucked down below the back deck in a stairwell surrounded by a three-foot cement retainer wall, it was going to be easy to take down the police officers who were coming to get him. He had planned his reign of terror down to the last detail.

Rich was alone on the deck of the home on Avenue Y. Alalouf was in the stairwell next door.

"I found the best angle I could and fired," Rich remembered. He was able to fire five or six rounds before his gun jammed. Luckily, he had gone to firearms requalification training just the week before, and the instructor, Chris Brandt, focused on the gun jam drill. His words rang in Rich's ears. "If your gun jams, get rid of it. Get rid of it. Get rid of it."

He dropped the gun and pulled his backup weapon. As he was getting ready to fire, Joe Ocasio appeared, completely out of breath. Rich found out later that one of the pit bulls had attacked Joe when he jumped over the fence. It took several minutes for Ocasio to deal with the dog and then weave his way back through the yard. As he cleared several obstacles, he realized he could not see Rich.

"Ocasio had a Mini 14," Rich recalled. "That is a very accurate rifle, and I thought from his angle Joe might have a chance to get him. I don't remember it, but Joe told me later I was screaming, 'Fire the Mini. Fire the Mini. Fire the Mini.'"

Ocasio fired the rifle, but he couldn't get Alalouf, who kept on shooting. A third officer, Bill Fisher, appeared. He was armed with a Mini 14 as well. Rich said the first time he realized there was a third cop was when he heard someone yelling at him to get out of the line of fire and pushing him up against the back wall of the house.

Despite the distractions, Rich kept his gun pointed at the stairwell. He pushed Fisher away and whispered over to him. "Wait. Wait. I think I can get him now." He kept firing but the rounds kept hitting the walkway around Alalouf. Knowing his magazine was almost empty, Rich decided to take the risk and reload. Hoping Alalouf wouldn't see him, he tried to move a barbecue grill for cover and get a better angle, but it was screwed into the deck and he couldn't budge it. Totally exposed, he dumped the empty magazine while yelling, "I'm out. I'm out." A year later when Rich became a tactics instructor, he realized this was a bad phrase to use. He was almost finished reloading when Alalouf rose out of the stairwell. His 12 gauge shotgun was pointed directly at Rich.

"I was just getting the bunker back in position when I saw him stand up and fire," Rich said. "I screamed over at Ocasio, 'Hit him, Joe. Hit him, Joe.'"

A split second later, another round smashed into Rich's ballistic shield. A desperate attempt to keep his hand clenched around the bunker handle failed. The shield, his only protection against the fusillade of bullets coming at him, went flying. At the exact time Rich lost his bunker, Joe Ocasio, who was crouching down on the deck to his right, started screaming.

"I looked to my right just in time to see Joe's hands flying up in the air," Rich said. "He was hit. The force of the rounds had him screaming in pain."

At that point Rich had no bunker, and he was almost out of ammunition. He summoned all his energy and tried to concentrate. He pushed himself up against the back wall of the house and looked down on the stairwell.

Billy Fisher crouched down and made his way toward the bleeding body of Joe Ocasio. The bullets were flying. Just as Fisher reached Ocasio, he felt a round tear into his leg. Holding his hand over the wound, he managed to drag himself and Joe to the front of the house where waiting ambulances rushed both officers to the hospital.

Now it was just Rich and Alalouf. Rich knew only one of them was going to get out alive.

The gun battle continued. Every time Rich stopped firing, Alalouf popped up and got off another shot. At some point Rich had to face the fact that at his present angle, he was not going to be able to shoot the gunman. He was running out of ammunition for his one remaining handgun, but he had one more thing to try. He hoped a flash-bang, thrown into the stairwell, might distract the shooter and give him a few seconds of cover. "I knew other Emergency Service officers would be coming," he said. "That's what they do."

Rich yelled back toward Parkway Court asking for someone to bring him a flash-bang so he could hurl it into the stairwell. But rather than deliver the flash-bang, someone threw it. It missed, landing against an exercise bike on the walkway before bouncing backward in Rich's direction. The explosion of light and noise was intense, and his ears were ringing. It took a few seconds for the air to clear, and when it did, the sight was unnerving. Rich saw his opponent sitting up against the storm door in the stairwell. "He was holding his rifle across his lap and laughing. Who knows why he was laughing. When the flash-bang went off, he probably thought we had blown ourselves up."

* * *

With his adversary sitting in that position, Rich hoped he had a better angle. He fired, but Alalouf quickly moved to his previous position, crouching down in the corner against the retainer wall. They were back to square one.

Rich stood there, alone, as Alalouf tried to reload. Their eyes met. Alalouf rose up a bit, and Rich could see he was totally exposed. Quickly, the gunman crouched down against the retainer wall in the stairwell, but most of his back was still visible. As Alalouf continued to try and reload his shotgun, Rich fired a shot. Alalouf groaned and slumped back down into the stairwell. Rich stood perfectly still looking down from the deck. Hoping it might be over, he looked around and wondered where Joe and Billy were. At that same moment, Alalouf rose up and fired again. The round whizzed by Rich's head.

At that point Rich knew he had no choice but to come at him from a different angle. As he ran past Officers Patty McGee and Greg Welch, he yelled over, "You can't get the motherfucker from here."

Rich hopped the fence to the neighboring yard where Alalouf was still crouching in the stairwell. Alalouf jumped up and fired a shot where Rich had been positioned just seconds before. The round came in below the deck right at McGee and Welch. Alalouf crouched down again, unaware that Rich, like a tailback running a Green Bay sweep, was coming at him from a wide angle. As he closed in, Rich hoped Alalouf would be distracted by McGee and Welch. In high school, Rich ran the forty-yard dash in 4.6 seconds. In his desperate sprint to come back up on the shooter, he is sure he broke his record even carrying all his gear.

Clutching his gun with both hands, he closed the distance to twenty feet. As he moved in, confident he could get an upper body shot, Alalouf turned his head and looked at Rich. Their eyes met. "You could see it in his face. He knew he was finished. He was like a deer caught in the headlights. I fired five or six times. I think every round hit him in the chest. When he finally slumped down, I knew it was finally over."

It was only minutes after the bullets stopped flying that word spread that five officers were wounded, and no one knew if any of them would survive. Everyone at the scene who could, took off for the hospital. When they pulled up to the emergency room entrance, reporters and camera crews were everywhere. The Police Commissioner and mayor had arrived along with distraught family members and friends of the wounded officers.

"By the time I got there, my ears were ringing really bad," Rich said. "I had a terrible headache, and I could barely hear. Once I checked in on our guys who were wounded, I asked if there was a doctor who could take a look at my ears."

It took a couple of years for his hearing to return to normal. Some days the ringing was worse than others. Over that time, Rich failed two hearing tests and suffered terrible headaches, but he never complained, and he never missed a day of work because of these injuries. Eight years later he said he never worried about the headaches and the hearing loss. "I'm still so proud to have ended it and that I was able to keep any more of my guys from being shot."

The wounded officers survived. Joe Guerra, Jimmy McGrath, and Joe Ocasio suffered the most serious wounds and were forced to retire because of their injuries. After several months of surgeries and recuperation, Greg John and Billy Fisher, both of whom wanted to return to work, were also forced to end their careers with the New York City Police Department.

* * *

By the time Rich got out of the hospital and returned to Truck Four in the Bronx to get his car and drive home, the sun was coming up. He had called his wife around midnight to tell her he was okay. Nevertheless, she was relieved when she heard the car pull into the driveway. When he opened his front door and went inside, he was overcome with an urge to make sure his three daughters were safe. He went to each of their bedrooms and watched them sleeping from the doorway.

He crawled into bed, hoping he could sleep, but the adrenaline rush was still intense and he couldn't relax. After checking on the kids again and pacing around the house, he laid down on the living room couch and shut his eyes. That was the first time he saw Arthur Alalouf. He was staring at him the same way he had right before he died.

Rich was raised a Catholic, and while he has had his issues with the Church, he has a strong faith in God. He has made it a habit to thank him when life is good, and he has prayed for help when times are tough. He did not know his new parish priest very well, but he had nowhere else to turn.

The next day he walked over to the church. Rich hoped the fresh air might help him clear his head. Every time he shut his eyes, Arthur Alalouf was there, staring at him. "It was spooky," he said. "It was like a ghost paying a visit."

Clutching the small pocket cross he carried since he was a rookie officer, Rich knocked on the front door of the rectory. A cleaning woman opened the door. "When I think back, I realized I must have looked disheveled. I hadn't had a shower or shave since early Saturday, but she didn't seem to notice. I asked if I could see the priest, and she showed me into his office."

Rich got to the point. He told the man he wanted to compose a prayer. "I explained that usually I had no trouble making my own prayers, but this time I needed some help." The priest recalled the front-page news reports and seemed eager to do what he could. Rich told the priest that first he wanted to thank God for letting him live. Then he asked for a prayer for his fellow officers who were still in the hospital recovering from their wounds. Finally he said he needed a prayer for Arthur Alalouf. He wanted to ask God to let his soul rest in peace.

The priest asked Rich to kneel. He stood above him and put one hand on his bowed head. He thanked God for keeping Rich safe. He prayed for the quick and complete recovery for the brave police officers who were wounded and still in the hospital. Finally he prayed to the Holy Father to let Arthur Alalouf's soul rest in peace. When Rich stood up, he felt calmer. His pulse had slowed, and his breathing was deeper and more steady. He shut his eyes. It was the first time since Saturday that Arthur Alalouf was not looking back at him.

* * *

When the gunfire stops and the assailants are dead, wounded, or under arrest, it should be over, but it's not. In many ways, for the officers who were involved, the hardest part is ahead.

After every incident where shots are fired and people are wounded or killed, every law enforcement agency has strict procedures and policies concerning the follow-up investigation. In New York City, everyone on the scene who fires his weapon submits a detailed report and is questioned at length by officials from the Department's Internal Affairs Bureau. It is the job of Internal Affairs detectives and their supervisors to determine that actions taken were warranted and in compliance with the strict guidelines all officers must follow when it comes to using deadly force.

After that comes the internal Department critique—a roundtable discussion that includes all the people who played a role in the incident, including all the supervisors up to the Chief of the Division.

The Department scheduled its first no-holds barred critique of the incident just four days later. Following a detailed, step-by-step review of the entire incident, officers discuss which tactics worked and which ones failed. Those found to be in violation of Department policies on the use of excessive force are reprimanded. Supervisors who made decisions must explain their actions.

It is a classic Monday morning quarterbacking scenario. Sometimes it is a productive process where a frank discussion of mistakes means a better job is done the next time. But just as often, the critique turns into an ugly slugfest replete with the recriminations and blame that inevitably occur when five officers are seriously wounded by one man in an incident lasting over six hours.

Difficult questions are raised. Who ran? Who stayed? Who left a wounded comrade because they were afraid?

Over the course of his career with the NYPD, Rich has been an enthusiastic proponent of these Department debriefings. But when the bosses wanted to sit down and hash out the Alalouf incident just four days afterward, Rich was adamant the timing was wrong.

"I've always believed that the only way we can improve is by talking honestly about our mistakes," he said. "It's the only way we get better at what we do. But there were a lot of things that went wrong on that job, and it was essential to have the key players talking about what worked for them and what didn't. Four days afterward, most of those people were still in the hospital. Their voices would not be heard."

Rich suggested to his supervisors, including the Commander of Emergency Service, that it might be wise to postpone the meeting. His warning went unheeded.

On the Wednesday after the gun battle in Brooklyn, the debriefing session was held as scheduled. Questions were raised about who left Joe Guerra after he was wounded. Someone else asked why so many cops were out in front of the house taking cover behind police cars or running down the street away from the mayhem once the shooting started. One officer said he heard someone say, "Don't go in there. They're shooting at us." The meeting degenerated into a barrage of hostile questions and defensive answers, most of which were never answered. One officer reported there was so much tension in the room you could feel it pressing against you.

Eventually Rich Miller was awarded the Combat Cross, the NYPD's second-highest medal, for his heroic actions the day Arthur Alalouf decided to kill New York City police officers. When the incident was further reviewed, everyone agreed he should have received the Department's highest award for courage and valor, the Medal of Honor, for stopping what is still one of the worst gun battles in New York City history.

*   *   *

With the exception of the face-to-face conversation with the reporter from *New York Newsday*, Rich has rebuffed countless requests for interviews. He admits that when Robin Moore, author of many best-selling books including *The Green Berets* and *The French Connection*, took him out to dinner and told him he wanted to write a book about his life, he was a little overwhelmed. Despite being an admirer of Moore's work and enormously flattered to get the offer, Rich turned it down. "I was never interested in that kind of attention," he said.

After his twenty-three years with the New York City Police Department, he has started to think about the next stage of his life. He knows the kind of police work he has excelled at is a young person's job, yet he is determined to stay as long as he can, injuries and all. "I love this city, I love this job, and I love the people I work with. I still look forward to going to work every day."

He has many options, but the one he's most enthused about is teaching younger officers about the tactics and nuances of police work. He has also cofounded a not-for-profit organization, the Post 911 Foundation, to assist first responders and returning veterans.

"There are a lot of us across the country who are concerned that the VFWs do not have the resources to handle the emotional needs of returning soldiers," Rich says. "Many of the special-ops guys are on their seventh and eighth rotations, and they need a lot of help when they return home. I'm looking forward to being a part of an effort that makes sure these heroes and all our first responders get everything they need and everything they deserve."

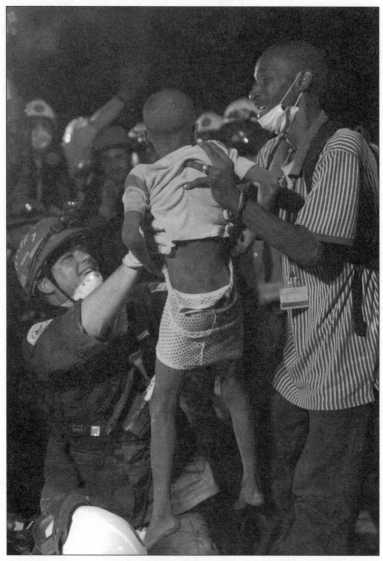

Following the devastating earthquake in Haiti, January 2010, Rich is seen here holding up seven-year-old "KiKi" following five hours of removing debris and tunneling underground with his FEMA Team, New York Task Force One. It was one of six live rescues during the team's deployment to Haiti. Photo by Charles Eckert, *Long Island News Day*.

Rich was five when this photo was taken with his Dad and younger sister Lynn. He was devastated when his father died when he was only 12 years old.

Rich joined the U.S. Marines when he was 18 years old. He says being a Marine was a great foundation and stepping stone for his life's work in the military and law enforcement.

Rich with his wife Theresa on their wedding day.

Rich and his family, summer 2009. Left to right: Theresa;
daughters Kristie,15; Nikki,13; and son Richie, 6.

Rich with Nikki and Richie on a day of river rock climbing in Connecticut.

When a citizen needs assistance, they call 911. When NYPD officers need help, they call the Emergency Service Unit. Above, left to right, Officers Rich Miller, Chris Knappenberger and Ray Neuman.

U.S. Army Senior Enlisted Advisor to SOCOM, Scott Neil (left), and Rich Miller have teamed up to form the Post 911 Foundation to serve first responders and veterans suffering from post traumatic stress disorder and other related disabilities. Rich says, "We are worried the VFW's do not have the resources to handle the emotional needs of returning soldiers who have done two, three and even four tours of duty in Iraq and Afghanistan. They are going to need a lot of help and I am committed to leading an effort that makes sure they get what they need." Below Rich and Theresa at VFW Post 39 in St. Petersburg, Florida, the oldest VFW in the South.

Rich Miller (right) and Richie Hartigan one year after the attacks of September 11. Miller and Hartigan raised the first flag at Ground Zero for their fallen comrades. Two days later there were hundreds of American flags flying at the place where the World Trade Center buildings stood. That proud symbol gave hope to Americans everywhere that we were strong and we would survive.

After serving as a personal body guard to the royal family of Jordan in the 1980's, Rich is reunited with His Royal Majesty King Abdullah during a 2003 visit to One Police Plaza. Here, Rich explains the tactical gear carried by ESU personnel. To the right, Commissioner Raymond Kelly looks on.

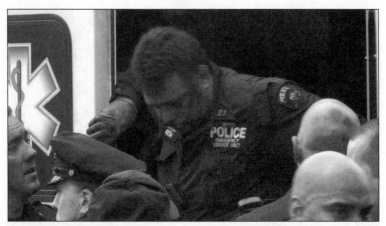

In May 2010, Rich Miller was severely injured trying to subdue an "EDP" – emotionally disturbed person – in a psychotic state. He and his team members, Lieutenant Mike Licitra and partner, Detective Roger Savage, chased the six-foot-two, two-hundred-and-seventy-pound man from the Bronx all the way into Manhattan, running on the train tracks. During the violent, physical struggle under a subway car, Rich tore his bicep. Following surgery to repair his left arm, Doctors indicated it would be at least nine months before he would experience only a near full recovery. These photos were taken just before Rich was rushed to the hospital in an ambulance. Photos courtesy Robert Stridiron/robsflashphotos.com.

Rich Miller raises the first American flag at Ground Zero the day following the terrorist attacks. Richie Hartigan, also assigned to the NYPD's Emergency Service Unit, is right below Rich on the ladder. The only sound that could be heard was an FDNY Battalion Chief yelling, "Present Arms," as Rich secured the flag on to the antenna which had fallen from the top of the Trade Center's North Tower. Photo courtesy Bill McNulty, NYPD/TARU (Ret).

Chapter Two

MIKE MORRA: The Rescuer

*"Without courage, there is no power on earth to
deter an aggressor, nothing to oppose the principle
that might is right." — John Percival*

One of Mike Morra's most vivid memories goes back to middle school. He was on his way to the cafeteria when he came around a corner and almost stumbled. There were books strewn everywhere. He looked around, and over in the corner he saw two older kids. They were punching and kicking a much smaller boy. "He was one of those small nerdy kids who loved school," Mike remembered. "Everyone made fun of him."

His reaction was immediate and impulsive. "They were way bigger than me, but I ran over and grabbed them by their shirts. I remember shaking them and yelling. I told them to get lost, to leave the kid alone."

Mike wasn't big or tough, and he's not sure why he felt it was his responsibility to get involved, but his mother wasn't surprised to hear the story. From the time she could remember, her son Michael would find the kids who were fighting and try to separate them. He was the boy who always stuck up for the little guy, someone who reacted instinctively when one of his classmates was being hurt or was in some kind of trouble. It was a trait that would lead him to a career in law enforcement.

Mike's courage and instinct to help would be called upon repeatedly during his years with the NYPD so far. One of those times occurred in 2006 on a cool overcast day in April. The call came in to the NYPD's 911 center, a massive room taking up a whole floor at police headquarters in lower Manhattan. Twenty-four hours a day, 365 days a year, hundreds of operators handle over thirty thousand calls a day. That's twelve million calls a year from people who are getting stabbed on a city street, robbed at an ATM machine, or just looking for directions.

It was a little after five o'clock in the afternoon on that April 2006 day. A power failure had knocked out the tramway going between Manhattan and Roosevelt Island. Two tramcars holding a total of sixty-nine passengers, including two infants, several children, and a disabled woman, were trapped on the tramcars. One car was dangling two hundred and fifty feet above the cold East River. The other cable car stopped over the congested streets of New York. It looked like a scene right out of a big-budget disaster movie.

In New York City, dangerous rescue operations like this are assigned to the Emergency Service Unit, a highly trained, close-knit division of four hundred officers working out of ten different squads called Trucks throughout the five boroughs of New York. Of the twenty-three New York City police officers who died saving people from the collapsing World Trade Center buildings on September 11, fourteen were from the Emergency Service Unit.

The day the trams broke down, Mike Morra had been a police officer in New York City since 1995, but he was a newcomer to Emergency Service. He had wanted the assignment to ESU from the time he began hearing the stories about cops rappelling off the Brooklyn Bridge to save a jumper or breaching a door in the Bronx to arrest a heavily armed bad guy. There is a saying about the Unit. "When a citizen is in trouble, the person calls 911. When a cop is in trouble, they call ESU."

Many NYPD police officers have their "ESU cop who saved my life" story, and after a few years on the job, Mike had his. The year was 2000. He and his partner had been patrolling in Long Island City in Queens when the call came over their radio. It was a 10-10—NYPD lingo for man with a gun or shots fired. The dispatcher reported there were five men involved. They were last seen at the Ravenwood Houses. Mike and his partner made a fast U-turn and sped to the scene.

"When we came around the corner, we saw five guys running," Mike said. "When they saw the police car, they broke into two groups. We jammed on the brakes and got out of the car. I took off after three of them, my partner chased the other two. When I got close enough so they could hear me, I pulled my gun and told them to get down on the ground. With those odds, one against three, there was no way I could search them or put them in handcuffs. I hid partially behind a dumpster so I had some cover, but one guy began getting fidgety, and that made me nervous. I couldn't tell if he was going to run or go for his gun. Then out of nowhere, somewhere behind me, I heard the sound of a round getting loaded into a shotgun and someone telling those three guys on the ground not to move. I turned slightly to my left. I saw a uniform. There is no way to describe how happy I was to see that officer and hear that round going into that shotgun."

The officer who saved Mike's life was Tom Langone, a veteran of Emergency Service and one of the twenty-three NYPD officers who died just one year later on September 11, 2001. Many years later Mike would say, "I wanted ESU so I could help other cops like Tom helped me."

Mike Morra speaks four languages, including Spanish, Italian, and Farsi, the most widely spoken language in Iran and Afghanistan and the second most prevalent tongue in Iraq, Yemen, and the United Arab Emirates. After the attacks of 9/11, when the Department learned that Mike spoke Farsi, there was enormous pressure for him to go to the Intelligence Unit. But he kept thinking about Tom Langone, and he held out for Emergency Service.

* * *

When the trams malfunctioned that April evening in 2006, it had only been six months since Mike finished Special Tactics School, a rigorous seven-month training program for all incoming ESU cops. The program covers everything from heavy weapons training to tips on how to deal with emotionally disturbed people who have gone off their meds. But he had been a cop for eleven years, and he had worked in Queens. He knew exactly where he and his partner needed to go to rescue the people in the disabled tram.

Many agencies responded to the tram disaster. Over one hundred police officers, scores of firefighters, the NYPD's Harbor and Aviation Units, the Police Commissioner, and even the Mayor showed up to help. However, ultimately, the rescue of the panicked people stranded in the tram would fall to Mike and Mike Iliadis,Ray Flood, and Dave Fiol, three of his colleagues from Emergency Service.

With almost seventy lives in jeopardy, scores of officers rushed to the scene. When an incident occurs with the potential for great loss of life, officers can usually tell by the dispatcher's tone. "You knew right away this was bad," Mike said. "She kept saying it over and over. 'Seventy people, seventy people, seventy people.' You could hear it in her voice. She was nervous."

A quick inspection revealed the diesel generator that powered the tramline had blown, preventing the haul rope from moving the two cars along the track. The backup diesel had stalled, the brake would not release, and the tram operator's radio was out. The officers discovered that the rescue cage had never been assembled by the tram company. It was still laying in pieces on the ground. That compounded the problem considerably.

The cops knew they could get the people stranded in the tram above the street down without much trouble; they could use a crane. But the tram stranded above the East River was going to be a more difficult challenge. With police boats circling in the river below, the four ESU officers began assembling the rescue cage. Three hours later, the last bolt was screwed in. The men were drenched in sweat as they loaded in hundreds of feet of rope, harnesses, safety nets, baby food, diapers, bottles, and baggies. All these things would be needed since the passengers had been trapped for so many hours. Once the officers torque-wrenched the cage up onto the cables and hooked themselves in with the harnesses, they were ready to roll.

It was ten minutes past eight in the evening and almost dark. The cops got into the rescue cage and began their slow trek on the cable line out over the river. "It was running on a separate diesel generator," Mike said. "Once we got that going, it started moving." A crowd gathered on the ground and looked on in horror as they watched the cage sway back and forth as it inched its way over to the tram.

Mike admits to having a few nervous moments when the tram's mechanic admitted he was unsure how the cage would get by the first tower. It was hundreds feet to the second tower, but the three officers with Mike were among the most experienced in the Emergency Service Unit. He knew if anybody could get those people back down on the ground, they would be the ones to do it. Contrary to popular myth, not all cops have the guts to run toward screams and gunfire, but if there was a test for bravery, a way to determine who will risk their lives for others, there's no doubt Morra, Iliadis, Flood, and Fiol would all score high.

"There's no one who's worked with Mike Iliadis who doesn't come away impressed," Morra said. "Nothing gets to him. Under pressure he stays real calm. Same with Dave Fiol and Ray Flood. When this incident occurred, Ray had been in ESU for six years. He's a rock when things get intense. Dave's a former Marine and extremely disciplined."

Mike explains that for cops to perform where there is a good chance of injury or even death, it's essential to have confidence in yourself and your equipment, but mostly you have to trust your partners. "You have to know your team will perform," he said.

As the steel cage moved out over the dark river, the terrified passengers were able to make eye contact with their saviors. For Emergency Service officers, dangling hundreds of feet above the icy East River is something they train to do. It's a little scarier for civilians suspended over the water two hundred and fifty feet up in the air.

As they got near the tram, the officers pulled the cage up as close as they could. The two Mikes put on their harnesses and hooked themselves to the cage. If they fell, they would still be attached. Morra leaned out and tried to pull the emergency cage closer, but there was still two-and-a-half feet between them, and the tram was a full foot-and-a-half lower than the cage. "I could barely reach it," Mike remembered. "Mike Iliadis was holding on to me. Finally I was able to grab it."

The two officers hoisted themselves over to the tram. Their first task was to create a safety net between the tram and the rescue cage. If someone slipped, the net would prevent them from plunging into the river below. Ray and Dave passed strips of webbed netting to the two Mikes. It was painstaking work that took close to an hour. Once they were convinced the net would do its job, they were ready to start moving people out of the tram.

Mike Morra instructed the passengers to get up one at a time and crawl out the window into the gap where Mike and Mike were waiting for them. As they came through the window, Morra and Iliadis grabbed each person as best they could and pushed them out and over to Ray and Dave, who were waiting for them inside the rescue cage on the other side of the net. One by one, the frightened, hungry, thirsty passengers made it over.

Then it was a young father's turn. He had a small baby clenched tight in his arms. The officers told him to hand them the baby. Once he was safely inside the rescue cage, they would hand him his child. At the time Mike Morra had two young daughters, and he knew what was going through the young dad's mind. "Can you imagine being stranded that far up over the East River?" he asked. "It's pitch dark and you have to hand your baby up to a person you don't know and can barely see? I'm not sure I could have done it."

Morra summoned up all his negotiating skills, but things were not going well with the man and his child. At some point he had to face the fact the man was not going to let go. He changed tactics. He stopped negotiating and began issuing orders. "I told him, 'My name is Michael. I'm trained to do these rescues. You have to hand your baby to me. We have everything under control. We've done this before. You have no choice. Give me your baby.'" The distraught father finally handed his little girl to Mike.

The entire operation took twelve hours. The cops were drained from the physical strain of the grueling work, but they were proud, too. Every one of the sixty-nine people was safely back on the ground. None of them had been injured.

* * *

Law enforcement is a profession that attracts people with deep reserves of courage who are willing to take big risks for the people they serve, but the cops assigned to Emergency Service take the notion of bravery to a different level. Nearly every incident they respond to is a high-risk, life-and-death scenario. They are regularly called upon to perform such tasks as dissuading a potential jumper perched on a high ledge, rescuing a child taken hostage, or freeing a family from the wreckage of a car accident. They will rush to help construction workers dying under scaffolding that collapsed or free severely injured office workers from an elevator that just plummeted forty floors.

Everyone in Emergency Service is a trained emergency medical technician, and every officer is a heavy weapons expert. A military background, especially a stint with the Marines or Special Forces helps, as does a basic knowledge of rope climbing, carpentry, and electronics. Staff are required to know the difference between a paranoid schizophrenic and someone with bi-polar disorder and the appropriate tactics to use in each case. As one observer said, "ESU folks are out there doing God's work."

The physical demands of such specialized work require these officers to be extremely agile and able to remain calm under tremendous pressure. Considering the fact that ESU officers respond to lots of calls that require them to get up on top of bridges and skyscrapers, good balance is critical.

During his career, Mike Morra has dangled and rappelled off tall buildings and bridges scores of times. He remembers one man who was determined to end it all off an overpass in the Bronx. He almost succeeded, but Mike and his partner, Anthony Mazza, made it there in time. "We grabbed him just as he pushed himself off the ledge," Mike said. "I had him by his belt and pants, and somehow we dragged him back up, which wasn't easy. He weighed over three hundred pounds." Since that incident in 2007, Mike has never missed a day of work, and no one has heard him complain, but his back still hurts and his doctor finally told him he may never be free of pain again.

It's not easy to get assigned to the Emergency Service Unit. One year there were four thousand applicants for fifteen positions. Officers must be on the job for at least five years and have many, if not all, of the skills previously mentioned just to be considered. There are twenty-two tests, including exams for mechanical aptitude and agility. Mike's family, including his father, was in the building trades, and his father had worked as an electrician. Mike was a serious runner, and months before the test he began swimming five times a week. "I did everything I could to score high on every one of those tests," he said.

Mike was a natural for police work. Along with compassion for victims and the courage to help them, he's gained a strong work ethic from his parents, a value they passed on to their four children. His dad, Alberto Morra, came to the United States from Italy in 1972, leaving his young family behind. He was a carpenter for the School District during the day and a landscaper at night and weekends. Every penny Alberto wasn't sending back to his wife, Lucia, in Italy, he saved for a down payment on a house. It took five years, but finally he bought his house, and Lucia, sons Vinnie and Mike, and daughters Maria and Lorena arrived in the United States.

Today Vinnie is the CEO of a health management company, and his sisters are both stay- at-home moms, but Mike had other ambitions. "The United

States is such an incredible place," he said. "There's so much opportunity here, but I think most people take it for granted. Maybe it's because I wasn't born here that I felt I had to do something with my life that would help my country."

Mike was hired by the New York City Police Department in 1995. After the six-month stint in the Police Academy, his first assignment was the 114th Precinct in Astoria, one of the most racially mixed neighborhoods in the world, located in the northwestern corner of the borough of Queens.

Mike remembers his first weeks on the street. "There were shootings, robberies, and drugs," he said. But even with all the violence and mayhem, Mike believed his most important weapons were his mouth and his brain. He's still proud when he can control a situation with his wits rather than his firearm.

One incident happened when he had only been on the job a year. Another rookie walking a beat spotted a young man with a large knife, breaking into an office building. He called for backup, and Mike and his partner, Rich Troise, were dispatched to the scene. By the time they got there, the suspect had entered the building, and two secretaries had barricaded themselves in the bathroom. As Mike and Rich approached the office, they could see the young man swinging the knife through the air. It was big, and it looked sharp. Mike was nervous, but something in his gut, some sort of instinct, told him to start talking.

There are close to one million law enforcement officers in the United States. During their training, every one of them learns the twenty-one-foot rule: if a potential assailant with a knife gets closer than twenty-one feet, you may not have time to draw your weapon to save your life. In those situations officers are trained to shoot, and that action is almost always considered justified. Despite the threat, Mike and Rich kept talking.

Mike explains that for police officers to be successful in situations like this, it's important to find something the person cares about so you can start a conversation. "We never pulled our weapons," Mike said. "We kept trying to think of things to say. We found out he had a girlfriend. We asked him about her. I remember Rich kept saying, 'Your girlfriend would not want you to be doing this. You need to call and talk to her.'" They knew the bonds were starting to develop when the man also told them his close friend had just died. They dropped the girlfriend and began to focus on the friend.

"We told him how disappointed his friend would be if he could see him now, that he would want him to drop the knife. You could see him start to calm down. Over and over again, we said, 'Put the knife down.'" It took over forty minutes. Finally he let it fall to the floor."

Most police officers never fire their guns during their entire careers. Every day, however, they negotiate and mediate often with desperate people in raged or psychotic stated. Mike's always felt his job is to calm things down. "If I have to make an arrest, I tell a few jokes and, if I have to, a few fibs. If I can get them laughing on the way to Central Booking, I'm having a real good day."

The fibs, Mike says, come in handy on any number of occasions. "If someone gets arrested late in the week, sometimes they get nervous if they realize they are going to spend the weekend in jail. I can't tell you how many times I've said, 'Hey, there's night court today. Don't worry. You'll get out.'"

The best cops out there will try everything to end a threat without using force, but sometimes there is no other option. "We got one call," Mike remembered. "A man locked himself in an apartment and was threatening to kill himself. We talked to him for hours, but right from the beginning, everyone on that call knew it was probably going to be hopeless. It turns out we were right."

Morra explains there's so much about law enforcement work that requires making your best judgment with the few facts you have. "Sometimes we have only seconds to decide what tactics to use. What's their age? What's the nature of the crime? Do they have hostages? Are small kids involved? If you decide to hold off and negotiate, you try to put yourself in their position. You try to find something in common to talk about."

The officers learned the man threatening to kill himself was a traffic agent. Despite the fact that they all worked for the city, he would not let the cops in. Mike talked to him through the door. "I told him I was a cop and I hated my job, too." But there was no response from the other side. After three hours Mike and his partner made the difficult decision to breach the door. The officers cut a hole, retrieved their body bunkers, positioned them in front of their bodies, drew their weapons, and went in. As one seasoned veteran said, "When you gotta go in, you gotta go in."

For most cops, "taking the door" is one of the most dangerous but exciting parts of law enforcement work. It is always accompanied by the adrenaline rush that comes when a situation can turn dangerous. Ed Conlon, the New

York City cop who wrote the best-selling memoir *Blue Blood*, says, "It's the most thrilling part of the warrant, and even of the job, as far as it can be predicted or planned. A moment that's a blur of adrenaline and instinct."

* * *

While a law enforcement career is often rewarding and exciting, there is a reason the job always makes the top five on any list of stressful occupations. The grueling pressure of shift work, working on holidays, seeing people at the worst moments of their lives, and coming face-to-face with heartbreaking cruelty and violence take its toll.

And there's the endless paperwork. Everything a law enforcement officer does has to be written up and filed, sometimes in many places. The complexities of getting a warrant, which some say is the most important skill in law enforcement, can be mind-boggling. A thorough understanding of the law is required, along with how the law has been interpreted and the ability to make the case in writing. Any officer who has worked hard on an investigation, meticulously gathering the evidence and building a case against someone they know is breaking the law, only to fail when it's time to get the warrant, will tell you it's one of the most frustrating and disheartening parts of the job.

"There's one case that still bugs me,' Morra said. "A bad guy who escaped justice. We needed a little more evidence and we would have had him, but our informant took off and he got away." It happened when Mike was working on a federal burglary team. The man they were after was stealing gold jewelry from people's homes, sending it in Colombia where it was melted down, and then shipped back to New York. He was running the operation out of a storefront that doubled as a pawnshop in Queens. Hundreds of thousands of dollars of gold was involved.

The cops were working with a confidential informant who was selling the stolen gold to the man. But after the second sale, the informant learned his cover was blown.

"We had one last meeting with him," Mike said. "I remember he was sitting in the backseat of our police car. He told us the Colombians found out he was working with us and they knew where his family lived. He was afraid they were going to kill them. He asked to be let out of the car." Mike pulled over, and their informant disappeared. They never saw him again. The case still haunts Mike. "We were so close. We almost had our warrant."

Every once in a while Mike puts a call into his old unit. He tells them if they ever find the guy, he wants to be the one to bring him in.

* * *

Over time, cops learn to tune out abuse from the public. After a stop for speeding or a ticket for illegal parking, the outbursts of, "Don't you have a terrorist to catch?" or "Isn't there a bank robber you should be chasing?" or that old standby, "Don't you know I pay your salary?," rarely get a rise out of a cop who's been on the job for a while. Yet there are times when even an easygoing and disciplined officer like Mike Morra gets annoyed.

Mike is still angry about the woman who came up to him when he was on patrol with a group of heavily armed officers outside Bloomingdale's. It was ten months after the attacks of September 11.

"You could tell she was upset as she walked over to me," Mike said. "She asked me what we were doing there. I told her we were part of a team that was working to stop another terrorist attack. She laughed. I asked her if she remembered 9/11, and she laughed at me again. She said there was no terrorist attack. September 11, she said, was a Bush ploy, an inside job. I pointed to the other officers who were there and said we had sworn to protect her and even give our lives for her. She just looked at me like I was crazy. She said, 'Why would you do that?'

"Just a short time after dealing with that woman at Bloomingdale's, I was patrolling on Wall Street. Along comes a group of men. They're waving signs that the U.S. government had planned the attacks on the Trade Center. It's hard to explain the emotions you go through dealing with people like that. I wanted to tell that woman at Bloomingdale's and those guys on Wall Street that fourteen of my friends died saving people like them from those towers. They were really good friends, and they are gone. But about all I could do was tell them to move along, that if they interfered with traffic, I would lock them up. When I find myself getting emotional, I try to remember some good advice I got when I first came on the job about how to deal with all the nuts you meet on the street. Treat them like you would your own mother, until they force you to do otherwise."

* * *

One of the most traumatic situations any officer will face is having to kill to protect their own life or someone else's. Mike Morra feels fortunate that he has never been in that situation. "Overall, I've been very lucky," he says. "I've been shot at, had my head opened up, and broken my hand, but so far I have never had to take a life. I'm really grateful for that. I don't know how I would react if I had to kill someone, and I hope I never have to find out.

"Having to kill another human being—even if you shoot someone who's trying to kill you—takes a terrible toll," he said. "I still think about this sergeant who got shot by a twenty-one-year-old. He returned fire. It was fatal. He would never admit that something was wrong, but everyone knew. He was never the same after he killed that boy.

"I don't think I've ever been afraid. Apprehensive may be a better word. My biggest fear is that someone with me will get hurt. Look, I'm not a big tough guy, and there have been a few times I've been scared. But I always knew it was going to be all right because I had such good people with me."

* * *

It's no secret that a career in law enforcement can be destructive for the people who choose that life. After several years in a job where there are hours and sometimes days of boredom punctuated by the worst terror imaginable, along with the unrelenting cruelty and violence that seem to be everywhere when cops go to work, it is understandable that some law enforcement officers will dull the pain by having too many drinks after work.

Although Mike Morra been as up close to all the rough stuff the job can dish out, his only indulgences are an occasional Tylenol PM if he can't sleep after a grueling day at work or a little red wine at his mother's house when he and his family go there on Sunday for dinner. "I have no police in my family, and none of my friends are cops," Mike says. "When I leave the job, I really leave it." His wife, Lori, teaches Spanish and Italian in a Port Washington, Long Island, middle school, and she is proud her husband is a cop. Mike loves to cook and read, he is a serious runner, and he takes great pleasure in coaching his daughters' teams. Marina is into basketball, Michaela plays soccer, and the youngest, Lianna, has started kicking her older sister's soccer ball around. On top of that, he's started to do some acting.

Despite his interests outside of law enforcement and the downside that comes with a life in the field, there's no way Mike would be anything but a cop. He says that those times when you help someone, save a life, or get a bad guy off the street make up for everything else.

He has had many rewarding moments, but one he still thinks about happened back in 2000 when he was assigned to the Robbery Task Force. "There was a guy in the neighborhood who had done over twenty robberies," Mike said. "He used knives, guns, and mace to hold up cabdrivers and rob them. My captain wanted this guy off the street so bad he offered to buy a case of beer for anyone who caught him.

"One night when we were out on patrol, my partner and I saw a cab drive off. There was a man in the back seat. He looked like he was lunging toward the driver, and we thought it might be the guy. We got into our car and chased the cab. As we pulled up, he was stabbing the cabdriver in the face. We tore out of our car, pulled open the door, and took him out at gunpoint. As they were taking the bleeding cabdriver away in the ambulance, the man reached out his hand to me. He said, 'Thank you so much for what you did. I never thought I would see my kids again.'

"The satisfaction we both got from saving that cabdriver and knowing he would survive and go home to his family—there is no amount of money in the world that can compare to that sense of accomplishment. It's the feeling every cop has after an experience like that—that we did something important, something that really helped someone else."

Mike and his future wife Lori on the proud day he graduated from the NYPD Police Academy, March 16, 1996.

Mike Morra and his three daughters on Halloween night, 2008. Left to right: Marina, Lianna and Michaela. All the girls are showing a keen interest in sports.

Above, Mike Morra and his fellow officers approach the disabled tram in the rescue cage. One tram was disabled over a city street but this one was dangling 250 feet above the East River. It took the cops 12 hours to get everyone over to the rescue cage and back on the ground. At right, officers bring a boy to safety. The youngster was trapped in the tram for almost ten hours.

Photo courtesy Matt Kobel: NYPD / Emergency Service Unit

Mike and his team the day after the Roosevelt Tram incident. Left to right: Dave Fiol, Ray Flood, Mike Morra, and Mike Iliadis.

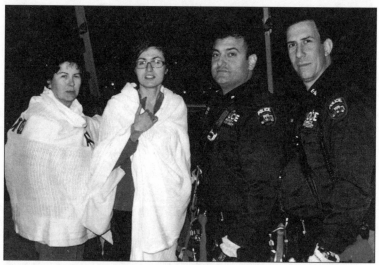

Mike Morra (second from right) and Mike Iliadis with grateful tourists from Portugal who were rescued after almost 12 hours in the tram above the East River.

Above, Mike Morra, on right, second row kneeling, and other members of the NYPD's Air Support Team. Below, Mike rappelling from an NYPD helicopter.

Mike and his team practicing high-rise rescues atop the Brooklyn Bridge. These skills are crucial for officers like Mike Morra who are frequently asked to rescue suicidal people who are attempting to jump off one of New York City's many high bridges.

Chapter Three

SAM PANCHAL: The Evidence Collector

"Courage is the art of being the only one who
knows you're scared to death." —Harold Wilson

Sam felt the waves of nausea rolling over him and knew he was going to throw up. He told his partner to pull over. Jimmy, a detective with the NYPD's Special Fraud Squad and a nineteen-year veteran of the force, thought Sam was kidding. They'd been working together closely for months, and the older detective had never heard his younger cigar-loving colleague complain he wasn't feeling well. He kept driving, Sam puked, and the sickening smell would linger for months.

Sam Panchal and Jim Feasel were investigating what they thought was an auto insurance fraud scam. Sam had gone undercover to collect the evidence the NYPD hoped would crack the case. He had been successfully passing himself off as someone who was looking for easy money. "I had become part of their operation," he said. "I'd worked for them for months, but they'd never invited me to go anywhere. Then out of the blue they tell me, 'Come on, you go with us. We'll go for tea.'"

He felt he had no choice. When you meet Sam, you can't imagine him afraid. Everything about him exudes self-confidence. As his former commander Louis Vozza said, "When I first met Sam, I thought, here's a guy who is absolutely fearless." But the invitation to the tea party had made him nervous. He had no radio, no cell phone, no pager. Worst of all, there'd been no time to tell Jimmy about the plan. If they figured out he was a cop, Sam would have had no way to call for backup.

Four Bengali men had driven him to a diner in Elmhurst, a section of New York heavily populated with Indians and Pakistanis. "They told me I had to go," Sam said. "They wanted me to meet the number one guy. I thought they'd found out I was a cop."

A Pakistani waitress had brought an assortment of things to eat—strange nuts and crackers and a really foul-smelling beverage. Sam had tried to pass, but they poured it and he drank it. The concoction was vile. "I never did know what was in that tea," he said. "But it was bad. I was sick for two days."

* * *

Sam had only been on the street two years when he got the undercover assignment. He was born in India, where his extended family is from, but some people assume he's Hispanic. But no one who talks to him for even a minute has any doubt that wherever his roots are, Sam is a New Yorker.

Sam explained that back when Jimmy called to see if he would consider taking on the undercover assignment, it helped he was a young guy with only a couple of years on the job. "I wasn't talking the talk yet," he said. "They could mold me so I wouldn't seem like a cop."

The NYPD got involved in the case after someone working on the inside of the insurance scam agreed to cooperate with the FBI. "The feds tried to introduce an undercover but it didn't work," Sam said. "He didn't speak their language. That's when they came to the NYPD for help."

About all they knew at the time was that the operation was run by a group of secretive well-organized Indian men. The insurance claims they filed were running into the hundreds of millions of dollars. Detectives assigned to the NYPD's Special Fraud Squad were familiar with all kinds of criminal scams run by Russians, Italians, and Asians. But Indians? In the early 1990s, this was something new.

The case ended up on the desk of Jim Feasel, a seasoned detective who had been working with the Organized Crime Control Bureau for five years. Detective Feasel was considered the NYPD's top investigator on insurance fraud. He knew he had to send in an undercover, but no one knew how many Indian cops they had. The detective searched the NYPD's massive database and discovered that among the Department's forty thousand sworn personnel, there were only three officers of Indian descent. Feasel called all three. Sam Panchal, a rookie officer still in his twenties, was the only one who called back.

On paper, Sam didn't look like he was ready for such a complicated dangerous assignment. He was young and had been on the job only a short time. The previous two years he'd worked in a radio car in the South Bronx. But like most people who meet Sam Panchal, Feasel was impressed. When he learned Sam speaks three Indian dialects—Hindi, Punjabi, and Urdu—it was even better.

"His grandfather was one hundred years old and spoke Hindi to him every day," Feasel said. "He had this big, outgoing personality. You could just tell he had guts. I thought right away he might be able do the job."

There are thirty-five different dialects in India alone. Bangladesh and Pakistan have their own languages. "Sammy can tell Sikhs from Hindus just from what they're wearing on their wrist," Feasel said. "As he sat there explaining to me what certain feathers meant in the turbans and a bunch of other obscure details about clothing and customs, I knew he was the guy."

But understanding a different culture is one thing, and being ready emotionally for work of this intensity and risk is another. Feasel admits he was worried about sending this young cop on such a dangerous assignment. But the insurance companies were demanding that something be done, and Sam was their only hope.

Once Sam was approved for the assignment, the NYPD began to construct his new identity. Every law enforcement agency goes to great lengths to protect its undercover officers, and the NYPD does more than most. Within weeks, Officer Sam Panchal of the New York City Police Department ceased to exist. His name disappeared from the vast bureaucracy, and for almost a year he picked up his paycheck in cash, always at a different location.

Sam had a new identity, but the job was in the same neighborhood where he lived with his family. That made everything much riskier. Ten years after he went undercover, Sam is married with two young children. "If I'd had the kids then," he says, "I would have had to seriously think it over."

For a year, his life was totally transformed and not for the better. He was forced to retreat into a shell, which was not easy for such a gregarious twenty-three-year-old who loved nothing better than to go out with his friends, have a few drinks, and smoke a cigar.

"For almost a year I had no life," Sam remembered. "I couldn't hang out with my friends or take my grandfather or parents shopping. After a while—probably because you're lonely—you start getting friendly with the same people you are working hard to lock up. I knew they were really bad guys, but when contact is that close, bonds develop."

Cops who go undercover say the hardest part of the job is the isolation that often leads to becoming friends with the enemy. Sam said Jimmy met with him almost every day and worked hard to keep his head on straight. "When I'd go weak and say, 'Are you sure we should be chasing them? They seem okay to me,' Jimmy would go crazy and tell me one more time all the bad things they had done."

The Department was worried, too. Jim Feasel was constantly summoned to meetings with the Chief of Detectives, a high-ranking commander who oversees the NYPD's massive five-thousand person Detective Bureau. "Everyone knew we were sending this kid into the belly of the beast," Feasel said. "It was a nerve-racking year."

* * *

The scam seemed simple: filing insurance claims on behalf of people who didn't exist for accidents that never happened. Thousands of claims were filed for visits to nonexistent doctors, travel expenses for trips that weren't taken, massages that were never given, and prescriptions that were never filled. A limousine company was the front.

Once he got his new identity, Sam went to the limo company and applied for a job. The scene was tense. Sam told them he was Pakistani, but they weren't buying it. "I think they thought I was Hispanic. They seemed very suspicious. But I spoke their language and I talked real fast. I could tell they were wondering about my heavy New York accent, so I told them I had come to this country when I was young. I kept saying, 'I'm here to make money.'"

As they went back and forth, at some point Sam sensed he had to take control of the interaction. "I told them to take it or leave it," he said. That approach seemed to work. Sam got hired.

In the beginning, the NYPD thought the only victims were the innocent people who were watching their insurance premiums go through the roof. The insurance companies were paying on the bogus claims, taking massive losses and passing them on to consumers. That injustice alone was enough to fire up Jimmy and Sam for the mission. But when Sam was told by the boss to find people on the street and offer them $25 for each X-ray and then tell them they had to do it five times a day, they realized there was another group of victims—people whose lives were threatened.

Sam said it was only when he was deep into it that he realized they were preying on illegal immigrants. "These people were desperate for money. I'm sure a lot of them were just trying to feed their families, and $25 for getting an X-ray must have looked pretty good. One guy got seven in one day. He went home with $175 in cash and a lethal dose of radiation. It was bad. We had to stop it."

When Sam and Jim learned people were getting zapped so many times a day, they wanted to call in homicide. "I still get angry about what they were doing to those people," he said. "There is no way a body could take all that radiation. I remember Sammy even tried to get the guys to use animals instead of people. They told him to forget it. The bone structure was not the same, and the X-rays would look fake."

Right up until the morning they were arrested, the bad guys never knew Sam was a cop. He had finally convinced them he was Pakistani, not an easy feat when you're Hindu. He had to keep reminding himself not to wear his om, a crosslike symbol of Hindu affiliation.

It hadn't taken long for Sam to start rising through the ranks of the criminal enterprise. He'd started out as a street-level guy—a runner looking for people to be X-rayed. By the end of the investigation, he was hanging out with the man who ran the whole operation.

His job description got more diverse. He no longer spent all his time hustling people off the street to get X-rays. He was setting up phony marriages and getting bogus green cards. "At least once a week, someone would ask me if I knew an American girl who would agree to marry one of his friends.

The price for a fake marriage to an American was ten thousand bucks," Sam said.

The organization was running five medical clinics in Queens. They processed people all day long. The phony clinics assigned phony names to the X-rays. Then they were sent to phony law firms who then filed claims with the insurance companies. It wasn't long before the cops knew this was going to be way bigger than a simple auto insurance scam.

* * *

Over the eight months that Sam was undercover, Jim Feasel watched over him like a big brother. One day the boss of the insurance fraud operation rented a yacht for a lavish birthday party for his five-year-old daughter. He insisted that Sam go. Sam was willing, but Feasel was opposed, and the department agreed. Sam would have been out on the water all by himself, and that was too dangerous. Together they came up with a plausible excuse why Sam was unable to go on the boat.

Sam knew the investigation was spreading and law enforcement agencies in other parts of the country were getting involved. What he didn't know was the FBI had put so much pressure on the Virginia wing of the operation, some of their top people had been sent to New York to avoid getting arrested.

Now people Sam didn't know were asking who he was and where he was from. "They patted me down, but I came right back at them. I asked who they were and what they were doing." The aggressive approach seemed to work again. After a few weeks, the Virginia contingent left him alone.

"From day one Jimmy always told me that if I felt uncomfortable, I could get out," Sam said. "'This case is nothing,' he'd say. 'It's your life that's important.' He kept telling me there were no second chances in this line of work. I felt the whole time the investigation was handled the right way."

When things got really intense, Jim Feasel was a master at calming Sam down. He knew his job was to try and keep the young cop relaxed and focused. "There were some times I would come out and I'd be off the wall," Sam said. "Jimmy would always be calm. 'What's up?' he'd say. 'Relax. Calm down. Let's go talk.' Sometimes we'd sit in his car for an hour just shooting the breeze while my heartbeat got back to normal."

The thrill of knowing they are getting close to taking a bad guy off the street or saving an innocent person from harm always makes cops' hearts race. When Jim and Sam realized they were about to blow the lid off a medical insurance fraud scheme that involved hundreds of millions of dollars and criminals from coast to coast, the adrenaline was definitely raging.

"Along with processing the phony accident claims, these people were selling alien registration cards, green cards, passports, guns, and drugs," Sam said. "It just snowballed. By the time we were through, the investigation had widened to eleven states with hundreds of suspects."

When it became apparent that the crime ring extended across the country, the FBI, state and local agencies, Immigration, and the ATF worked together to coordinate the arrests.

"When most people think of Indians, they think of engineers or computer scientists, not organized crime figures," Sam continued. "No one ever expected such serious crimes to be taking place in the Indian community."

As officials made plans to arrest the suspects, Sam went into hiding. "It was an emotional roller coaster from beginning to end," he said. "Two days before the arrests went down, I hadn't slept in a week. The whole thing got to be an obsession. I was calling Jimmy in the middle of the night. But he always took my call, and he was always patient and generous with his time."

Sam accumulated an overwhelming amount of evidence. "We had pictures, we had videos, we had tapes of phone conversations—over a hundred in all," he said. The evidence was so overwhelming that when the arrests went down and the suspects found out that Sam Panchal was a New York City cop, every person arrested pled guilty. The case was a prosecutor's dream.

When the operation was over, a $100-million scam involving much more than auto insurance fraud had been uncovered. Over one hundred people were arrested by federal and local officers in an eleven-state, predawn sweep. "It took only eight months," Feasel said. "Sammy got them on audio, he got them on video, and he had a firsthand account."

Sam says his relationship with Jim Feasel made a big difference in his career. "A lot of cops don't want to be bothered," he said. "They have the attitude, 'Great, now I have to watch my partner and the bad guy.' But Jimmy was never like that. He showed me the ropes. He taught me how to talk to people, how to relate to people. Without those skills, you can never do good detective work."

As Sam bounced back from his eight months undercover, he was promoted to detective and assigned to one of the NYPD's most exclusive units, TARU, the Technical Assistance Response Unit. For the next decade he would set up surveillance equipment, bug the offices and homes of mobsters and other criminals, and wire up cars for audio and video.

Dave Fitzpatrick, a twenty-year veteran of the NYPD, headed up the Photographic Division of TARU for many years. Dave said when Sam joined TARU, it was like getting the first pick in the NBA draft. "The guy is amazing," Fitzpatrick said. "When it comes to electronics, there's nothing he can't do."

Lieutenant Louis Vozza also worked closely with Sam during his stint at TARU. "Sammy came across as very savvy for someone so young," Vozza said, adding that during his two-decade career with the NYPD, Sam was the only person he met who could do the technical stuff and shine as an investigator as well. "It's very unusual to have both those skills," he said. "Sammy could do both. It wasn't just video. He did audio and tracking, too. No one did it faster or better."

When he got a surveillance assignment, the first thing Sam did was check out the location. He would look for an object where he could insert a camera or an audio or tracking device. None of this equipment can be bought in stores, so once he cased out the location, he went back to his workshop at TARU headquarters, designed the equipment himself, and then planted it so no one knew it was there. "Keep in mind that he was doing all this stuff physically by himself," Vozza said. "He'd assess the situation, get all the different equipment he needed, and then build these things—cameras, audio machines, and tracking devices."

When they watched Sam work, his colleagues would just stand there in awe. Louis Vozza said that if he was honest, he would have to admit that no one had any idea what the young detective was doing. "But Sammy was patient and generous with his time," Vozza said. "He always tried to explain, and he always delivered. No matter how complicated it was, he did the job."

Because Sam was fast, most jobs went off without a hitch. But there were times things got tense. "I remember one job where Sammy was installing cameras and recorders in a well-known organized crime figure's social club," Vozza said. "We were almost done when a commander called on his radio and said the suspect was unexpectedly returning and we had to clear out. We all left the building, but Sam didn't make it out. As the suspects were coming in the door, Sam was running down to the basement, where he hid for hours.

Those guys were right above him, and that was dangerous."

* * *

Sam's choice of a career in law enforcement came as a shock to his family. "It's not acceptable in the Indian culture," Sam explained. "You are supposed to be an engineer, a doctor, or a professor. Police officer is not on the list."

But Sam had always dreamed of being a cop. Like so many people who are drawn to law enforcement, it was more of a calling, a passion, something deep in his soul that drew him to this dangerous and stressful life. "It's all I ever wanted to do," he said.

When he signed up for the police exam, he was twenty years old. He was working as a technician for the phone company and living with his parents. It wasn't long before his boss realized he had a special knack for electronics and he started to get promotions. But Sam was bored. He kept thinking about the police department.

Despite being extraordinarily close to his family, Sam never told them what he was doing. For months he hid his uniform in the car and changed his clothes on the way to the academy. He knew his father, who had come to this country with nothing and twenty years later was a senior vice president at MetLife, would never understand his desire to go into law enforcement. All the time that Sam was training at the police academy, his parents thought he was still working at the phone company.

Finally Sam had to tell the truth. His mother was getting suspicious. She knew something wasn't right. Once they got over the shock that their son was going to be a police officer and would be making only half of what he did at the phone company, they began to worry. Sam said they thought he was going to get killed.

His first assignment out of the Academy was the midnight shift at the 43rd Precinct in the South Bronx. For Sam's parents, that was the worst district they could have put him in. But for the rookie cop, getting assigned to one of the toughest precincts in the city was a dream come true.

"I went to work at night and got off duty at eight in the morning," he said. "Every shift we were out there nonstop. There was crack cocaine, heroin, and other drugs. We were called out to a lot of shootings. One of my first nights on patrol, we responded to a call for shots fired. When we got to the location, there was a man lying on the street. I got there just in time to see him take his last breath. Twenty years later, I can still see him, all alone, lying on the sidewalk.

"While we were in the South Bronx, we saw a lot of violence, people wasted by drugs, poor people getting preyed on. It was almost overwhelming at times. But there's a thrill to taking the bad guys out that's hard to explain to someone who has never been a cop. Getting a criminal off the streets—it's as great a feeling today as when I first came on the job."

But there's a lot more to police work than the thrill of locking up bad guys. A lot of the work is emotionally devastating, and every law enforcement officer in the United States would agree it's the calls where kids have been hurt—whether they've been in a car crash, injured by parental neglect, or become innocent victims of violence—that haunt them the most.

One call Sam still thinks about was a domestic violence call. Ironically, it was an Indian couple. "It was pre–OJ Simpson, and things were a little different then," he said. "We got to the scene, and this guy had beaten his wife pretty badly. Despite being really banged up, she kept yelling at us, 'No, no, please. Don't take him to jail.'

"My partner took the guy in one room, and I took the woman in the other. He started yelling at her across the rooms in an Indian dialect that he would beat her even more if he got locked up. He had no idea that I was Indian and could understand everything he was saying. Later I found out he thought I was Hispanic. We ended up locking him up, and I took great pleasure in telling him a few things in his native language while we were driving to the booking center."

* * *

For pure excitement, not much beats a career in law enforcement in New York City, and Sam still gets fired up when he talks about his work. "My run has been unbelievable," he says. "This job has given me so much opportunity and I still have such a passion for it. I love the thrill—the good guy–bad guy thing—and I still want to help people. Where else could I get to work hostage jobs and kidnappings? Where else could I break into suspects' homes and set up hidden cameras and microphones? Where else but being a cop could I be out here doing battle with the real bad guys and get paid for it?"

Everyone who knows Sam Panchal agrees his legacy is secure. For those who have had the pleasure of working with him, he is known as a guy who gives 100 percent, the one who does his best, the one who always takes that extra step.

Jim Feasel (right) and Sam are deep in the middle of their undercover project but they were able to take some time to attend Sam's brother's wedding in January, 1994. Sam remembers the wedding as a brief moment of normalcy in the midst of the most stressful, intense eight months of his life. Sam credits Feasel with keeping him calm and committed on his worst days.

When he's not working, Sam is off having fun with his wife Alisha and his children – son Jaan and daughter Aniah, pictured above. Sam likes to brag the family has been to every amusement and water park in the Northeast.

Sam Panchal says the day he was promoted to the rank of First Grade Detective in September, 2006, by Police Commissioner Raymond W. Kelly, was one of the highlights of his life.

Sam and his wife Alisha. Panchal says his wife is proud he's a cop and has been enormously supportive of his career despite all the times the job took him away from her and their children.

New Year's Eve, 1997. Left: Detective Jose Manjarrez, Sam's first partner when he got assigned to TARU. Center is Sergeant Louis Vozza, who was Sam's supervisor for several years.

A few weeks after his undercover assignment ended and over 100 people were arrested in 11 states, Sam (third from left) shaved his head, grabbed his buddies and a box of cigars and went to Puerto Rico to relax.

Sam (right) with his Dad Rati Panchal (left) and brother Raj Panchal. Sam is unusually close to his family so it was traumatic when he hid the fact that he had taken a job with the NYPD from them. After his mother became suspicious, he came clean. Many years later, his family is proud of Sam and his career in law enforcement.

Celebrating Sam's promotion to Detective, Second Grade, in December, 2000. At left, Sam's mother and father, Rati and Kamla, and grandfather Asa Panchal, 100 years old. Center is Lieutenant Louis Vozza, Sam's longtime sergeant. Sam and his wife Alisha are at the right.

Sam Panchal, right, spent months working at Ground Zero following the attacks of September 11. Sam is pictured here with Detective Dave Fitzpatrick. Sam and Dave were both assigned to the NYPD's Technical Assistance Response Unit (TARU) in 2001. Dave Fitzpatrick's extraordinary photos of the disaster were published in the best selling book, *Above Hallowed Ground*.

Chapter Four

Ann-Margaret Lyons and Pete Tetukevich:
When Love Crashes In

*"You need two things in life to be happy—love and work
that you love. But you need them in that order. If one of
these goals eludes you, stick with love."* —*Sigmund Freud*

It was a clear, dry night in the early fall of 1985. Pete Tetukevich and his partner had just grabbed coffee before they hit the streets for their eight-hour, midnight to eight a.m. shift patrolling one of New York City's most crime-ridden public housing projects.

The four thirty-story apartment buildings at 155th Street and 8th Avenue in the heart of Harlem had been built on top of the Polo Grounds, the storied field that had been home to the New York Giants and their dedicated fans from 1883 to 1957. But by the 1980s, the cheers of thousands of people rooting for their favorite baseball team were a distant memory. Embattled residents had no time to enjoy sports. They were doing their best to cope with the robberies, burglaries, and murders that were destroying their neighborhood.

Pete, like the other cops who patrolled the area, rarely had a quiet night. On a typical shift, he might have to lock up people who were carrying guns without permits, break up marital fights and bar brawls, take burglary reports, and do his best to calm down emotionally disturbed people who had misplaced their meds. As they sat sipping coffee, Pete and his partner had no way to know what the night ahead would hold. All they could count on was that it would be busy.

Twenty minutes into their shift, the dispatcher's voice crackled over the radio. Someone called 911 to report a man had been stabbed. As it turned out, Pete and his partner were in front of the very building. Pete radioed back that they were available to take the call. When the elevator door opened on the seventeenth floor, they were greeted by a trail of blood. It led directly to the apartment on the far end of the hall.

"It looked like someone had slaughtered a lamb," Pete said. "We could have been in the Colosseum in Rome right after someone had been torn apart by lions."

Pete knocked and a woman opened the door. He remembers the apartment was spotless. There were lots of books around, and he assumed the family must be educated. As soon as she saw the cops, the woman broke down sobbing. She led the officers into the living room, where they found a clean-shaven and well-groomed, light-complexioned black male covered with blood. "He couldn't have been more than twenty years old," Pete said.

A quick glance indicated he'd been stabbed in the jugular vein. He was still alive but barely. His mother told the cops her son had said only one word. "Chucky." Chucky, it turned out, was her son's friend. He lived on the thirteenth floor.

Pete called for backup, and the two officers headed four floors down to the thirteenth. Sometimes only four cops patrolled this large dangerous neighborhood at any give time. They knew they didn't have the luxury of waiting. They were going to have to deal with Chucky.

"It was amazing," Pete said. "The trail of blood went down the hall, down the stairwell, and directly to an apartment on the thirteenth floor. To be honest, I can't remember whether we had our weapons out or not, but I do remember we gave each other 'the look.' That's the eye contact we use to gear ourselves up. The look that says, okay, here we go. We are going to deal with this."

They knocked and a woman came to the door. She asked, "Can I help you?" Pete said she sounded more like a salesperson at the local supermarket than someone harboring a murderer. "We asked her if Chucky was home. She told us he was in the back bedroom getting dressed. She seemed as if she didn't have a care in the world."

Unlike the apartment on the seventeenth floor, this place was a vision from hell. "When the front door opened, an army of cockroaches ran out," Pete remembered. "I'd seen some filthy places, but nothing like this. I swear it looked like the walls were shaking from all those cockroaches."

The officers rushed to the bedroom and opened the door. It looked like a war zone. There was blood everywhere, including an oversized plastic container so full it was overflowing. It was everywhere except on Chucky. He was spotless.

The cops got him in cuffs and took him back to the precinct. When they received confirmation that the twenty-year-old man was dead, they booked Chucky for murder. When he was told to take off his clothes as part of the arrest process, officers found his body covered with blood. The thick globs had clotted into a dark purplish-black crust.

Homicide detectives discovered later that the victim and Chucky were involved in a sexual encounter when things got out of hand. Both men were nude, and the victim was handcuffed to the bed. Chucky was wearing his favorite gorilla mask, and at some point his buddy got stabbed in the jugular. He claimed he couldn't remember how it happened. He did admit when the blood starting gushing out like a broken water main, he tried to catch it in the plastic container. The handcuffs, it turned out, belonged to Chucky's mother.

By the time the incident report was filed and Pete and his partner had finished with the detectives, eight hours had gone by. Their shift had ended hours ago. They both knew, with the adrenaline rush that's always a companion after incidents like this one, it would not be easy to fall asleep once they got home.

* * *

In 1988 Officer Ann-Margaret Lyons was on patrol hundreds of feet underground in the New York City Subway. She was twenty-one and had been out of the Academy for only two weeks and was happy to be finished with the six-month training. Lyons's shift was eight in the evening to four in the morning, five days a week. Like all subway cops at that time, Ann-Margaret worked alone.

A week before, someone had doused a token booth clerk with gasoline and set him on fire. The clerk was burned over 80 percent of his body. Despite the valiant efforts of the burn doctors, he died later that day. It was a particularly vicious crime, and the Department doubled the number of police officers patrolling the subways. Officers were instructed to spend their shifts riding the subway cars and walking through stations in hopes of spotting the criminal who killed the clerk.

Around two in the morning, Lyons was almost at the end of her shift. She was riding on a subway car in East New York near Kingston Avenue and the Eastern Parkway.

"The door opened and I got off," she said. "Right away I heard screaming from the back of the train. Then I saw smoke."

Ann-Margaret ran toward the screams. Everyone else was running in the opposite direction. "I was almost at the end of the train when I saw a man running," she said. "He's on fire, and smoke is pouring off his body. Then I see two kids running along the platform. They were big. I pulled my gun, pointed it at them, and yelled, 'Freeze.' Just then another guy came running up. He was pointing at the kids and screaming, 'They robbed me, they robbed me.'"

Ann-Margaret had two suspects she was pretty certain had set a man on fire. She had the man who was on fire and another man screaming that the suspects had just robbed him. On top of all that, she was in a subway tunnel. Her radio wasn't working, and she had no way to call for backup.

"I knew I had to deal with the boys first," she remembered. "When I ordered them to freeze, they began running. I ran after them. I had my weapon out, and I was yelling at them to stop. As I got closer, they saw the gun, and I think they got scared. I told them to get their hands up over their heads and put them against the wall."

This time the boys followed the officer's instructions, but it was still two against one. There was no way Lyons could get them in handcuffs with those odds. "Thank God they were cooperative with the gun pointed at them." She tried her radio again, and fortunately this time it worked. She described her position, and the dispatcher told her to hold on. Backup was on the way.

With her gun pointed at the two suspects with their hands spread up against the wall, she could look around to see what else was going on. It turned out that the man who had been set on fire and who appeared to be homeless put out the flames himself. His arms looked badly burned, but he told Lyons he was taking off.

"I couldn't believe he wasn't going to give us a statement," she said. "I told him, 'You've got to be kidding. You almost died and you don't want to help us?' I tried to hold him there, but he was scared, and I had to keep my focus on the kids until backup showed up. At least the guy who got robbed was willing to testify. Otherwise I would have had to let those kids go."

Looking back on her first arrest, Ann-Margaret says the experience was really scary. "It was my first collar, and I was all alone in that subway tunnel. When it was over, my whole body was shaking. I remember thinking, 'Holy cow, is this how it's going to be? But to be completely honest, there was something really exciting about it, too. I know the thought went through my mind that this job was looking pretty cool. But what has bothered me all these years was that I could only get them on the robbery. To charge someone for an assault I didn't witness personally, I had to have a statement from the victim. The man who had been set on fire wasn't willing to testify. It was over twenty years ago, and it still bugs me."

* * *

Even when their shifts have ended, cops are never really off duty. This was a reality Ann-Margaret experienced during her first year on the job. It was four in the morning on a frigid January day. She was driving home after working a double shift of sixteen hours. "All I wanted to do was get home and go to bed," she said.

As she pulled out from the precinct parking lot in Brooklyn and headed toward home, something caught her eye. She pulled over to the side of the road to get a better look, when she saw a building on fire. She grabbed her radio and raced toward the flames. A small crowd had gathered in the street, but no one had thought to call the police or fire department.

She radioed it in and then stood back to take in the scene in front of her. The building was completely engulfed in flames. Right next door was a newly renovated apartment building. Ann-Margaret guessed there were probably at least eight families asleep in there. "Those apartments were only one foot from the building that was burning down, and I could see flames coming from the top floor."

She knew she couldn't wait for the fire department. She ran to the front door and was relieved when she found it open. She raced from floor to floor, screaming, "Your building is on fire. You've got to get out." She banged on doors. She kicked them in if there was no response. Within minutes, she was sure everyone was out of the building. By the time the firefighters arrived, the fire in the apartment building had spread to the lower floors. Her actions that night saved many lives and earned her a distinguished service award.

* * *

When John Wayne said, "Courage is being scared to death but saddling up anyway," he could have been talking about Ann-Margaret Lyons. She went on to earn her second award for meritorious service that same year, an honor almost unheard of for a rookie cop.

It was right before Labor Day in 1991. The No. 4 Lexington Avenue train derailed before entering the Union Square Station at 14th Street. On that day the 4 train was operated by Robert Ray. He derailed while switching from the express to the local tracks about one hundred yards before he entered the station. Transit Authority rules require motormen to travel no more than ten miles per hour when switching from one track to another. Ray had been traveling close to fifty.

Ann-Margaret was in a police car near the station when she heard the 10-13 come in over the radio. "It was something about two cops injured at the rear of a subway train," she said. "There was a lieutenant with me. We flew up to 14th Street and ran down into the station."

What awaited Ann-Margaret and the other first responders was shocking. The carnage made the station look like a junkyard that had just been bombed. Everything was upside down and burning.

The first car of the ten-car train jumped the tracks as it was clearing the switch. It veered to the right, slamming into the wall. Then it veered to the left slashing through a dozen metal beams. The car was sheared cleanly in half. The next four cars derailed, with the third and fourth cars sustaining the most damage. The force of the crash propelled them up into the air, where they collided together with enormous force before they fell back down in a tangled mess. Some of the cars were sticking straight up at a 90° angle from the tracks. Five people died, and scores were taken to local hospitals with serious injuries.

Ann-Margaret said when she got down there, the scene was like a horror movie. She could see people were still inside the train. "One person was holding on to a pole. Somehow it was still upright. The man was staring straight ahead. He'd gone into total shock."

She climbed into the one of the cars. "There were wires hanging everywhere. Somehow I got to the man clutching the pole. I think a few of us pushed him through a hole, but I can't remember exactly."

When the doors wouldn't open on the second car, Ann-Margaret squeezed through a small opening. Once she got inside, she was able to get several more people out of the wreck. By this time the fire department was on the scene. There were bodies lying everywhere, and the temperature had soared over 100°.

"We were trying to get them onto stretchers and carry them to the triage area for initial treatment before they were evacuated to the hospital," Ann-Margaret said. "There was one thing that happened down there I've never been able to forget. I still dream about it. There was a man pinned to the roof of the subway. His head was wedged up and completely crushed by the metal."

For her work that day, Ann-Margaret received an award for meritorious service.

* * *

Pete Tetukevich and Ann-Margaret Lyons were both police officers who enjoyed their work serving and protecting the people living, working, and visiting New York, no matter the risk. In 1991, they had yet to meet, but both were developing reputations as gutsy, active cops, and their respective bosses were starting to take notice. By that time Pete had been transferred to the NYPD's Emergency Service Unit. He was assigned to Truck Two which covers the neighborhoods of the Upper East Side and Harlem.

Among their varied tasks, Emergency Service cops respond to calls when someone is threatening to jump off a bridge or a tall building. One cold day in December, Pete and his team were doing their best to keep a distraught man from jumping from his apartment balcony on the seventeenth floor.

When a would-be suicide call comes in, the police who respond know they have to negotiate. "It is a skill," Pete says, "that you learn on the street and from the way you were brought up. They try and teach this stuff at the Academy, but personally I think you really learn how to interact with people—calming them down and convincing them to do what you say—by dealing with them in real circumstances and by watching cops who have been on the job a long time. I learned a lot from those old-timers. Some of them were brilliant when it came to dealing with all kinds of people."

Saving a jumper is an exercise in finding common ground. It's an effort to find something the person cares about and get them talking about it. That's not an easy feat when someone is determined to end his or her life. If negotiations aren't working and their instincts tell them the person is going to jump, the officers will try to physically prevent the person from making the leap. It's called "going for the grab," and that's when it gets dangerous.

When they arrived at the distraught man's apartment, he was out on a narrow ledge off his balcony. Pete remembers him as a well-dressed black man who looked like he was in his late twenties. "It was a weird scene," Pete recalled. "He was wearing an expensive suit and a full-length, dark gray wool overcoat. He had his back to us and was staring off into the distance. He had one hand on the railing. That was all that was keeping him from falling to the street below."

In the dining area, glass doors opened onto the balcony. Pete moved slowly in that direction. He tried to start a conversation, but there was no response. "He said very little to me all the hours we were up there trying to help him. At some point we knew I was going to have to grab him and pull him back over the railing."

The other cops hooked Pete into his harness. "I had no idea when that happened. My total focus was on the jumper. This is a time you have to have complete trust in the people behind you. You have to believe they won't screw up. If they do, the stakes are pretty high."

Pete used a tactic he had tried before. He told the man he had a problem and he needed his help. "I had been squatting for over an hour and my legs were cramping up," he said. "On top of that I was freezing. The doors to the balcony were wide open. It was a cold day, and I'd started to shiver. I knew one of my guys left me a jacket, but I didn't want to reach around to get it. I asked the jumper for permission to get up, stretch my legs, and put on the jacket. I was completely focused on his body language to see if he was responding to what I was saying. It seemed like a pretty long time, but finally he looked in my direction and told me it was okay to stand up and put on the jacket."

Now Pete had an opening. "I told him I wanted to tell him something, but I didn't want the other guys to hear me. I asked him if it was okay if I moved a little closer. By then, I think I was about five feet away. He agreed. I moved out a little farther on the balcony. Every time he looked away, I would get a little closer. I was near enough to talk to him, but he wouldn't look at me. That's a bad sign. He was just staring off into space. At some point I realized I had to face the fact that I wasn't going to get him to come in. He didn't have the courage to jump, but he wasn't listening to me either. I was afraid we were going to lose him. I put my right hand behind my back so he couldn't see it, and I gave the signal to the cops behind me."

Time was up. Pete was going to grab the man and bring him back up over the balcony where he would be safe. With as little movement and noise as possible, Pete's team attached a lifeline to his harness. If the man decided to jump and take Pete with him, the officers would pull him back with the lifeline. Pete's life was now in their hands.

Pete was waiting for the moment when the man lost his focus. He didn't have to wait very long. "In that split second, I sensed he wasn't concentrating, I reached both my arms over the railing and grabbed him around the waist. It was a big, bear hug–type embrace. But he was a lot stronger than he looked, and he pulled me right over the railing. Now I'm over on his side, on a small ledge, seventeen stories above the street."

Pete's fellow officers had to move fast to pull him back up. The lifeline lived up to its name, and the cops came through. They pulled Pete, whose arms were still wrapped around the suicidal man, back up over the railing. As Pete tumbled to the floor and the man fell on top of him, the team moved in quickly.

"Once I calmed down," Pete said, "I looked at the guy. He was in cuffs staring at me. I told him he was going to be all right, but I could see the hatred in his eyes. He had wanted to die, and I had stopped him. In all my years as a cop, that was one of the most draining jobs I ever worked."

* * *

During her career with the NYPD, Ann-Margaret responded to dozens of calls when people had thrown themselves under an oncoming subway train. "These calls are horrible," she said. "Body parts are everywhere. A lot of cops throw up the first time they go to one of these scenes. Some people never get used to it.

"One man jumped in front of a train at the Queens Plaza stop. He was crushed from the waist down. I had to tell him he was going to die when we got the train off him. It's so hard to know what to say. I asked him if he wanted a cigarette. I told him we were going to do everything we could for him. It was terrible.

"Another guy was at the 14th Street stop on the R train. I'm not sure what happened, but he was cut in half. The train never stopped. When we got there, someone had put the man on a stretcher. We picked up all the body parts we could find, put them in a bucket, and carried them up to the street where an ambulance was waiting. When we were going up the stairs, this little girl walked by. We tried to block her view, but she saw the guy's leg sticking up out of a bucket. She looked at us, then back to the leg. She totally broke down. We didn't have time to deal with her, but I still remember her face and her tears. The man was just a torso, but he lived for four hours. We watched the doctor trying to save him in the emergency room. I've had three of these cases. It's a very hard part of this job."

* * *

Approximately 150 law enforcement officers are killed in the line of duty each year in the United States. When a police officer dies doing his or her job, the community pays a dramatic tribute. Hundreds, if not thousands, of law enforcement officers in their dress uniforms attend the funeral to show their respect. For days, details about the slain officer and his or her family are the main feature on local television stations and in the newspapers. But there are also thousands of officers who are injured every day. The media rarely show much interest in these men and women who survive but spend the rest of their lives recovering after being shot, stabbed, assaulted, or run over.

During his years with the NYPD, Pete Tetukevich was in the hospital so many times he lost count. One injury occurred when he was with Emergency Service on the Apprehension Team, a group of highly trained officers who serve warrants and arrest heavily armed people wanted for serious, mostly violent, crimes.

One night his team's assignment was to go to a bodega in Queens and bring in a man wanted for several killings.

"We arrived at the address where this guy was supposed to be," Pete said. "My partner and I were the last people on our eight-person team to enter. As soon as we were inside, we saw a man behind the counter reaching down to get something. We assumed it was a gun. Without saying a word, we both reached over the glass counter, grabbed the guy, and pulled him back up. Everything was going great. It looked like we had our bad guy, but as we dragged him across the counter, the glass broke over my left leg. A large dagger-like shard went right through my calf. My leg was bleeding pretty badly, but somehow we got the handcuffs on the guy. I didn't even have time to check the bleeding when I heard a commotion in the back of the store. I was the cuff man, so I figured I'd better go see what was going on. I was dragging my leg and holding my hand over the wound, trying to stop the bleeding."

When Pete got to the back of the store, the sergeant was standing in the doorway. He was alarmed to see the blood gushing from Pete's leg. Quickly, he instructed two officers to get Pete to the hospital and do it fast. "It seemed like we hit every red light, and the bleeding was getting really bad," Pete said. "It turned out the glass had hit an artery."

The doctors stitched him up and sent Pete home with instructions to keep his leg elevated. The four-inch wound needed to clot, and the swelling had to go down before he would be allowed to go back to work.

Two days later Pete was bored, and he drove to the station. No one wanted to see him back so soon. The swelling was still bad, but the NYPD doctors could see he wanted to get back to work, so they ordered him to work the desk for at least two weeks. Fourteen days later Pete was back on full duty. It took his leg a long time to heal, and later he admitted he told the doctors he was feeling better than he really was. He figured his leg would get better sooner or later, and he wanted to get back out on the street.

Those who knew Pete's dad, for whom he was named, would not be surprised to hear this story. Pete Senior served seventeen years with the NYPD. He spent fifteen of those years in the Emergency Service Unit. Pete had just turned thirteen when his father became ill. The doctors thought he had lung cancer and ordered radiation treatments. But it turned out the diagnosis was wrong, and the treatments destroyed his heart. His dad died over thirty years ago, but Pete's voice still gets shaky when he talks about him.

"My father wanted me to join the Air Force and become a pilot," he remembered. "But I'd spent so much time listening to my dad and his friends talk about being cops, that's all I wanted to do. They were really great guys, and I looked up to them. One thing I admired, even as a little kid, was that they knew how to work hard. On their days off, they would work on their own houses, work on their partners' houses, help each other build new houses. They were always working to make better lives for their friends and families.

"For a long time my father's partner was a Japanese guy, Eddie Yano. Eddie was a small man, and my father was big. Everyone called them Big Pete and the Indian. Right before Eddie died, he called me and said he wanted to come over and tell me about some of the things he and my dad had been through." Eddie seemed especially eager to talk to Pete about an incident in Washington Heights in the late 1960s.

"There was a call about a man holding a woman hostage," Pete said. "When the patrol cops showed up, he began firing at them with a high-powered rifle. They called in Emergency Service, and when my dad and Eddie got on the scene, they could see the rifle pointed right at them through the opening in the doorjamb. Bullets were flying, so they dove for cover in a corner of the hallway. Eddie wasn't sure exactly how long they waited before they decided to go in and get the gunman. The plan was for Eddie to grab the end of the rifle that was sticking through the door. At the same moment, my dad would enter the apartment and tackle the guy. They rushed toward the door, but just as Eddie grabbed the end of the rifle, the suspect got off a shot. The force of the round burned Eddie's hand, but somehow he was able to keep his grip on the gun. My dad kicked in the door, tackled the gunman, and broke his hold on the rifle."

At Big Pete's funeral in July 1975, two of his closest cop friends found thirteen-year-old Pete and took him aside. "One of them put his hands on my shoulders," Pete recalled. "They told me they knew someday I would join the NYPD and be an Emergency Service cop."

The day he turned eighteen, Pete signed up for the test.

* * *

Ann-Margaret's path to a law enforcement career was not as direct. Her only contact with the world of law enforcement when she was growing up in

Brooklyn was when they showed up to talk some sense into her parents after they'd had a fight. "My father drank a lot, which caused a lot of problems," she recalled. "The cops were great. They'd try to talk to them and get them to calm down. If it was really bad, they'd take one of them out for a walk. You could tell they just wanted to cool things down. I always thought of them as people who were there to help."

After graduating from high school, Ann-Margaret got a job working in the accounting office of a factory. The work she says was extremely boring. Every hour seemed like six.

Despite the fact that law enforcement was still a man's world and she didn't know anyone who was a cop, Ann-Margaret signed up for the police test. She was eighteen-years-old and weighed 125 pounds. She said she never thought about how a woman would survive in the male-dominated culture of the law enforcement. When she was growing up, her friends had all been boys. She preferred climbing trees to playing with dolls, and she had become pretty competitive on the football, softball, and soccer fields. When the New York City Police Department called to tell her she was accepted, she quit her job and began the mandatory six months of training in the Police Academy.

* * *

The first time Ann-Margaret saw Pete was in 1992. "We were going for a routine training exercise in the subway. When I came down the escalator, he was sitting up on a turnstile. I definitely noticed him. I said hello, but he blew me off. I don't think he even looked in my direction."

Pete doesn't recall seeing Ann-Margaret that day. He says the first time they met was a year later when she walked into Truck Two. It was her first day at her new assignment with Emergency Service. "She was wearing a really tight jumpsuit," Pete recalled. "I said to myself, 'Wow, she looks pretty good.'"

Both admit it was not love at first sight, but Pete was curious about the new cop on the team. Once he learned she shared his love of motorcycles and owned a 1993 Harley-Davidson Low Rider, he began pestering her to go on a ride. It took several weeks, but she finally agreed.

The day of the ride was cold and rainy, but Pete was looking forward to his first date with Ann. Rain or no rain, he didn't want to cancel. "I decided we'd ride to Connecticut," Pete said. "We left around ten in the morning, and it seemed to be getting colder. When we got over the state line, I told Ann I was worried she was getting cold. When I suggested we find a motel and have a hot shower, she looked disgusted." Pete had to face the fact that Ann-Margaret was not going to accompany him to a motel on their first date. They ended up in a local pub for lunch instead.

When they took that motorcycle ride, Pete and Ann-Margaret were both married, but neither was happy. "My wife was a teacher," Pete said. "It seemed like we had less and less in common. She thought life was great, and why wouldn't she? She worked with beautiful young children all day. My view of life was the exact opposite of hers. She never could understand why cops have such a bad view of the world and most of the people in it."

People who do marital counseling say there are many things that can be done to improve the situation when couples have sexual problems, conflicts over money, issues with the kids, and different ideas about how to spend leisure time. The situation is harder to fix when partners look at life in totally different ways. Having different world views could be the reason so many law enforcement officers end up divorced when they marry people who don't understand their jobs.

While Pete and his wife's differences were making communication hard, Ann-Margaret wasn't doing much better. She had been with the same person since high school. Looking back, she says she never should have married him. Everyone expected them to tie the knot, and they did, even though she had deep misgivings. The marriage lasted four years.

While it may not have been love at first sight, it wasn't long before Ann-Margaret and Pete realized they were falling in love. A year after their first motorcycle ride, they were both divorced.

Along with a love of high-risk police work and motorcycles, they looked at the world the same way. Pete says, for him, the best part of their relationship was they liked the same people and laughed at the same jokes. "We'd be sitting around talking, and I'd be amazed she felt the same way about things I did. At work, all the people who bugged her, bugged me, too."

After their divorces were final, they moved in together. While no one had seen anything in writing, every cop in the NYPD knew the Department did not like officers who were married, or even dating, to be working together. Ann-Margaret was determined to keep their relationship a secret. They both had their dream jobs assigned to the Emergency Service Unit, one of the most exciting, prestigious divisions in the entire Department. They knew it might be better if they weren't in the same squad, but it was what it was and they were confident they could deal with it.

For a while everything was fine. Pete and Ann-Margaret continued to do great police work, and no one paid much attention when they always showed up to work together. "We told them we were carpooling," Ann-Margaret said with a grin.

To this day, Pete says Ann was the better cop, mostly because she always stayed focused. "I remember this one night when we were sitting on the corner of Broadway and 61st Street on the Upper West Side. It was the first thing in the morning and the beginning of our shift. We ordered some ham and eggs and coffee."

As most cops learn, it's best to eat right when you are about to go on duty. If you wait and it gets busy, chances are good it'll be eight hours with no time for food.

"We'd just started to eat when we got a call about a possible suicide," Pete said. "We were right in front of the building, so we threw the food on the seat of the truck, grabbed the tools we would need to get into the apartment, and ran into the building."

Pete explained that with suicide calls, it's crucial to get in there right away. "Even then it may be too late," he said. "We used the rabbit tool, a small portable hand pump that spreads the door away from the door jamb. It pretty much wrecks the door, so we use it only when there's a serious emergency."

They forced the door open, looked around, and walked toward the back bedroom. There wasn't a sound. They pushed the bedroom door open. There, lying on a queen-size bed, was a naked woman with a two-inch stab wound in her sternum. She was sprawled across the bed, and she looked dead. The knife was laying at her side.

Pete still doesn't understand why he reacted the way he did, but he found himself completely distracted by the woman's wound. "I'd been a cop for years, and I'd seen a lot of this stuff. Who knows why I reacted this way. I just kept staring at the hole in her chest and thinking, 'Wow, that must hurt.'"

While Pete was staring at the woman's stab wound, Ann-Margaret was checking the other rooms. Cops are trained to never assume someone is dead, unless they have absolute proof. She took it for granted that Pete would make sure the woman with the knife would not pose a threat.

"When I went back to the bedroom, I could see he was distracted," Ann-Margaret recalled. "She could have easily grabbed the knife. It was laying right next to her hand. I started yelling at Pete, 'Grab the knife, grab the knife.' It's a good thing he snapped out of it because when the woman heard my voice, her hand moved toward the knife. She wasn't dead. It just looked that way."

For cops to be distracted like that, to lose their concentration for even a second, is extremely dangerous. It had never happened to Pete, and it made him nervous.

Ann-Margaret got on her radio and called for an ambulance. The woman was rushed to the emergency room, where the doctors did their best to save her life. "We never knew if she made it," Pete said, "or why she wanted to die. When you watch TV shows, sometimes the victim will contact the cops who saved them. The person cries and thanks the officers. It's all very emotional. I'm not into worrying about getting pats on the back, but it would be nice to know what happened to some of the people you worked so hard to help. In all my years on the job, I only heard from one victim. A woman I had pulled out of a really bad car accident tracked me down to say thanks."

The only time Ann-Margaret ever heard from a citizen was after she spent two hours on top of the cables of the George Washington Bridge, trying to talk down a suicidal man and he finally agreed to come down. A week later she received a letter from a nephew of a New York City police officer who was killed attempting to talk a jumper off the Brooklyn Bridge in 1908. Robert Fitzgerald wrote: "Congratulations on a courageous and successful saving of a life. God bless and protect our police officers. This incident reminded me of my uncle, Robert J. Fitzgerald. Patrolman Fitzgerald lost his life on the Brooklyn Bridge in 1908, trying to save a young man from jumping. While climbing on the bridge ironworks, my uncle was hit by a trolley car and was knocked from the bridge. His body went through the ice in the East River and was found three months later."

* * *

One day when Ann-Margaret and Pete arrived at work, a lieutenant told them he had a problem. A homeless man had built a little shantytown in an open lot in the 28th Precinct in Harlem. In addition to his self-constructed village, over thirty of his dogs were running wild around the neighborhood.

The residents were not happy. The night before, a group of them had met with the police and demanded something be done. The lieutenant assured them he would look into the matter.

Ann-Margaret and Pete, along with two precinct cops and two lieutenants, loaded up their tranquilizer guns with vials of Ketaset, an anesthetic used to subdue animals. They drove to the lot. "When we got there, it was total chaos," Ann-Margaret said. "Dogs were barking and running everywhere. The stench of dog shit was horrible."

The police had worked out their plan on the way to the site. They would tranquilize the dogs and, once they were down, load them into the truck. When the situation was under control, they would drive the dogs to a shelter. When Ann-Margaret saw the number of dogs they needed to tranquilize, she called for a paddy wagon on her radio. They were going to need a bigger vehicle.

"Pete and I both started tranquilizing the dogs," she said. "Once they went down, I picked them up and loaded them into the wagon."

Despite the stench and the chaotic scene, Ann-Margaret remembers being impressed with the little makeshift village the homeless man had made for himself. "He had made a small house with scraps of sheet metal for the roof and plywood for the walls," she said. "He even had small hot plates for cooking. It was actually set up pretty well. The dogs were causing the problem."

Several hours later Pete and Ann-Margaret had tranquilized close to thirty dogs and moved them into the wagon. There were only a couple left. Pete told Ann he was going to climb up on the sheet metal roof. He thought it would be easier to tranquilize the last few dogs from up there.

"I remember looking up at Pete on the roof of the shack," Ann-Margaret said. "I saw him walking out to the edge of the roof. He couldn't see it, but at the edge, it was just the sheet metal, with nothing underneath for support. I was looking up at him thinking, 'No, he's not going to walk to the edge, is he?' Before I could say anything, he was out on the end of the roof. A second later the sheet metal comes flying, and Pete is sailing through the air. With an incredibly loud thump, he landed on the ground."

"I looked around," Pete said. "I was lying in piles of dog shit with the sheet metal all around me. I could tell I was hurt. All I could think was, well, it's back to the hospital."

* * *

On Friday, December 8, 1995, Ann-Margaret and Pete were working the day shift. It was a clear, brisk, sunny morning, and they had enjoyed their ride into the city. Both recall when they crossed over the George Washington Bridge on their way to the West Side Highway, the Hudson River looked like someone had scattered millions of sparkling diamonds over the top of the water. They parked their Jeep Wrangler and went into the station. The other members of their squad were already there. That day Ann-Margaret and Pete were teamed up with Henry Medina, Seth Gahr, Pete Conlin, and Kevin Flanagan.

Kevin had cooked up some eggs in the small station house kitchen and was making a pot of coffee when Pete and Ann-Margaret arrived. By the time they got their gear and checked and locked their weapons, it was just after 8:30 a.m. One hour later, they had heard barely anything of the dispatcher's voice over their police radios. It was eerily quiet, prompting Pete to announce it must be Sunday, not Friday. Sundays in New York City, especially for cops working the day shift, were the quietest time of the week. Little did they know that in less than two hours, they would be dealing with one of the worst crime scenes in New York City's history.

The call came in around 10:15 a.m. "Confirmed robbery in progress, shots fired" and the words all cops dread most, "Officer needing assistance." The location was 272 West 125th Street. It took them only seconds to get suited up. The team donned their Kevlar-reinforced helmets and heavy tactical vests. They went to the large Emergency Service truck where the semiautomatics, submachine guns, and high-powered rifles are stored. They unlocked the weapons and made sure they had extra rounds.

A man armed with a bottle of lighter fluid and a gun, yelling, "It's on now," had gone into Freddy's Fashion Mart, a discount clothing store on Harlem's bustling 125th Street. Someone called 911, and when two precinct cops showed up, the gunman fired at the officers, pinning one of them down. One officer got away, ran to the street, and called in on his radio.

Pete said when their team got to the scene, it was pandemonium. "The gunman was shooting, but visibility was bad, so we couldn't pinpoint his position."

Their first task was to make sure the cop who had been pinned down was out of harm's way. As patrol officers crouched in the doorway with their guns drawn to provide cover, Ann-Margaret and Pete put their ballistic shields in position and walked toward the gunfire. With bullets whizzing by, they managed to get to the officer and drag him back to safety. Then they took cover.

The suspect was still firing from inside the store. "It's hard to know when it happened because your sense of time gets distorted," Ann-Margaret explained, "but at some point Pete and I saw flames start to come out of the building."

They knew they had to find the back door of the store to make sure the gunman could not escape out the back of building. As they ran toward the rear of the building, they could still hear the crackle of gunfire. Smoke was pouring out of Freddy's. The whole place looked like it was on fire. They were concerned about getting the shooter, but first they had to make sure people in the adjacent buildings knew there was a fire. If necessary, they would help them get out. Ann-Margaret rushed to the hair salon on one side, and Pete ran through the apartment building on the other. Both officers were alerting everyone about the disaster occurring nearby.

Once they were sure everyone was safe, Ann-Margaret and Pete started again to the rear entrance of the store. By this time, scores of police cars and hundreds of officers, sergeants, lieutenants, captains, and even the Police Commissioner himself, were on the scene. There were fire trucks and ambulances, reporters and photographers, camera crews and helicopters. Smoke was everywhere. Someone cranked up a boom box with rap music blaring, and you could still hear gunfire. No one knew if the people inside Freddy's were alive or dead.

Experienced law enforcement officers agree that at scenes like this, if you get distracted and lose your concentration, you get scared. It's a vicious cycle, with fear leading to confusion that leads to more fear. That's when the instinct to run from the danger rather than toward it can kick in. It takes enormous discipline and concentration to block out everything except the task at hand.

At some point Pete realized he'd lost track of Ann, but there wasn't time to think about that. He had to cover the rear of the store. At the back of the building, he saw a stairwell with a slightly open doorway. He hurried down the stairs and pushed open the door. It took a few seconds to adjust to the lack of light. Then something caught his eye. "As I got closer I realized it was a man sitting on a milk crate," he said. "I figured he was still alive because he was sitting up. I asked him if he was okay, but there was no reaction. I bent down to get a closer look, and I see blood on his T-shirt. Then I see a hole near the blood. Then I see gunpowder. I said to him, 'Buddy, you stay here. You've been shot. You stay here. I'll be right back.'"

Pete ran back up the stairs and out of the building. The first people he ran into were two EMTs. He was relieved to see Ann-Margaret right behind them. Pete told the EMTs to follow him. "I led them back into the basement to where the wounded guy was still sitting. I told him not to worry. The EMTs would take care of him."

Ann-Margaret and Pete took stock of the situation. It looked as if the man who had been shot crawled out of a space between the ceiling and a water pipe. But the hole was small and they didn't think it was big enough for someone to squeeze through.

Pete got on his radio, described his position and called for tools, sledge-hammers, heavy vests, and more powerful weapons. Armed with sledgeham-mers and rifles and joined by Kevin Flanagan, Pete and Ann-Margaret made their way to the wall. They hoped, once they broke through, it would lead them into the store. They began hammering away. It was giving way when all of a sudden, they hit something solid. "It felt like a heavy piece of metal," Pete said. "We didn't know what was on the other side, but it wasn't budg-ing."

They kept at it. Looking back they both say it could have been seconds, or it could have been hours. They were operating on pure adrenaline. Finally they broke through.

Smoke engulfed them as it billowed out through the opening they'd made in the wall. They began to choke. "We had to get in there," Ann-Margaret said. "We knew there were people who might still be alive. And there was the gunman to deal with."

Once they got through the wall, Pete couldn't see Ann. The smoke was too thick. But he could hear her. "I started screaming at her to get out. She yelled back, 'I can't move. I can't move. I'm caught on something.' It turns out her heavy ballistic vest was caught, and she was trapped. All of a sudden it hit me. Ann could die."

Neither Pete nor Ann-Margaret is sure what happened next. The lights had gone out, smoke was everywhere, the heat was soaring, and the police were disoriented. Ann-Margaret was frantically tugging on her vest, trying to get it off. Finally it broke free. She made her way over to Pete, who was completely enveloped in smoke and still screaming for her to get out.

Looking back, Ann-Margaret said it's hard to describe how hot it was once they got inside Freddy's. "The heat was just unreal," she said. "All the winter jackets had melted, and there were down feathers flying everywhere."

Punching a hole in the wall had created a draft, which made the smoke even thicker. The officers had no fire gear. Pete explained that the firefighters had been told to stay away because of the active shooter who was still present. Until that threat was over, even though there was a fire, it was considered a tactical job for the police. "But there was a fire, so firefighters were shooting water on it from outside the crime scene perimeter. You had two different agencies fighting two different problems. By putting water on the fire, they were forcing the heat and smoke back toward us. From our perspective, they were creating even more problems."

The fire department decided the floor might collapse, and they wanted the officers to leave the building. But the cops were determined to find victims who might still be alive. "There was no way we were leaving," Pete said. "They were telling us to get out, and we're telling them we're not leaving. I remember yelling into my radio, 'No way. We're not coming out. We have victims in here.'"

With only their helmets to protect them, Ann-Margaret and Pete forced their way through the heat and smoke into the store. It was only seconds when she came across the first grisly scene. Two young men and two young women were wedged in behind a palette of cinder blocks. They were all dead. As Ann-Margaret and Pete walked up the stairs to the second floor, the heat was even worse. Gasping for air and making their way through the life-threatening smoke, they found a badly burned man lying on the floor in the middle of one of the aisles. They knew immediately they had their gunman, He was dead. The gun was still in his hand.

Still choking, they stepped over his body. By the cash register they could see what looked like a pile of bodies. When they got closer, they saw three young girls. The Medical Examiner determined later they died of smoke inhalation.

The man in the basement, who had been shot five times, was an Irish immigrant who had been doing some construction work at the store. After the contractor was wounded by the gunman, he managed to find an opening around the water pipe in the basement and squeeze himself through. He tried to get the other people in the store to go with him, but no one would follow him. Eventually he recovered from his wounds. He was one of two survivors of the massacre at Freddy's.

Once the fire was out and the last victim was taken to the morgue, it was determined that seven innocent people perished. The gunman, a fifty-one-year-old unemployed man named Ronald Smith, was also dead. When detectives questioned people in the neighborhood about Smith, they said he was angry that Freddy's, a Jewish-owned clothing store, was refusing to renew the lease of a popular black-owned record shop next store. Freddy's wanted the space so it could expand. Pete said it was ironic that only minority workers who lived in the neighborhood died that day. "We did our best under the circumstances," Ann-Margaret said. "We wish we could have done more. It really hurt that we couldn't save those people."

It was now early evening. The flames were out, but the cops were still hyped up. They needed to find a way to try and get back to normal. Covered with soot and grime from the fire and heartbroken at the tragic loss of life they had just witnessed, they went back to the station.

"We decided to stay in quarters," Ann-Margaret said. "It was completely against the rules, but I'm not sure any of us even cared. We hunkered down in a corner of the kitchen. Someone had a bottle of bourbon. We found some Styrofoam coffee cups and poured ourselves a drink. We took turns talking about what had happened, how we reacted, and whether there was anything we could do better the next time. We were amazed we'd all survived."

* * *

By now, Ann-Margaret and Pete were deeply in love. It had been three years since they had met. They loved their work, their divorces were final, and they were living together but were confident that no one knew they were a couple. At that time any one of their bosses would have agreed they were two of the toughest, bravest cops on the force. But something changed after their near-death experience at Freddy's. They began to worry. It was the beginning of the end of their careers in law enforcement.

Pete felt it first. "Before Ann and I met, I never thought about dying or even what it would be like if I got seriously hurt. I just focused on the task at hand and took care of business. I started worrying almost from the time I met her, and it just grew from there. I realized I'd met someone I loved and wanted to be with. I thought about her all the time. The biggest surprise for me was

I'd started to enjoy life.

"At first the anxiety was subconscious. But as soon as you start thinking, 'I could fall and get hurt,' that's when you start second-guessing yourself and thinking about what might happen. You start to worry, you get shaky, and then it's time to go."

Pete said that during his entire career, he never worried about his safety. "Neither did Ann. We just went out and did the job. But my attitude changed. I was more cautious, and after Freddy's, I was especially anxious about her. If I was out on patrol and I wasn't with her, I felt this anxiety. I wasn't in control. If you know you can control the situation, you can do the job 100 percent. If you don't feel that, you can panic. If she was in Manhattan and I was in Queens, I knew I couldn't help her if she got into trouble."

Pete would admit later that his fears were irrational. If anyone he'd worked with could handle herself, it was Ann-Margaret. "There was one time she got involved in a car accident out in Queens. I'm thinking I want to go and be with her, but I can't because nobody knows we're dating. All they knew was that we were carpooling, and I knew they would find it suspicious if I ran to her bedside."

"We were going to a 10-13," Ann-Margaret said. "A cop was trapped in a car after a bad accident. We took the bridge from Manhattan into Queens. It was around nine o'clock at night. I was driving, and it was raining. We were going down 43rd Avenue. We stopped at a light, and when it turned green, I hit the gas. A cab coming into the intersection ran the red light, and we broadsided him. We started spinning, and I remember hitting my head. I got out of the truck, but I felt like I was going to pass out. I called in the accident on my radio, and that's the last thing I remember. When I woke up, I was in the hospital. It was weird. We were on our way to an accident, and we ended up being the accident."

The ambulance arrived within minutes after the collision, and Ann-Margaret was rushed to Bellevue Hospital. After going through a round of X-rays, they brought her back to her room. She was only there a few minutes when Pete came barging in. "He was really upset and saying something like, 'I just knew you were going to get hurt.' I remember looking at him and thinking, 'What is he doing?' I just wanted him to leave."

Pete tried to explain. He had cover. Back at the station, when the sergeant asked for someone to volunteer to take Ann-Margaret home from the hospital, Pete said he'd do it. But Ann was still angry. She was alarmed at Pete's behavior in the hospital room. She knew if anyone heard what he was saying, they'd know they were doing more than carpooling.

Pete didn't care. He was distraught when he learned she was in an accident, and he had reason to be nervous. Even in the macho world of ESU, Ann was considered a real go-getter. "I always looked at her and wondered how she could do it," Pete said. "She always went way out of her way and put so much energy into everything. It was like she had to prove to the guys that she was as good as they were. I knew that might be the reason she was always taking so many risks. I told her she should stop being so aggressive. She was a way better cop than most of the people we worked with. They should have been the ones trying to prove they were better than she was. But she never paid any attention to me. She just focused on the job, 100 percent."

After his outburst in the hospital room, Pete made a serious effort to keep his worries about Ann at bay. But it was a losing battle. His behavior on the job became more erratic.

Three months after the shooting rampage at Freddy's, Ann-Margaret and Pete got a call for a burglary in progress in Washington Heights. "When we arrived on the scene, there was a K-9 officer there with his police dog," Pete said. "We decided to send the dog in first. He came out wagging his tale, a signal no one's home. I looked at Ann, she nodded, and we went in for what we thought was one last search.

"Ann went to the bedroom with Henry Medina. Seth Gahr and I went to the living room," Pete continued. "All of a sudden I hear her screaming, 'Let me see your hands, let me see your hands.' She had a fully loaded, automatic submachine gun. If that wasn't scaring this guy, it was probably about to be a real bad scene. I ran in and I see her. She's got this guy at gunpoint. He's in a closet. I don't know what came over me. It was all instinct. I barreled across the room, threw myself into the closet, and tackled the guy."

Pete would admit later that he had let his emotions get the best of him. "I was under a lot of stress trying to hide our relationship. Emergency Service cops are a very macho group of police officers. The quarters are tight, and you're always in very close contact with the other cops and the bosses. You've got people bringing in all their baggage to work, and I didn't want to be adding to the mix. But the truth was simple. I was possessed with the notion I had to do something to save her. I was terrified she was going to get hurt."

For those not knowledgeable about the tactics that should have been used during this incident, let's just say that Pete had violated several NYPD protocols. No one was more aware of this fact than Ann-Margaret. If a supervisor had been there, he might have recommended that Pete be disciplined. When they got home that night, Ann-Margaret looked at Pete. She asked him directly, "What is your problem?"

"There had been many emotions building up over a long time," Pete said. "We both had had to deal with our divorces, and both of us felt the pressure of trying to hide our relationship from the cops we worked with. And, of course, I was worrying about her. It was a long list. Increasingly, I couldn't talk to her about all the things that were on my mind. So, as people do, I began to hurl insults and angry tirades at her."

Ann-Margaret remembers that night as a watershed moment. Pete said later that on some level, he knew it was over. "The world changed for me when I met Ann," he said. "Now, above everything, I wanted to know she would be there in the morning and that she'd be there in one piece."

He began to face the fact that his lack of focus and inappropriate behavior could jeopardize the lives of his colleagues. That was something he couldn't live with. He had to decide between the only two things he had ever cared about in his life—his career with the New York City Police Department and Ann-Margaret. They talked all night about the unthinkable: leaving their jobs with the NYPD.

The next morning Ann-Margaret went to work. Her first call was at Ft. Washington Avenue and 176th Street. Someone called 911 to complain about an emotionally disturbed person who was throwing things out the window. When Ann and her sergeant arrived at the scene, they could see a man sitting in the window of his apartment with a rottweiler sitting next to him.

With guns drawn, Ann-Margaret and her partner ran up the stairs. "I banged on the door, and the dog starts going nuts," she said. "It's bad to antagonize a dog before you make entry, but that's what happened."

Two more officers arrived on the scene, and quickly they set up teams. Ann-Margaret and her partner would corner the snarling, barking dog in the living room while one of the officers would shoot him with his tranquilizer gun. But he missed, and the dog went into a bigger rage. Ann had a noose. She decided to rush the dog and try to get it on the dog. As she moved in, the dog bared its teeth, leaped up, and attacked her.

"The dog went after my hand," Ann-Margaret said. "Thank God, I had on a thick leather glove." As the dog attacked Ann-Margaret, her partner got off a second shot. This time the dart hit the dog.

With the dog temporarily stunned, Ann-Margaret could focus on her hand. She looked down and saw blood pouring out of her glove. She waited until she got in the ambulance to remove it. She worried if she took the glove off back in the apartment and the finger fell onto the floor, the dog might be faster and would no doubt enjoy eating her finger. On the way to the hospital, she took the glove off, and her index finger fell out. She warded off the feelings of nausea, picked up her finger, and held it firmly onto the stump on her hand.

When the rottweiler bit off Ann-Margaret's finger, Pete was at Truck One. "I'm sitting there listening to this scene going down on the radio," he said. "I hear there's a dog involved, but I know that day she was assigned to drive the truck, so I wasn't too worried." But as Pete sat there listening, he got a bad feeling. "I was overcome with fear it might be Ann who had been bit."

Seconds later a lieutenant got on the air. His message struck Pete right in the heart. The lieutenant reported that a female officer with a dog bite was on her way to Columbia Presbyterian. "To this day I can still hear his voice and his words."

Holding her finger onto her hand, Ann-Margaret took her seat in the hospital waiting room. It would be over five hours before a doctor could see her. The X-rays showed that the force of the dog's bite smashed several bones in her hand, and they needed to reattach her finger. Henry Medina called Pete to tell him the good news. The doctors said there was a chance Ann would not lose her finger.

"They sent her home with painkillers," Pete recalled, "but they weren't working. There were so many emotions going back and forth between us. Ann is right-handed, and now she's injured a finger on her shooting hand. Despite the fact that the doctors were able to save her finger, within a year, the Department told her she had to retire. She turned in her badge and gun in May 1998."

Four years later, in February 2002, Pete retired.

* * *

Ann-Margaret and Pete now live a one-hour drive north of New York City. They have a charming house on a tree-lined street, an eight-year-old son,

Peter, whom they dote on, and a thriving landscape business they started the week after Pete retired from the NYPD.

While they're not pushing Peter into a career in law enforcement, both parents say there are signs he may be headed in that direction. "One time I took Peter down to Lower Manhattan to the Police Museum," Pete says. "There's a shield on display, and I was explaining to my son how we use that to protect ourselves in certain situations. I went over to look at it more closely, and I realized it was Truck Two's shield. I'd used it many times. I recognized the bullet holes. It was ten years later, and there was my son standing next to that shield in the New York City Police Museum."

Ann-Margaret and Pete both say they're too busy to think about the past. But when you ask them if they miss the job, it's clear they do. "Before I started worrying, the job was so much fun you can't imagine," Pete says. "And there is no more rewarding career than law enforcement. But there are times in your life when the risks are just too big, and you've got to get out. As hard as it was, Ann and I had no choice. We had to go."

Ann-Margaret Lyons and Pete Tetukevich, 1995. Both Ann and Pete had just been assigned to the prestigious Emergency Service Unit.

Pete (left) with his partner, on top of the Brooklyn Bridge.

Ann-Margaret and Pete shortly after Ann was forced to retire in May, 1998. A vicious Rottweiler bit off a finger on her shooting hand when she was responding to a call for an emotionally disturbed person in Washington Heights.

Above, Ann-Margaret on Pete's beloved Harley Davidson, 1992. When they met, both Ann and Pete rode Harleys.

Left to right, ESU cops Pete, Ann-Margaret and Rich Miller after fires were finally out and the last body had been brought to the morgue following the massacre at Freddy's Fashion Mart in Harlem on December 8, 1995.

In the late 1960's, Pete's Dad, Pete Senior, worked with Eddie Yano in the NYPD's Emergency Service Unit. At left, Yano and Tetukevich are pictured after the officers subdued a gunman with a high powered rifle who was holding a woman hostage. Pete says it was his Dad and his friends who inspired him to be a police officer.

Photos by Michael Schwartz, *New York Daily News*

During her career with the NYPD, Ann-Margaret Lyons found herself on top of the city's highest bridges many times. Here she's atop the George Washington Bridge trying desperately to keep a suicidal man from jumping. It took over an hour but finally Ann-Margaret was able to convince the man to let her put on a lifeline.

When everyone was back down on the ground with no injuries, Ann noted, "Whatever I said worked. It feels great to save a life."

Pete assembles his scuba gear before a training exercise. In the NYPD, all scuba rescues are handled by officers assigned to the Emergency Service Unit. All 400 officers assigned to the Unit are scuba trained.

Ann-Margaret and Pete get some liquid after the massacre at Freddy's Fashion Mart.

Ann-Margaret and Pete's son, Peter, the day his parents took him to visit the New York City Police Museum in the summer of 2008. Pete was explaining to his son how the shield works when he realized it was the one he used for many years. He recognized the bullet holes.

Chapter Five

BOBBY HOM:
Heroin, Heroics and Death in a Briefcase

*"It's important to know that words don't
move mountains. Work, exacting work, moves
mountains. —Danilo Dolci*

Bobby Hom, a New York City detective, worked with the Southeast Asian Heroin Task Force since 1988. The Task Force team of twenty-four seasoned law enforcement officers from local, state, and federal agencies was investigating a number of illegal narcotics and human trafficking operations in countries as faraway as Burma, Hong Kong, and Thailand. Along with investigators from the New York State Police and the New York City Police Department, the team included special agents from Immigration; IRS; Customs; Alcohol, Tobacco, and Firearms; and the Drug Enforcement Administration.

Bobby remembers one investigation. The team had nothing to show but dead ends after six months and endless hours of work. But the Task Force's luck turned when a confidential informant called to report that one group they were watching had just received a large shipment of heroin. It was the fall of 1990. Bobby realized that if they were careful and planned everything well, it could be one of the largest drug busts ever.

Within hours of receiving the informant's call, Hom and his partner, DEA Special Agent Wayne McDonnell, set up a surveillance post near the home of one of the suspects. After an hour, he came out of the house and got into his car.

"Now the fun began," Bobby said. "We followed this guy for days. We learned where he and his crew hung out and who they did business with."

A week later, based on information they'd picked up from following the first suspect, Hom, McDonnell, and a couple of other investigators were back in their unmarked cars patiently watching a different home in a quiet neighborhood in Brooklyn. The cops suspected the occupants were involved in the operation.

It wasn't long before a car pulled up and double-parked. A man opened the driver's side door, got out, walked over to the sidewalk. He stared for a couple of minutes at a two-family home in the middle of the block and then walked back to the trunk. He opened it and tried to lift something out.

Trying to get a better angle, he stepped up on the bumper. Bobby knew from the way the man was struggling, whatever it was, it was heavy. Finally he got a canvas duffel bag up and out of the trunk. It landed on the bumper of the car before falling with a thud onto street. They were sure inside there was going to be a lot of heroin.

The man dragged the duffel bag up the stairs and disappeared inside the house. A few minutes later, he was back. Now the adrenaline was flowing as Bobby and Wayne watched him take a second bag out of the trunk. This one looked even heavier than the first. He almost had it to the top of the stairs when it broke open. The cops saw something white. They could not be absolutely sure, but it looked like a brick of heroin. The man looked around, stuffed it back into the bag, and disappeared into the house.

The investigators put a call in to Cathy Palmer, the assistant U.S. attorney in Brooklyn for the Eastern District. She would prosecute the defendants if they made an arrest. When they told Cathy where they were and what they had seen, she told them to stand by while she called the judge. She hoped she could convince him there was probable cause for a search. If the judge was even slightly dubious, he would not approve the warrant. Palmer made her case that the chances of seizing a large amount of heroin were high, and the judge signed off on the search.

Quickly, Bobby and the other members of the team worked out a tactical plan to enter the house. Once everything was in place and they were sure the suspect was gone, Bobby, Wayne, and several other agents entered the house. In the bedroom, jammed between the wall and the bed, they found several duffel bags identical to the ones the man dragged into the house. When they opened the bags, there was no heroin. It was all money.

"There were thousands of $50 and $100 bills," Bobby remembered. "They'd been pressed into bricks. Some were wrapped in stacks with rubber bands."

Over the next twenty-four hours, the team searched three other locations and several safe-deposit boxes. At one location, members of the Task Force seized 1,400 grams of pure heroin. Each brick was sealed with the Double U Globe Brand label with pictures of two lions leaning on a globe of the world. Underneath the lions, written in Chinese, were the words, "Beware of Counterfeits. Guaranteed 100 percent."

When all the money was accounted for, they had intercepted close to $9 million in cash. Along with the heroin and the money, the Task Force officers seized a machine gun, a press for compressing the heroin into bricks, and three pistols, including one outfitted with a silencer. A follow-up investigation traced the drugs back to Burma. At the time, it was the largest seizure of heroin drug money in DEA history.

For two decades spanning the 1980s and 1990s, 85 percent of the heroin purchased in the United States passed through New York City. The demand among Americans for illegal drugs has been so great for so long that it virtually guarantees a limitless market for the world's suppliers. Bobby Hom and the team at the Southeast Asian Heroin Task Force were busy.

Bobby never ceased to be amazed at the inventive ways criminals found to smuggle drugs. "They look for places where drug-sniffing dogs cannot pick up the scent," he said. "They break it up into small quantities and hide it in the most unexpected places. We found narcotics stashed in Chinese vases, wooden picture frames, and PVC pipes. They pack the heroin and cocaine in airplanes, cargo ships, luggage, headboards of beds, steel frames of tractor trailer trucks, cars, and furniture."

* * *

By the 1990s, Cathy Palmer had built a solid reputation as a fierce prosecutor of Asian gangs. It was early in 1992 when someone decided to make it clear that he was annoyed with Cathy Palmer and the U.S. Attorney's Office for the Eastern District. Detective Hom and Agent McDonnell were waiting for Cathy in her office when her secretary came in with a package. When she arrived for their meeting a short time later, Bobby pointed out the package. She opened it, and when she saw the new briefcase, she assumed it was a belated Christmas gift from her parents. When she started joking that it might be a bomb, Bobby asked to have a look.

Together Bobby and Wayne removed the briefcase from its box and opened it a fraction of an inch. That's when Hom saw a spring-operated rattrap inside. Carefully, he pressed his finger against the trap to deactivate it. Once he was positive it posed no danger, he opened the briefcase. Inside he found a sawed-off .22 caliber rifle connected to the trap by a string that was rigged to fire as soon as the case was opened.

David Kwong, who worked on and off as an informant, had sent the package. At his trial, jurors learned that his plan was to kill Cathy, frame a drug suspect, and then take credit for providing information that would solve the case. When detectives searched his apartment, they found several books on weaponry, booby traps, the creation of fake documents, and a manual on disguises.

At his trial for attempted murder, the prosecutor told the jury Cathy Palmer had been sent a "gift of death." They deliberated two hours before finding David Kwong guilty on all charges.

* * *

Bobby Hom was born and raised in the Bronx. "My mother worked in Macy's and Alexander's," he recalled. "My father, who immigrated to the United States from China, ran a Chinese wet wash. He started his day at four in the morning, making his rounds, picking up clothes from other laundries, and bringing them back to his shop, where he washed and pressed them before returning them before the end of the day. If there was one thing that stood out about my parents, it was their work ethic."

During the week, the workday for Bobby's father never ended until seven in the evening, and he always put in a half-day on Saturday. The few times the family took a vacation, his father stayed behind so he would not miss work. He retired when he was seventy.

Bobby was ten years old when he got his first job. "I did odd jobs for a florist. I raked his lawn and cut his grass," he said. At eleven, he began helping the driver, Arnie, with deliveries of flowers and plants to homes, businesses, and hospitals. When he wasn't in school or working for the florist, Bobby helped the owner of the local candy store by unloading sodas, sweeping the floors, and stocking the shelves. The owner always stuffed a couple of bucks in Bobby's pocket at the end of the day. By the time he was fifteen, he was helping out on construction projects.

"Growing up, I got to know a couple of police officers who patrolled my neighborhood," Bobby said. "They made it their business to make sure we were behaving. If some lady complained we were throwing a ball against her house, they told us to get in the back seat. Then they drove us around the neighborhood and talked to us. There was never a time I was afraid of them. They were positive role models, and I looked up to them. These days people think cops don't do this kind of thing, but they're wrong. Keeping kids on the right path is a big part of our job."

After he graduated from high school, Bobby and his older brother, Russell, signed up for the civil service test to become police officers in New York City. They walked over to a high school in the Bronx to take the four-hour exam with questions on everything from U.S. history to mathematics. At the time, Bobby had a desk job in a supermarket. "I almost went crazy being confined to that desk all day," he said. "After six months, I said, 'That's it. This is not for me.'"

Bobby was twenty-four years old when he entered the New York City Police Academy. He said it was like being back in high school, except you had to wear a shirt and tie. "It was very regimented. I was amazed at how many people had no idea how to put on a tie or iron a shirt. Looking back, I can see that all that structure was probably a good way to do it for people coming into that environment who were not disciplined or motivated. Once the instructors began teaching us about actual police work and all the laws we were going to enforce, I was fascinated. We learned about very complicated police procedures as well as forensic science, social sciences, and the law. I began to see what a complex environment I was going into."

His first few years on the job, Bobby was assigned to A-Houses, precincts in neighborhoods with a lot of crime and a lot of victims. Bobby and his part-ners found themselves rushing to calls for burglaries, grand larcenies, and domestic violence as well as shootings, stolen autos, assaults, and firearms violations.

Like most rookies, he was distressed to see the terrible conditions some people live in. He remembers one call. The apartment was one small room that served as home to a woman and her six children. "There were cock-roaches crawling everywhere," he said. "The kids were lying on the mattress, and several of the younger ones were in dirty diapers. You say to yourself, 'Is this how people live?' You want to help them, but there's only so much you can do. You've got to keep your perspective. You learn you can't change their lives, but you can find small ways to help them. Sometimes just treating them with respect is enough."

* * *

Everyone in the business of policing knows that enforcing the law often comes down to a power struggle. During his years on patrol, Bobby made it a point to study the demeanor of older, more experienced cops. He learned that to be effective, you have to earn respect, and that takes time. He says he will always remember the incident when he knew he had mastered the art of not backing down.

"I was up on 181st Street and Broadway in Washington Heights. I was standing on the sidewalk in full uniform when a van pulled up and the driver got out to unload some boxes. The van did not have commercial plates, so he was not allowed to unload in that area. I told the driver he needed commercial plates to do that and when he was finished, he had to move.

"He took some boxes up the stairs to a nightclub. When he came back down, I warned him again. A few minutes later, a man from the club followed him out on the street. He was nicely dressed in a suit and tie. He glared at me. He said, 'Excuse me, did you just tell my guy he had to move the van?' Then he took his finger and jabbed it into my chest. 'Do you know who I am?' he said. 'I'm the manager of this club and a community leader, and you are go-ing to stop asking my guy to move.'"

Bobby told him to calm down. He pointed out that the illegally parked van was already causing a traffic jam.

The man went into a rage. He threatened to get Bobby transferred. A large crowd started to gather. Bobby got on his radio and told Central he was about to make an arrest and that he needed backup. He put on the cuffs and waited for the other officers to arrive so they could drive him to the station.

"He yelled and screamed the whole way," Bobby said. "When we got there, an old-time lieutenant was manning the desk. He always wore his reading glasses down over his nose. When we came in, the man was still screaming and demanding to talk to the captain. The lieutenant calmly looked up over the top of his glasses and asked what was going on.

"I told the lieutenant I had tried to give the man a summons for disorderly conduct, but he had refused to give me his name. The lieutenant rose up out of his chair. His face was beet red. You could tell he was furious. He told him that he was the captain there today and that he had better give me his name now. You could see the guy was scared. He gave me his name, and I handed him his summons."

Bobby is a firm believer that the uniform has to have respect. "If you treat people respectfully, they should return the favor. That man could have said, 'Okay, I'm so-and-so. If you have a problem with my van, come and talk to me.' Then we could have had a conversation. Cops learn pretty fast that if you don't take the bull by the horns, this type of person will walk all over you. If I hadn't put him in handcuffs and taken him off the street, the people looking on would have known I was too weak to exert my authority as a police officer."

* * *

There are a lot of skills to master and lessons to learn before law enforcement officers excel at what they do. Along with acquiring negotiation skills, developing empathy, demanding respect, and winning power struggles, cops have to learn to never take personally what happens on the street. Finding the fine line between asserting one's authority and letting some things go by is key.

One time one of Bobby's partners let her emotions get the best of her. She took something that happened personally, and the results almost ended in disaster. "We were driving down the street, and some people flagged us down. They told us that up the block in the middle of the street, a man and woman were fighting. They weren't sure if either party was armed, but they were going at it.

"We drove up there and jumped out of the car," Bobby said. "I grabbed the man, and my partner took the woman. I told the guy, 'Hey, let's just forget about this. There are no injuries here. Let's you and I take a walk. You can tell me what happened.'"

Bobby's partner took the opposite approach. "I'm not sure what happened, but she began screaming at the woman. A crowd started to form, and soon they were yelling obscenities. Seconds after that, bottles started coming at us. I called in a 10-85 for backup. There must have been close to one hundred people on the street, all trying to get at my partner. It all happened in a couple of minutes, and it was very scary."

Bobby explains that it only takes a couple of minutes to incite a crowd. "The group can get very big very fast, especially in warmer weather in these tightly packed neighborhoods where everyone is hanging out on the street. Think about it. There were just two of us and hundreds of them moving in, all because my partner reacted emotionally when someone on the street insulted her."

* * *

As time went by, Bobby was amazed to learn how much people depend on the police for a whole range of things outside law enforcement. He began to recognize the ability cops have to help people.

"Some of this stuff really makes you laugh," he said. " People run up to you on the street and expect the world. Some think you know everything. There's a bus stop right in front of them, but they want you to tell them where it is. If you worked in the Bronx your whole career, you don't know too much about Manhattan or Staten Island, yet if you're in a uniform, they think you know everything about every part of the city."

A rookie officer has much to learn, and Bobby holds that without the intense supervision and mentoring from older, more experienced officers, it would take a lifetime to learn how to be a good cop. "When you get out of the Academy, they put you in a car one day and make you walk a beat the next. When you're in the car, there's always a field training officer with you. We call them FTOs. The walking beat you do on your own.

"One time we got a call for a burglary in progress. My field training officer was with me. We drove to the location, jumped out of the car, and ran up the stairs. I went over to the door and tried to listen in. It turned out to be nothing. When we were back in the car, the FTO told me I had made a big mistake: You never stand in front of a door. He explained there is absolutely no protection if someone comes charging out the door with a knife or shoots through it with a gun. I learned that day that when you approach a door, you never do it head-on.

"If you're book smart, that's great, but in this line of work, street smarts are more important. When I came on the job in 1981, there were still guys working who had begun their careers in the sixties. They had fifteen or twenty years on. Back then there was a height requirement, and they all seemed like huge men—and Irish. If you took the time to listen to them, you learned a lot. It takes years of watching and talking to learn how to do this job well."

Bobby had only been a cop a little more than two months when he had his first homicide. "That day I was working alone in the 26th Precinct in Harlem," he said. "I was walking a beat at 112th Street and Broadway when I heard that unmistakable sound. Pop. Pop. Pop. The gunfire seemed like it was coming from right around the corner, and I ran toward the sound. As I turned the corner, I saw a man crouching down. There was a body lying at his feet. I don't know if he saw me or not, but he turned around and started walking. I got on the radio and told Central that a man had been shot. I said I needed an ambulance and backup and reported that the possible shooter was a Hispanic male around five-foot-five who was carrying a gun and walking northbound on the west side of Broadway. I followed him, all the while giving Central a running commentary. It was only a minute or two when several Anti-Crime cops and a field training officer were by my side. They ran ahead, caught up to the suspect, grabbed him from behind, and got him in handcuffs. As the precinct cops got the suspect into the backseat of their car, I ran back to where his victim was lying in the street. The man was huge, I guessed around six-foot-seven and 350 pounds. There was blood all over him, and he appeared to be dead.

"A crowd had gathered on the street, and all the women were cheering. They told us that every day, the dead man picked on the shooter. He would wait outside the shooter's door until he tried to go out. Then he beat him and stole his money. I guess the shooter finally snapped.

"After medical personnel tried and failed to save the victim, his body was taken to the morgue. I was standing there in the street thinking to myself, 'Boy, this is amazing. I just got myself a great collar—a homicide arrest and a gun arrest all rolled into one.'"

Bobby's sergeant pulled up and offered to drive him back to the precinct. On the way back, the sergeant broke the news. The Anti-Crime cops had more experience. They were going to process the arrest.

A month later Bobby got his second homicide, or lost it, depending on your point of view. He was working the day shift. He was waiting by the front desk for his FTO when a woman in her late twenties came into the station. "She was crying," Bobby recalled. "She walked over and told me she had just killed her baby. I was stunned that anyone would come into a police station and say something like that. She said she put the baby in a box and buried him under a tree in the park a couple of blocks away. I told her to sit down and try to relax. I would be right back. I ran upstairs to find the FTO. I told him, 'Freddie, there's a woman in the lobby. She says she just killed her baby.'"

Freddie and two detectives jumped out of their chairs and ran down the stairs. The woman was crying harder now. They talked to her for a couple of minutes before leaving for the park. They found the baby boy exactly where she said he would be, buried under a tree.

Once they were back at the station, Bobby's field training officer told him that the two detectives were going to arrest the woman for the death of her son. "I thought to myself, 'Hey, is this how this job goes? I'm the new guy, so other people get the credit?'"

After he had more experience, Bobby came to understand that homicide investigations are complicated. Detectives would interview the mother and try to find out if her story stayed consistent. As best they could, they would try to determine her state of mind when she killed her child. They would explore the possibility that maybe she didn't do it. Perhaps someone else killed the baby, and she was taking the blame. With only two months on the street, there was no way a rookie had the skills for such complex tasks.

* * *

Looking back at his two-and-a-half-decade career, Bobby has no trouble recalling his most amazing experience. It was 1985. He had been on the force for four years, and his rank was patrol officer. "I had finished my shift and was home watching television when my sergeant called me. He told me to get a suit and tie and report the next morning to the twelfth floor of One Police Plaza for an interview. The Chief of the Organized Crime Control Bureau wanted to see me."

Bobby was incredulous. The sergeant sometimes pulled these kind of pranks. He thought it must be some sort of a practical joke. The sergeant must have realized Bobby wasn't buying the story because he called back. He explained that it was no joke. "Organized Crime wants you down there for an interview," he told him. "And I have no idea why."

The next day Bobby drove down to the southern tip of Manhattan to NYPD headquarters. He took the elevator up to the twelfth floor.

He was mystified. "Organized Crime is one of the most elite units in the NYPD," Bobby said. "You need at least five years of experience working in plainclothes to even be considered. I'd never heard of anyone making the leap from where I was on the totem pole—patrol officer in a precinct—to Organized Crime. I couldn't figure it out."

The interview was tense. Seated at a rectangular table were two lieutenants, a captain, and an inspector. Their questions ranged from what strategies Hom would use during investigations of particular crimes to inquiries designed to determine if he had any tendencies to be corrupt.

At one point the captain looked at Bobby. "You're sitting in a diner. You pay a dollar for a cup of coffee. They hand the dollar back to you. What do you do?" Hom replied that he didn't drink coffee. "I told the captain I would order a cup of tea, leave a dollar for the tea and another one for the tip. Then I would say, 'Have a nice day.'"

The lieutenant asked him what he would do if he was asked to respond to a robbery in a liquor store. Bobby said he would interview the people involved, write up a detailed report, and go back to the precinct, and hand it in.

"I barely got the words out of my mouth when the lieutenant told me I was acting like a cop. He wanted to know what I would do as a detective."

Bobby didn't want them to see he was nervous. He tried to respond quickly. "I would interview everyone," he said. "But I would also find out who had been fired or if there was anyone who might want to retaliate against the store, its owner, its manager, or any of the employees. Then I would try to determine what was going on outside when the suspects left, and I would get descriptions and license plate numbers of the cars that were parked outside the store."

The New York City Police Department was starting up a new unit at the Organized Crime Control Bureau to focus on crimes plaguing the Asian community. Twenty-five people were interviewed for the new unit, but only a handful were chosen. Bobby Hom was one of them. Two weeks later he was transferred from the 40th Precinct in the Bronx. The Nontraditional Organized Crime Task Force III was his new assignment.

On his first day with the Task Force, Hom was greeted by his new sergeant and a mountain of paperwork. He was anxious to get to work, but first he needed a security clearance from the FBI. That could take up to three months.

"There were several criminal gangs operating in Chinatown at that time," Bobby explained. "We had the White Eagles, the Black Eagles, the Ghost Shadows, and the Flying Dragons. They were into drugs, extortion, and kidnappings. The Ghost Shadows and Flying Dragons were bitter rivals. They had staked out separate five block areas in and around Chinatown and extorted money from small, legitimate Chinese business owners in exchange for protection."

Bobby explained that the 5th Precinct, which covers the Chinatown area, had a plainclothes unit known as the Jade Squad. These officers focused exclusively on Chinese gangs, but it was next to impossible to infiltrate these groups, and the crime and violence was getting worse. NYPD officials were hoping that Bobby Hom and the team at the Nontraditional Organized Crime Task Force could get things under control.

"You can't get close to Chinese gangs," Bobby explains. "They're similar to the Italian Mafia in that way. They have to know you personally. The only way we could get information was to wait until someone we arrested flipped. They all have different reasons for working with us. Some are tired of the system. Others want revenge. We make them an offer. If they accept, they go back and infiltrate their own gang."

The gangs were ruthless. Small business owners who could not pay up when the extortionists came calling were frequently beaten. Their businesses were trashed and their families threatened. To avoid these repercussions, the typical small business paid an average of $100 every week.

"I'll never forget one small herbal medicine store," Bobby said. "The owner either wouldn't or couldn't pay, so they completely destroyed his store. Then they came back and told the guy, 'Hey, you won't pay one hundred? Well, now you owe us two hundred.'

"These small merchants are reluctant to call the police. One of the victims—a guy who paid every week—said to us, 'Look you're here now, but soon you'll leave. I have to be here alone, fifteen hours a day, by myself.' It's sad. The police cannot be there all the time. You can understand why they pay."

Some of the investigations focused on illegal gambling operations that went on in the back of storefronts and other businesses that appeared legitimate from the street. "There were several on Mott Street," Bobby said. "To someone walking by, it looked like a Chinese grocery store. But down in the basement or out in the back, there were high-stakes gambling operations under way. If you're not Asian, you are not going to get in."

The Vice Unit would request Asian undercovers for these assignments. "We did some of the entries for the gambling parlors," Bobby continued. "These places all had double doors. The first undercover goes through the first door and leaves a newspaper in the door jam. That way the door can't shut, leaving us trapped in the passageway between the first and second doors. There is always a guard at the second door. You've only got a split second to grab him and get him under control. Your backup hit team is coming right in behind you. If you hesitate at all, the guy at the door will ring an alarm, and their guys will exit out of a back room and be gone."

The adrenaline was always flowing when it came time to make the entry. Bobby is part Chinese, and frequently he was picked to be the first one in. He'd get to the second door, show his shield, and tell whoever was guarding the door that he was the police. "Chinese gangs are reluctant to take on a police officer," Hom says. "You've got to make it clear immediately that you are a cop. If they think it's another gang out to rob them, there's trouble."

One time the operation went haywire. Bobby got buzzed in at the first door. "I dropped the paper down so the door would not shut behind me. I got to the second door, and a nineteen-year-old kid opened it. He had a thirty-inch fan sitting next to him, and before I could say anything or get my shield out, he threw it at me. I ducked, then I tackled him. We ended up rolling around on the floor. That's when I saw the gun roll out of his pants. It was a .25 automatic. I knocked him against the wall. I was yelling, 'Police. Police. Police.' I heard the troops come in behind me. One of the worst things you can do, tactically, is get in their way, so I tried to step back. Once our team gets through those doors, if the people downstairs see what's happening on their security cameras, it's all over. The money disappears, the receipts disappear, and the people disappear. You've wasted your time because you have no evidence. Without evidence, you can't arrest anybody.

"We kept struggling at the door. I had my back up against the wall, and I was still holding onto the kid. The other cops came in, grabbed him, and forced him down to the floor. When I looked over, I could see one cop crouching over him, struggling to get the handcuffs on. We were sure all the guys in the back would be long gone, along with the evidence. Lucky for us, they were still there, and we made several arrests."

The next raid went better. Bobby again went in first. When he got to the second door, he pulled his shield and grabbed the guy by his shirt. "It must have been just a second when the other guys came in behind me," he said. "They raced down the stairs to the room where a high-stakes game was going on. Everyone at the table was arrested."

Bobby says it's a myth that gambling is a victimless crime. "These places were hotbeds of serious crime. That much money passing hands in unregulated businesses outside the reach of the law is always a recipe for disaster. If someone incurs big losses and can't come up with the money, the gang goes after them. Sometimes people are brutally beaten and family members are threatened. Others are kidnapped and held for ransom, and legitimate businesses are trashed.

"We will never eliminate illegal gambling. It's too big a business. But you can make the people who are running these operations afraid that if they beat, kidnap, or threaten someone, the police will be there enforcing the law."

One time Bobby and Wayne McDonnell asked a confidential informant if he had any leads on people involved with robberies, illegal firearms, or hijackings. "He said no," Bobby recalled. "Then he asked, 'What about kidnappings?' He told us his friend was in a car downstairs and that some guys had kidnapped his cousin. She was a young girl, barely eighteen years old. That night he and his friend were going to meet the kidnappers and pay them $40,000 to get her back."

Kidnappings fall under the jurisdiction of the NYPD's Major Case Squad, and Bobby and Wayne told them what they knew. Major Case investigators, along with Detective Hom and Agent McDonnell, another detective with the Organized Crime Control Bureau, and two DEA agents, followed the informant as he drove to the prearranged meeting spot to drop the money and pick up the girl. "The suspect showed up," Bobby recalled, "but he didn't have the girl with him. We weren't too worried because the informant knew where she was being held."

The informant gave the man the $40,000. Earlier the officers had put a bug inside the bag of money so they wouldn't lose him. They let him drive three or four blocks. Then they put on the lights and sirens and pulled him over. "He must have thought it was a motor vehicle stop," Bobby said.

Once the suspected kidnapper was under arrest, Bobby and Wayne Mc-Donnell drove to the place where the girl was being held. "She had burn marks all over her," Bobby said. "It looked like they had taken lit cigarettes and pressed them into her skin until the cigarette went out. She'd been badly beaten and raped, most likely repeatedly. They treated her like a rag doll. She spoke no English, and even with a translator, she was afraid to talk to us. We called in a female detective in hopes that might help us get some information, but she was too frightened to speak. The subsequent investigation revealed that these people had been kidnapping illegal immigrants and holding them for ransom. They know their victims are so terrified of being deported that they will never call the police, no matter what happens to them."

Bobby still remembers one young man who came to the United States illegally to find work. "Once they got him to the United States, one of the principals in the smuggling ring knew he had no one to protect him. He imprisoned the boy in his home and used him as a slave. Eventually the kid got desperate and jumped out of a fifth-story bathroom window. He hit an air conditioner on his fall down to the street. That was probably the only reason he survived."

When detectives talked to him in the hospital, the young man told them he was being held hostage. He had no place to go and no one he could ask to pay the ransom demanded by the man he had already paid to smuggle him into the country. At that time, the going rate for what the victims believed would be safe passage to the United States, was $40,000 to $50,000. Hopeful immigrants were told that housing, jobs, and even cars would be waiting for them. But the reality was that they were more likely to end up working as prostitutes until they could pay back the fees. If they could not come up with the money, the smugglers beat and tortured them, turned them over to Immigration, or tried to find a family member who would come up with the money.

Bobby says it's important not to underestimate the important role played by confidential informants. "If people didn't flip and agree to work with us and inform on their own people, it would be much more difficult, if not impossible, for us to know what is going on. Asian communities are very insulated. They don't talk to non-Asians. There were only a few times when law enforcement was able to infiltrate the groups.

"One of the cases we worked was on the West Coast back in the 1980s. A major breakthrough occurred when two NYPD detectives went undercover and managed to get inducted into the gang. They did the whole bit—even cutting their fingers as part of the initiation ritual. But it was a rare occurrence for law enforcement officers to get on the inside. Mostly we relied on confidential informants for information to make our cases."

* * *

Bobby retired as a First Grade Detective in 2006 after twenty-six years on the job. Today he's the director of security for a company in the city. His new position is challenging, but he admits he misses being a cop with the NYPD. "When you're a police officer, every day is different, and every day is interesting. And you are doing important work. I miss all that."

His many hobbies and interests keep him busy in his spare time. He loves restoring cars from the 1960s. He's an avid fisherman and hunter and is still involved with martial arts, a lifelong passion. He has a daughter, Tara, who works in the medical billing department of a local hospital and she moonlights during baseball season at Yankee Stadium working with its security team.

Deciding to become a police officer is still the best decision Bobby made in his life. "Working for the police department is a great experience," he says. "You're out on the street, lots of things are happening, and you're helping people. How can you beat that?"

When people ask him if he would go back, he doesn't even stop to think before answering. "I would go back in a minute," he says smiling.

Bobby was promoted to Second Grade Detective in 1988. Above, left to right: John Martin, Bobby's partner on the Drug Enforcement Task Force; Bobby's wife Denise; brother Russell; Detective Ida Rosenblum; Sergeant Lenny Lemer. Denise (left) still recalls how proud she felt that day. But Bobby's career didn't stop there. They celebrated again in April, 2001, when he was promoted to Detective First Grade.

Heroin bust nets $5M

By DANIEL HAYS
Daily News Staff Writer

Displaying a 4-foot, $5 million mountain of greenbacks, anti-drug cops yesterday announced they had seized a record amount of cash during a raid on a Brooklyn rowhouse used by a Southeast Asian heroin ring.

The operation, which involved searches of three homes in Brooklyn, led to the arrest of four men and the seizure of a machine gun, three pistols, a press for making blocks of heroin and 13 steel canisters said to have contained 150 pounds of heroin.

Much of the heroin originated with Chang Chi Fu, the Burma-based, Chinese druglord the Drug Enforcement Administration calls a self-proclaimed "king of opium," said Agent Robert Bryden, speaking at DEA's Manhattan headquarters.

Bryden was joined by Police Commissioner Lee Brown and representatives of the U.S. Customs Service, Immigration and Naturalization Service, Internal Revenue Service and State Police as well as Mayor Dinkins and Rep. Charles Rangel (D-Manhattan).

Guaranteed 100%

Seized material included labels used to identify the heroin as the "Double U Globe Brand." Picturing two lions leaning on a globe of the world, the stickers state in Chinese, "beware of counterfeits — guaranteed 100 percent."

In Brooklyn, Assistant U.S. Attorney Cathy Palmer called the four men who were arrested "pretty significant players."

She said the Double U brand was a variety of heroin produced by Chang and it was "very significant and rare to find heroin presses."

The four arrested were identified as Ken Lee Sak, of Elizabeth Place; Siu Chuen Chung, 32, of E. Ninth St.; Kam-Far Lee of 70th St., all of Brooklyn and Tak Chew Chiu, 30, of Glendale, Arizona.

The task force has been tracking the operation for six months with intense surveillance, officials said.

The investigation took six months, but when Bobby and his team raided four locations in Brooklyn, all the hard work paid off. At one location members of the Task Force seized 1400 grams of pure heroin. When all the money was accounted for, they had collected close to $9 million in cash. At the time, it was the largest seizure of heroin drug money in DEA history. Above is one of the many news accounts of the bust.

Above, a photo of the sawed-off rifle connected to a trap that was rigged to fire when the case was opened. The target was U.S. Attorney Cathy Palmer, a prosecutor of Asian gangs. Luckily, Bobby Hom was in Cathy's office when the deadly package arrived. Detective Hom was able to deactivate the spring before it could cause any damage. The jury deliberated two hours before finding David Kwong, the man who sent the package and was charged with attempted murder, guilty on all charges. Both the print and broadcast media ran numerous news stories on the incident and the subsequent trial.

Bobby with his
daughter, Tara, at his
retirement party from
the NYPD. Tara works
in the medical billing
department of a local
hospital and moonlights
during baseball season
at Yankee Stadium
working with their
security team.

Bobby spent several years with the Southeast Asian Heroin Task Force.
During the 1980's and 90's, 85 percent of the heroin purchased in the
United States passed through New York City. The demand among
Americans for illegal drugs has been so great for so long that it virtually
guarantees a limitless market for the world's suppliers. Bobby Hom and
his team at the Task Force were always busy.

Bobby and his good friend Glen Bressan on the day they graduated from the NYPD Academy in 1982. Bobby and Glen have stayed close friends for three decades.

At right, Bobby in 2006 right before he retired. This may have been Detective Hom's last time in uniform after a long, successful career with the New York City Police Department.

Chapter Six

John Busching:
The Man Who Wouldn't Leave Ground Zero

"True heroism is remarkably sober, very undramatic. It is not the urge to surpass all others at whatever cost but the urge to serve others at whatever cost." —Arthur Ashe

Hurricane Isabel, which formed from a tropical wave in the warm waters of the Caribbean on September 6, 2003, was gathering strength. Five days later it was packing winds of 165 miles per hour. As the storm churned up the Atlantic Coast, emergency management officials from South Carolina to Massachusetts activated disaster plans. The Navy ordered forty warships and submarines in Norfolk, Virginia, to go out to sea. The Air Force ordered fighter jets at coastal bases to fly inland as far as Oklahoma, and the Governor of Virginia declared a state of emergency. In New York, Governor George Pataki urged residents to purchase emergency supplies and fill their gas tanks. The state's National Guard began to mobilize, the Army and Air National Guard started reviewing their lists of personnel and equipment, and the New York State Police deployed troopers throughout the state to secure buildings with sandbags. By September 20, almost two weeks later, Isabel had moved past New York. The storm had weakened on its path, but the seas were rough and the winds were still gusting up to sixty miles per hour.

On that day, John Busching, a veteran New York City cop, made the forty-five-minute commute from his home on Long Island to his current assignment at Floyd Bennett Field in Brooklyn. He knew the former Coast Guard base at the southeast tip of Brooklyn, now home to the Emergency Service Headquarters, would not close down. The weather was the last thing on his mind as he drove down the Belt Parkway toward his office. Floyd Bennett Field is the location of the special training school for the NYPD's Emergency Service Unit. It also serves as a storage facility for the Department's additional extra large equipment and vehicles including several multimillion-dollar mobile command vehicles and rescue trucks. Across the roadway is the Department's Aviation Unit.

As John was preparing material for an upcoming training session, the phone rang. A pilot with the Aviation Unit was on the other end of the line, and when he realized he'd reached John Busching, he must have been relieved. The pilot knew John was a paramedic, one of only 15 officers out of close to 40,000 in the entire Department who could start an IV, connect a heart attack victim up to an EKG machine, or insert a tube into someone's trachea to help them breathe. The pilot was going to need someone with those skills. He told John to find a partner, get his rappelling harness and medical kit, and hurry over to his office.

John Busching and John Murphy assembled their gear and went over to Aviation. Murphy, a lieutenant with sixteen years on the force, never hesitated even though he had no information about the mission and was still on light duty because of an injury two years earlier when he was on a search and rescue mission at Ground Zero. It had been just hours after the attacks of September 11, 2001, and falling debris had almost amputated his hand. He had undergone several surgeries and countless hours of rehab, but scar tissue had developed and his hand was still messed up.

The Commander of the NYPD's Special Operations Division greeted them at the door. Cops know something major is happening when the guy who heads up many of the specialized units of the NYPD, including Aviation, Harbor, Emergency Service, and K-9, just to name a few, is the welcoming party. John remembers the Commander's first words were not encouraging. "He started out saying, if we think it's too windy, too risky, too dangerous, we shouldn't do it. I think he even said something about not wanting us to go out there and get killed. John Murphy had the right response. He said we should get focused, figure out the mission, and then decide if we could do it."

The Commander explained an urgent call had come in to the Coast Guard. A container ship, registered in South Africa on its way to New York from the Congo, had someone on board who was bleeding to death. The ship was eight miles out, with seas approaching ten feet. The Coast Guard decided a ship-to-ship rescue was too risky. They called the New York City Police Department to see if they could help.

The Commander told Officer Busching and Lieutenant Murphy they would be flown out to the ship and lowered one at a time onto the deck. They would find the injured person, patch him up, and get him into a rescue stretcher so he could be hoisted back up to the helicopter. The crew would fly the injured man to the hospital, refuel, and then return to get Busching and Murphy. A big Bell 412 aircraft was all gassed up and ready to go along with a pilot, copilot, and two crew chiefs, one more than usual due to the heavy weather.

People in Emergency Service live for assignments like this, and despite the unknowns, Busching and Murphy agreed to take on the mission. But there were serious drawbacks. John Busching had practiced being lowered out of a helicopter only once, and John Murphy had never been lowered with the hoist—not much experience for an operation of this sort. And then there was the problem of Lieutenant Murphy's hand. Murphy said later the thought crossed his mind that his bosses might wonder why he was being lowered out of a helicopter in high winds and rough seas when he was still recovering from a serious injury, but there was a life to save and he decided to deal with the consequences later. Busching and Murphy got their gear, climbed into the 412, and lifted off.

"We were on the scene less than five minutes," John recalled. "As far as we knew, we were there for a rescue mission of a person who was bleeding to death."

Exiting a helicopter that's hovering eighty feet above the designated land-ing spot when the winds are blowing hard requires focus, balance, and fearlessness. "After you step off, you're tethered by that one cable," John explained. "You've got to be very careful you don't shock-load the cable when you step out onto the skid of the helicopter. You have to let go very smoothly. If you jump, the cable will shear off to keep the helicopter from crashing." Both officers were well aware an Israeli military helicopter had had the cable snap when a soldier jumped out with too much force. That was an experience they were not eager to replicate.

As the pilot got closer and was able to look down on the deck, he could see they had a problem. There was almost no place on the crowded tanker deck for the officers to land. Containers stacked as high as a five-story building were packed in tight from bow to stern. There was no room for error.

They decided Murphy would go first. "Because of the way the cargo containers were stacked, they had to drop us from eighty feet in the air," John continued. "They just couldn't get closer."

Lieutenant Murphy got out on the skids and double-checked that his cable was secure. The scene inside the helicopter was tense. The pilot was working hard trying to hold the aircraft steady against the winds, and the crew chief was in the back trying to control the swing of the cable. The lieutenant with the injured hand was getting blown all over the place as he was being lowered down. In addition, the ship was riding up and down on the waves.

"No one remembers how long it took, John said "It might have only been ten minutes, but it seemed to go on for hours."

Busching was weighted down with a backpack filled with medical supplies and an oxygen tank. When it was his turn to jump, he had to be extremely careful because of the extra weight. "As soon as you left the helicopter you could feel how strong the wind was blowing and you just knew you were in for the ride of a lifetime. I forced myself to concentrate on the task at hand, not all the things that could go wrong."

* * *

When police officers begin their extensive training at the Police Academy, they're taught there's no such thing as a routine call, that no matter what they've been told to expect by the dispatcher or whoever has relayed the information, they had better be prepared for a surprise when they get to the scene. That was certainly true for John Murphy and John Busching on that day in September of 2003 eight miles off the coast of New York City. John said whoever called the Coast Guard indicated someone had cut himself and was bleeding badly. "Unfortunately for us, that wasn't the entire truth."

The real story was the captain had discovered two stowaways from the Congo onboard when the ship was thirty miles outside the New York Harbor. The captain made the decision to lock them inside one of the cabins until he could get the ship closer to shore. One went peacefully, but the other guy fought back, so they tied him up and put him in a separate cabin. Ironically, it was the compliant one who would pose the threat. He understood U.S. laws well enough to know that if he needed medical attention, he would be in the system and then he could apply for asylum. He found a screwdriver and stabbed himself in the leg. So instead of an injured crew member, the cops were out at sea facing an armed stowaway who was bleeding. "We had no special equipment," John recalled. "No Tasers, no heavy ballistic vests. Nothing. On top of all that, he was from Africa where the threat of AIDS is really big. I looked at John and said, 'Okay, here we go.'"

The first thing they did was call the pilot on the radio. They told him they had run into a glitch. The bleeding guy was a stowaway from Africa and he was barricaded and armed. They promised to call with updates every ten minutes and reassured the crew circling in the helicopter they were aware the fuel was burning.

Busching explains when cops are faced with the unexpected, they revert back to their training. The first thing New York City cops are trained to do when a mentally ill person barricades him- or herself in a room or building is to secure the door so the person can't open it and shoot or throw something out. "Once the door is secure and we've minimized the threat from the other side, then we start negotiating," he said. "John found some webbing and we took some big hooks from our rappelling gear and somehow were able to secure the door."

The bleeding stowaway spoke very little English, so negotiations were a bit of a bust. In addition, they were pressed for time. The helicopter could stay hovering over the ship for only a limited amount of time. The officers decided to try and get a look to see what they were dealing with. They felt if the stowaway was acting crazy, he would be too dangerous to deal with since they had minimal manpower and limited equipment. They would have to wait for backup.

"I opened the door just a little," John said. "I could see he was on the far side of the room lying down on the floor. There was blood all around the cabin and he was completely naked. He spoke a little English—about as much as I speak French. Murphy kept telling him if he decided to fight with us, bad things were going to happen, but I'm not sure how much he understood. We told him to throw the weapon across the room toward us, and after a few minutes he did push it over in our direction. Murphy was behind me in the doorway, so he didn't have a good view inside the cabin. He had no idea the guy was naked. He kept asking me how I could be sure he didn't have any other weapons on him. I told him not to worry. We got him dressed in one of the crew member's clothes, and I bandaged and dressed his wound. Then we handcuffed him, put him in the rescue basket, and raised him up to the helicopter."

Neither Busching nor Murphy was happy they had to remain on the boat, but there wasn't room for all of them in the helicopter. The pilot told them he'd get back to the ship as quickly as possible after the trip to the hospital and refueling the aircraft. "Still we felt relieved to see the door to the helicopter close and fly away to the hospital." John said. "We had done our jobs and nobody had been hurt."

John explained that some of the misunderstandings they encountered on the ship could be attributed to a language barrier. Most of the crew did not speak English. "We actually were treated very well while we waited to be picked up by the helicopter," he remembered. "We shared a soda with the captain in the galley." John felt bad the captain was probably going to lose his job because of the stowaways. "It was a huge ship and he only had ten crew members. Think about that. We had six highly trained people in that helicopter and that captain only had ten men to run that huge ship."

When the helicopter touched down back at the NYPD's Aviation Unit, Busching and Murphy were tired. It had been a three-hour ordeal. They had had nothing to eat and the adrenalin rush left them exhausted. All they wanted to do was go home. But in law enforcement work you don't control your work time. Frequently cops have to keep working long after their shift officially ends. John said they were almost out the door when they got a call from the NYPD's Public Information Office. They were told they couldn't go home just yet. Reporters were on their way to interview them for the ten o'clock news.

* * *

When people make the decision to go into a life of public service, whether they choose to serve in the armed forces, teach our young people, save people from burning buildings, ride in the back of an ambulance, or enforce the laws so we can live in peace and safety, many things can influence that decision. Some are looking for a secure job with health insurance and a pension, others are committed to doing something with their lives that will help others and make the world a better place, and then there are the people whose mother or father was a teacher, firefighter. or cop and it never occurred to them to be anything else.

John's father, Warren, spent thirty-six years with the New York City Fire Department. "He still is the person I look up to the most," John says. "He never talked about the fires he fought or what went on at work, but you could tell he loved what he did. He never came home in a bad mood. I always appreciated that."

There was only one time John and his family remember their dad being upset. "We were all at home, and as soon as he got in the door, he found me and my brother and my sisters, and he hugged each of us for a long time. To be that emotional was very out of character for him. We found out later that several children had died in a fire that day, and he had helped bring their burned bodies out of the building."

In the spring of 1983, as John approached his high school graduation, his father began to talk to his eldest son about taking the police exam. John said his father never forced it on him. "He always told me that working for the Police or Fire Department was more than a regular job. You had to really want to do it. Because I looked up so much to my father, all I ever really wanted to do was be a firefighter," John confessed.

The fire service was in the Busching genes. Along with his dad, John's grandfather was an auxiliary fireman during World War II, and his younger brother started out as a cop but soon quickly switched over to the FDNY. The Fire Department wasn't hiring and the Police Department was. John signed up for the civil service test required for all Police Department hopefuls. A few months later he learned he passed. His Academy class of one thousand recruits began a few months later.

* * *

After seven months in the Academy, John's first assignment was patrolling the New York City subway system. At that time, it was the largest public tran-

sit system in the world. With 468 stations and 656 miles of track, the system
has inspired music, poetry, art, drama, and comedy. Jennifer Lopez named
her debut album in 1999 "On the 6" after the train she rode from her home
in the Bronx to her dance and music lessons in Manhattan. *Seinfeld, I Love
Lucy, All in the Family,* among the most popular television programs of the
last half-century, all had episodes taking place in New York subway cars. One
of America's most famous jazz compositions, "Take the A Train," written by
Billy Strayhorn for Duke Ellington in the 1940s, was inspired by the train that
runs from Harlem down to the southernmost tip of Manhattan.

At the same time that New York's subways provided fodder for the arts,
they were also a magnet for criminals. During the past several decades and
especially after the terrorist attacks of September 11, the city has maintained
a strong law enforcement presence on the cars and platforms of the vast system.

John's first assignment was the Tactical Patrol Force out of District 20 in
Queens. The assignment entailed riding the trains back and forth from one
end of the line to the other—alone. His tour of duty was from 7:30 p.m. to
4:00 a.m. You could call for backup only if the radios worked, and the communications system underground was notorious for not working. To survive,
subway cops learn to be self-reliant, and they learn how to talk to people.
About those days, John says, "It was you and them.

"Early in my career I stopped a young man—probably in his early twenties—for smoking on the train," he recalled. "I asked him for identification
and he started to act very nervous. I looked in his back pocket and could see
he had an open knife sticking out. He went for the knife and I went for my
gun. As I was taking him off the train at gunpoint, the conductor closed the
door of the train on my arm. The gun was outside along with my suspect and
I was still inside the car. Luckily, I kept hold of my gun. The door jerked open
and I proceeded with the arrest."

But John was shaken up. The first chance he got, he told the story to another subway cop hoping for some sympathy. "Welcome to the Transit Police,"
the other officer replied with a shrug.

As the years passed, he learned about a specialized unit called the Emergency Medical Rescue Unit, better known as EMRU. EMRU cops respond to
all the medical disasters that occur in the massive subway system. He remembers that from the minute he learned of its existence, he had one goal: to do

whatever was necessary to be accepted into that unit.

John's passion to combine law enforcement and medical work developed when he was still assigned to patrol. One call was pivotal. A body was trapped under a subway car, and when he got to the scene, he jumped down off the platform and crawled under the train. "I saw this young woman—she probably was in her early twenties. It looked like several trains had run over her. I talked to her but she never answered. I called for help and tried to do what I could. I bandaged her wounds, administered oxygen, and held her head and neck tightly in my hands. I tried to pull her close to me so she would be supported while I waited for the EMRU cops to arrive. When those guys got there, I watched them in action. They completely took over and did everything possible to save that girl's life. I was really hooked. I said to myself, 'Whatever it takes, I'm going to be part of this.'"

John spent the next five years on regular patrol while making repeated requests for a transfer. He prepared himself for the extensive tests and interviews that are required before winning an assignment to the EMRU. He realized his goal in 1991 when the department assigned him to the unit. In April 1995, the New York City Transit Police Department was merged with the NYPD, and Transit's EMRU merged with the NYPD's Emergency Service Unit.

John began ESU's rigorous training program, but he turned out to be no ordinary trainee. It wasn't long before he began to jot down his thoughts in a notebook. "I was surprised there were no lesson plans," he said. "Things were not taught in an orderly way. Everything seemed like it was done by the seat of the pants."

After filling countless notebooks over the next six years, John was asked to help teach a class of new people coming into the unit. A few months later he was given the go-ahead to develop a comprehensive training curriculum for the NYPD's Emergency Service Unit.

He worked three months developing a new program. He eliminated the parts he thought were weak and added segments he knew would make the program stronger. After three months of work and proofreading the document one last time, he called the NYPD's Commissioner of Training and asked for an appointment.

"I had everything on a disk," he said. "I had detailed lesson plans, suggestions for training aides and props, and a recommendation that all the instructors become certified by the State of New York so we could receive college credits."

The curriculum was well done, and slowly ESU began to incorporate John's ideas into the rigorous training program required of all new officers coming into the unit. He cannot remember getting a pat on the back or any higher-ups acknowledging his work, but he knew he had done a good job when he learned months later the Department was using his curriculum for several other specialized units.

* * *

John's first assignment with ESU was Truck Seven in Brooklyn. Right off the bat it was everything he dreamed of. His third day with the unit, he was sent on a call for a barricaded perpetrator with hostages. An armed robbery had gone bad and patrol called for ESU. The job ended with the suspect in custody, no injuries to the hostages, and the cops exhilarated knowing they had done the job well.

After a year with the unit, Emergency Service officers are allowed to request a transfer to the ESU Apprehension Team where their only assignment is serving warrants against suspected felons who are almost always assumed to be violent.

In his first months on the A-Team, John and his fellow officers executed over seventy warrants. Mostly they did it without ever firing a shot. Their work took multiple perpetrators into custody and got hundreds of guns and tens of thousands of pounds of illegal narcotics off the street. It was after seeing close-up the risky assignments ESU officers routinely handled that John became interested in the concept of ESU personnel developing the skills necessary to provide medical support to officers who might become injured doing this dangerous work.

It was obvious to John that having some ESU officers who were trained as paramedics was going to save lives. Neither the Fire Department, the Emergency Medical Services nor private operators allow their people to enter situations where lives are at risk from active shooting or other threats. Until the scene has been neutralized, these first responders are not allowed inside the perimeter. Everyone knew of officers whose injuries were much worse because they had had to wait for medical help until the threat was over. John found out that many other big-city SWAT teams had had tactical medical programs up and running for years. John was confident the decision makers would agree that the busiest tactical team in the country should have a program of its own.

Spending about $4,000 of his own money during his off-duty time, he began the thirteen hundred required hours to become a paramedic: 162 eight-hour days of clinical and classroom training with stints in the neonatal unit, the morgue, the ICU, and the CCU. During the time he studied to become a paramedic, John was still working full time as a cop. For weeks his shift at the Department would end at midnight. Paramedic classes began eight hours later, at eight in the morning.

He wrote a report about the benefits to the Department if it established a Tactical Medical Program. He was at the beginning of his journey, with no clue about the obstacles that lay ahead. Looking back, John remembers sending the report off with high hopes it would be approved. He got a letter back with just two words. Request Denied. He knew he would have to fight harder.

John convinced the Department to let him and his partner, Dennis Healy, go to a training program where they could earn their tactical medic certification. "We paid for it out of our own pockets," he remembered. "The school was great. We came back all pumped up. I sent in another a report saying it was excellent training and it would be useful to the busiest tactical team in the country."

But disappointment arrived again in an envelope. Request Denied.

But this was all before Saturday, August 12, 2000. On that afternoon, Arthur Alalouf, a man who could not pass the psychological test for admission to the New York City Police Department took several semiautomatic weapons and thousands of rounds of ammunition and crawled down into a stairwell in a quiet neighborhood in Brooklyn. His plan was to kill as many cops as he could. By the time senior ESU snipers arrived on the scene, five New York City police officers lay seriously wounded on the ground. To this day, it is still one of the worst shootings in Department history. It was six hours when the first officer was hit to the time the suspect was shot and killed. Because none of the cops were approved to operate as paramedics, and the firefighters and EMTs were not allowed in while there was still gunfire, no one tended to officers' injuries on an advanced-life-support level.

John says he remembers every detail like it was yesterday. "I thought that's it, they are finally going to see the value of having dedicated medical support for all those people who got shot and could not get help because things were still active. Because we were not certified, our guys got no treatment until they got to the hospital. If Joe Guerra had been shot a little more to the center of his face, he would have had an airway blockage and died needlessly. Two other officers were severely injured and were forced to retire. One had nerve damage to his face. The other developed a blood clot in his leg."

A colleague of John's, Officer Tom Rowe, submitted the recommendation again. This time they were confident. Ron Wasson was now the Commander of Emergency Service. The word on Wasson was he taught EMT classes and understood the value of the program. Their hopes were realized when Wasson signed off on the proposal. Tom retired a few months later, and John took over the effort to establish a Tactical Medical Program. But approval required that the proposal follow a slow journey up through the endless chain of command. From the Emergency Service Unit, it went to the Special Operations Division, and then on to the Chief of Patrol, and finally up to the Chief of the Department. The next stop was the NYPD's Legal Bureau. Once the Department lawyers looked it over, they wrote a two-page endorsement saying the Department would be more liable for injuries to their officers if it did not have officers trained as tactical medics and that similar programs were already running in most of the big agencies in the country. From Legal, the proposal went to the First Deputy Commissioner's office, the second-highest ranking person in the Department. After he signed off, it went to its final destination—the desk of the NYPD Commissioner. When the Commissioner signed his name on the dotted line, it had been five years since John submitted his first proposal. He thought it was time to celebrate.

But notions of celebration were a bit premature. John found out he had several more rounds to fight, and the hassles within his own agency would turn out to be the least of his problems.

To get approval for the NYPD to have some of its officers perform more advanced medical work, the Department would have to get approval from the State of New York's Department of Health. In New York City all the emergency medical services are run by the FDNY, which meant John would have to make an alliance with the Fire Department. Then he learned that every organization that was even remotely involved with medical care would have to be briefed and then agree to sign off on the proposal. That included the

911 system, the city's Fire and Police Departments, all the private hospitals, all the public hospitals, and the city's Regional EMS Council right up to the Department of Health State EMS Council.

The written work required was mountainous. John went to countless meetings and hearings. At one point he was told by the New York City Regional EMS Council that he had to send out certified letters to every one of the eighty hospitals in New York City and get a statement in writing if there were objections. He wrote eighty letters to the hospitals and went to the post office and got the return receipt cards to fill out. He enlisted some of his fellow officers to help him fill out the return receipt cards by hand.

During all this time, John continued to meet with the Fire Department, assuring them the Police Department did not want to encroach on their turf. He told them the Police Department was only interested in getting the certification so officers could provide medical help in a tactical setting where one of their own was hurt and waiting for an ambulance or trip to the hospital.

John says every time he thought he was close, he'd hit a wall. Twenty-page forms that took days to fill in only to be told they were the wrong document. Meetings that never happened. Meetings that did happen but weren't the right forum. Requests for paperwork that had never been mentioned. It went on and on.

John put his head down and kept on slugging. He was forced to muster endless reserves of self-control not to fly into a rage when he was asked for another form he had already submitted, or another letter of approval from the Police Commissioner that had been done months before, or a request to do a presentation to a group he had already spoken with. It was endless months of one step forward and five steps back.

One day, when John thought he was close to getting approval, he was thrown another curveball. This one was out of the blue. He was testifying at yet another public hearing when a bureaucrat announced that approval was being held up until the police cars and trucks carrying the cops who had been trained as medics were certified by the State Department of Health. For John, this was the last straw. It was as close as he would come to giving up.

"I stood up," he said. "I told him fine. I'll be a pain in the ass for five more years. I'll come back to every meeting you have and I'll sit here in uniform until you approve this thing. I kept telling them I would never give up. I would keep raising my hand. I would keep asking why can't we do this? Why? Why?

Why? I'd already been in their face for almost a year, I doubt they wanted me around for five more."

As the battle raged on, John was determined to be the one left standing. The New York City Regional EMS Council convened endless meetings and John was asked endless questions.

"They were adamant that we would only operate in the tactical environment," he said. "The minute we got out of the tactical environment, we would revert back to EMT status. They kept asking me the same questions over and over again. Did I understand that we could not give medication except in the tactical situation? I told them the same thing again and again. We do not want to do that. I said if they voted against us, the Fire Department was not going to come in and train their own people to do this work. Then we'd go round and round about who was I to speak for the Fire Department? I'd tell them, just take my word for it. No way is the Fire Department going to train its EMTs to enter active shooting scenes to give life-supporting treatment to injured cops. It was an arduous journey. Every time I thought I was there, they'd throw something else at me. I still don't know why they made it so hard."

When he looks back, John wonders whether the program would have ever been approved if it hadn't been for the attacks of September 11. That event had a major impact, and one of the biggest opponents on the Regional Medical Advisory Committee gave an impassioned speech before announcing he would approve a Tactical Medical Program for the NYPD. The final approval came in June 2002. Now New York City cops who become hurt while executing warrants, dealing with barricade jobs, engaging in shootouts, and rescuing people from subway crashes, building collapses, and car wrecks can get medical care from trained fellow officers when there is still a risk that someone could be hurt by a criminal element.

Tom Purtell was the Commander of the NYPD's Special Operations Division, which oversees the Emergency Service Unit, during some of the time John was fighting to get approval for a Tactical Medical Program.

"John Busching thought outside the box," Purtell said. "He had the discipline and motivation to take on the bureaucracy. This program means the difference between life and death for a cop who's been injured or shot. We have him to thank for that."

* * *

In the fall of 2001, New York City was home to over eight million residents as well as more than a half-million commuters who made the trek in every day to go to work. With close to 60,000 employees, the New York City Police Department is the largest law enforcement agency in North America and bigger than most countries' standing armies. New York cops witness more in a week than most of us will see in our lifetimes.

The thousands of NYPD officers who raced to Ground Zero were overwhelmed with the enormous loss of life and the catastrophic devastation after every one of the seven buildings in the huge World Trade Center complex collapsed. But there was something else that was hard to deal with.

Wherever they work, law enforcement officers are the consummate rescuers. Nothing pleases them more than to lock up bad guys who prey on innocent victims. To find themselves in the middle of the worst crime scene in United States history—an attack that took the lives of close to three thousand innocent people including 341 firefighters, 2 FDNY paramedics, 6 volunteer hospital EMS workers, 37 Port Authority police officers, and 23 members of the NYPD—and have no witnesses to interview, no one to arrest, and only a few people to rescue, was not only frustrating and disorienting but profoundly depressing as well. The hijackers were dead, and only twenty people would be pulled out alive after the towers fell.

* * *

On that clear September morning, John Busching had been at home getting ready for work when the first plane hit the North Tower at 8:46 a.m. John said it wasn't much past 9 a.m. when a friend, Detective Louie Franco, called and told him to turn on the television. "I had just turned on the TV when the second plane hit. I sat there stunned, looking at the screen. I had responded to the Trade Center bombing in 1993 and knew how bad that was. It was obvious this was going to be much worse."

He knew Floyd Bennett Field, headquarters for Emergency Service, would not shut down. He gathered a change of clothes, kissed his wife and three-year-old son good-bye and rushed out the door. The roadway, usually jammed with traffic at that time of day, was eerily quiet. As John drove toward Floyd Bennett, he saw a Port Authority SUV ahead. "I went right in behind him," John remembered. "When I got closer, I recognized the driver's face in the sideview mirror. It was George Howard, a Port Authority cop I knew. We'd trained together for the Police Department and the Volunteer Fire Department in my town. I tried to get his attention, but he didn't see me."

John turned off at Flatbush Avenue. He found out later that day that Howard arrived in Lower Manhattan just as the first tower fell, at 9:59 a.m. He was crushed to death by a falling air conditioner. Four months later, at his State of the Union address, President Bush held up George Howard's badge as he spoke to the nation about the sacrifice made by cops and firefighters on that terrible day.

When John pulled into the parking lot at Floyd Bennett, it was almost empty. He walked across the road to Aviation where he found a group of officers talking about the "high-rise rescue plan." It would be a joint operation, developed in the early 1980s, between the NYPD's Emergency Service Unit and the Fire Department. Firefighters would bring the people who were trapped in the burning towers up onto the roof after Emergency Service cops, carrying high-powered saws, bolt cutters, and medical supplies, rappelled out of helicopters down onto the roof and cut down the vast array of transmission antennas so the aircraft could land and begin to evacuate the victims.

The cops in the room had no way of knowing the immense fireballs ignited by the eight thousand gallons of fuel that came gushing out of each airplane after impact caused the temperature on the roof to soar to thousands of degrees Fahrenheit. It was 9:59 a.m., and they were ready to head out when the 110-story South Tower of the World Trade Center fell. In less than one minute the South Tower collapsed into a mass of dust and rubble. The North Tower came down at 10:28 a.m. Before it was over, seven buildings and almost fourteen million square feet of space had been transformed into a vast wasteland of twisted steel, concrete, and dust.

Back out at Floyd Bennett Field, the ESU team came up a new plan. They would transform their two big Bell 412 helicopters into a flying hospital, a sort of air ambulance as one officer described it. One of the commanders decided there would be one paramedic and one EMT in each helicopter. All four would be Emergency Service officers. They knew there could be up to fifty thousand people working at any given time in those towers. The buildings had fallen, but they still hoped there would be a lot of lives to save.

It was a relief for the four officers, EMTs Tom Kirklava and Tony Conti and paramedics Darrell Summers and John Busching, to have something to focus on. They were all anxious to get to the site and get to work.

"We sat there making our plan when the Commander, Deputy Inspector Joseph Gallucci, came into the room," John said. "The Inspector had a strange look on his face. He was very somber and serious. He told us, almost apologetically, that we would not be taking people out. We all sat there dumbfounded. Finally I asked if we shouldn't try to land or be lowered onto whatever top floor is left? He just looked at us and said, 'There is nothing left.' "We all knew then how bad it was. We were going to lose a lot of our friends."

John's premonition was accurate. Throughout the day, reports kept coming in about friends and coworkers who were injured, missing, or dead.

It's hard to explain how difficult it was for that roomful of cops to accept the fact that they weren't needed, that they would not be able to rescue people from the rubble, that there would be no need for medivacs. "I remember it took longer for the more senior guys to come to terms with it," John said. "One of them just couldn't comprehend it. He kept repeating over and over, 'We gotta get in there. We gotta get in there.'"

The New York City Police Department runs like a well-oiled machine when catastrophe occurs. Despite the fact that cell phones weren't working and communications had broken down between the Fire and Police departments, the NYPD chain of command remained intact. The officers at Floyd Bennett were told by the Commander of Aviation to stay put until they heard from Headquarters. Finally the word came down. The officers were to be flown by helicopter to Lower Manhattan. They would get their orders once they landed.

As they approached Battery Park, the officers looked down on the smoke billowing up hundreds of feet in the air from the rapidly spreading fires. The area where the towers had fallen looked like a nuclear bomb had been dropped. Once they landed, the ESU officers were met by the Commanding Officer of the Emergency Service Unit, Inspector Ron Wasson. Scores of firefighters and ESU cops were showing up, and Wasson split up the officers arriving on the helicopters into two teams.

For John and his colleagues, it was a relief to finally have something useful to do. They gathered every portable rescue tool they could carry and began heading to the pile to begin their assigned tasks. "We'd only been working for a few minutes when the orders changed," John said. "We were told to move fast to assist an ESU rescue team that was working to free two Port Authority police officers. They were buried in the rubble. They were still alive, but nobody had been able to reach them.

"We were told to get our gear and meet up with a search team that was waiting for us somewhere between Three, Four, and Five World Trade," John continued. "There were fires everywhere and they were spreading. We were trying to figure out where our group was gathering when we saw several firefighters and some ESU cops staggering down off the pile. They were covered from head to foot with grime and a coat of thick white dust. You could barely see their faces. They looked completely wiped out, mentally and physically. One of the guys was the other medic I rode with on the helicopter. He started to walk in my direction but when he was only a few feet away, he passed out and collapsed on the ground. He was a really big guy but a couple of people were able to pick him up and bring him to a medical aid station."

John remembers the conversation was focused on getting to the two buried cops. "I remember hearing someone say they had a better idea of how to reach them," he said. "Someone else said one of the cops needed an IV. I felt good because I had that with me."

John's team was split in half and his group was ordered to stay in the back. His Captain, Gin Yee, radioed to Sergeant John English, who was up on the top of the pile. Sergeant English knew John was a paramedic and would have his medical kit with him. "I could hear him up there yelling to send me up," John said. "I wasn't sure what to think. I had just seen a really big guy collapse in front of me. The smoke was so thick you could barely see. There were fires everywhere. Everyone was telling me not to go up to the top of the pile. It was too dangerous and I wouldn't be able to do anything. But Sergeant English was calling. I didn't have a choice."

Once John decided he would try to climb to the top of the pile to see if he could help, he had to stop and think. How would he get up there and what would he find? The pile was a massive wreck of crushed concrete blocks and steel beams. The whole place was a smoldering, smoking fire. He would have to crawl along the beams and hope he didn't fall into the abyss below.

"It was like looking up into hell," John remembered. "Dante's Inferno could not have been worse."

"I thought about what I might encounter. I crawled up the pile. It took about fifteen minutes to reach Sergeant English after climbing up and over large amounts of debris and avoiding voids that dropped from a few feet to more than sixty and seventy feet down. When I got to the top, the Sergeant told me I was going to be sent in to give the trapped Port Authority cop some medical attention. He told me he had been buried at least thirty feet down. No one had been able to get to him."

English told John he would have to shimmy down a steel I-beam from the top until he hit the concrete flooring. Then he'd have to squeeze down another couple of feet where a Battalion Chief from the Fire Department would be waiting. The Fire Chief would guide John the rest of the way in.

"Climbing down the I-beam, I had to pass under two pieces of concrete flooring that had formed a tent," he remembered. "I didn't want to fall off that beam on the right side. It looked like a really long drop."

When John found the Battalion Chief, a paramedic from the Fire Department was already there, but he had gone down without his medical bag and the trapped officer needed an IV. "He offered to try to get to him first to see what the trapped officer needed," John said. "I told him it wasn't necessary, that I was a paramedic and I had my equipment with me."

It's no secret that in New York City there's an intense rivalry between the Police and Fire Departments, and the animosity can be particularly intense between firefighters and ESU cops who frequently respond to the same disasters. John said it really hit home that we were dealing with a very unusual event when the Battalion Chief announced he was sending John down, not one of his own guys from the Fire Department. "I remember standing there thinking, 'Oh man, if he wants me to go, this must be the end of the world.'"

The Fire Chief instructed John to focus on what he was doing and block out everything that didn't have to do with the mission. Then he told Busching to hand over his medical kit. He said the pathway to the officer was so small the medical kit might impede his progress. John would have to crawl down on his stomach. There was no room for the kit.

John thought for a moment trying to figure out what he should do when another ESU officer, Eddie Reyes, crawled out from the hole. "When he saw I had no one with me, he volunteered to go in behind me," John said. "Eddie Reyes was a registered nurse, but the Fire Chief didn't like the idea. Eddie had just come out after twenty minutes of exhausting labor, and he didn't look well. But Eddie insisted he wanted to go with me, and I was relieved to have some help."

John handed his medical bag to Reyes and got down on his stomach. As he began to inch his way over to the injured officer, he had to exhale deeply to pull himself through the small space. He laid on his stomach and crawled twenty-five feet. When he came across another steel beam laying across his path, he had to exhale even harder to squeeze under it.

Finally John saw the man. He was lying face down and completely buried under massive chunks of cement and steel. From his waist down to his feet, he was completely crushed under the rubble, but he was still conscious.

"He told me his name was John McLoughlin," John said, "and that he was a Port Authority cop. He'd had some medical training, so he knew the situation was bad."

At that moment John Busching began to face the fact that he was probably going to die. "The most you could move was to push yourself up a couple of inches," he said. "You couldn't move to your left or your right." John thought about his wife and son at home and realized he might never see them again. As he began to inch his way out, John looked over at McLoughlin and realized there was no way he could leave him there. "I couldn't do it." he said. "I stopped backing out. I remember thinking, 'I'm screwed, but I have to crawl back and stay with him.'"

John inched his way back to McLoughlin and tried to come up with a plan. The hole measured about three feet across and was eighteen to twenty-four inches high. Due to the tight quarters, only one rescuer at a time could have direct contact with him. There was no natural light, and when the wind shifted, putrid smoke filled the hole where the rescuer was positioned. Everything was burning and collapsing. The space where McLoughlin was trapped was next to an elevator shaft. John says there must have been an updraft of air in that spot because no one remembers McLoughlin complaining about the smoke.

Once Busching made the decision to stay, he approached the task like everything he decided to take on, with total discipline and the expectation that everything was going to be okay. Eddie Reyes came back with John's medical supplies. Eddie crawled in behind him, but the space was so small the cops were worried there might not be room to get the IV out of the bag. McLoughlin was nauseous and getting dehydrated, and John knew he had to start an IV and get him some fluids soon. "A doctor at the top of the hole told me I could give four milligrams of morphine and I wanted to get that going too, but my hands were trembling pretty badly. That's not good for starting IVs. I remember thinking, God, I'm going to need some help. But for some reason, right at that moment, my hands stopped shaking and I was able to get the IV into McLoughlin's arm on the first try."

McCloughin was in enormous pain, but John never could get him the morphine. It came in a delivery system that wouldn't fit in the IV tubing. "McLoughlin didn't want it anyway." John said. "He thought it would cause his blood pressure to drop and he would die."

"Once the IV was working, Eddie began backing out and I inched my way backward behind him. I was face down the whole time sucking in my breath to make myself smaller. To get from where McLoughlin was buried back up to the top of the pile took about twenty minutes, but it seemed like hours."

When John finally got himself back to the top of the pile, he spoke to John Chovanes, a former EMT and doctor who'd had a lot of experience treating trauma victims. When Chovanes realized the towers had fallen, he got in his car and drove to Lower Manhattan from his home in Pennsylvania. The doctor was alarmed when Busching described McLoughlin's condition. "Dr. Chovanes decided to go down and give him some morphine," John said. "When the doctor came out, he had the same look as everyone else who had gone down there. Absolute horror."

Chovanes and John decided to take turns going back down to try to keep McLoughlin alive. When Dr. Chovanes crawled out after his fifth trip down, he was visibly distraught. The doctor told Busching if McClaughlin's condition deteriorated any more, they would have to amputate both his legs. When John asked Chovanes how he could possibly take off his legs down in that hole, he replied, "I'm a surgeon, so I have to do it. And you're the only one around who has medical training, so you have to help me. I'll come up with a way to get his legs off. You look in your bag and figure out how to keep him from bleeding to death."

John was aghast at this prospect but he rummaged through his bag and came up with cloth triangular bandages to make tourniquets. The doctor took one look at the bandages and said there was no way that would work. He needed to find something else.

"Chovanes asked me if I had any clamps." John said. "He'd been a paramedic and he knew we don't carry clamps. He told me to keep thinking. Like every ESU cop I had a Leatherman tool that looks like a small pair of pliers on my belt. When I asked if that would work, the doctor seemed relieved. He told me he knew I would come up with something."

Chovanes had a plan, but when John heard what it was, he felt nauseous. The doctor said if things got critical, he would have to take McLoughlin's legs off with a cordless saw. "You," he told John, "will clamp the wounds closed with your Leatherman tool." The doctor said they would not be able to anesthetize him, it would be too dangerous.

"I decided right then, there was no way this was going to happen," John said. "When I told the cops and firefighters who were digging that if we couldn't get him out soon, we were going to amputate his legs, they began to dig a lot faster."

As they were making plans to save John McLoughlin's life, a team of thirty people were being rotated in to dig him out. The only tools they could use were their bare hands. They had to dig under the trapped officer. Everything above him was a solid mass of concrete and steel. About thirty firefighters and ESU cops made up the team. Two firemen and two cops worked fifteen-minute shifts before being relieved. It took almost twelve hours. They dug out John McLoughlin one handful at a time.

The Port Authority officer was crushed at ten in the morning on September 11. When the last piece of concrete was removed from under his body and there was enough room to slide him out, it was seven o'clock the next morning.

"They brought him out in a Stokes basket, which is a kind of metal stretcher," John said. "A long line of firefighters and cops, going all the way back to Church Street, passed the stretcher from one person to the next until the severely injured officer reached the waiting ambulance." John Busching said watching John McLoughlin brought out of that hole alive is the most remarkable thing he ever witnessed.

* * *

McLoughlin was in a coma for over a month. The doctor in charge of the trauma team overseeing his care told John Chovanes and John Busching they saved his life. When someone is crushed, they must be treated before they are freed. Otherwise, once they are unencumbered, all the toxins will be released when the pressure is relieved, and death is nearly always the outcome. John and Chovanes were aware of this and had given McLoughlin sodium bicarbonate, which neutralized the acidic toxins in his body. It was only fifteen minutes of paramedic training, but John had just read an article about the subject in a medical journal and, luckily for John McLoughlin, he remembered it.

McLoughlin now lives in Upstate New York. His life since that day has been an arduous series of surgeries, followed by grueling and painful physical therapy. He lost a lot of his muscle mass due to the extended time he suffered without oxygen. He had to learn to walk again using a set of different muscles.

John says they bump into each other every once in a while and McLoughlin seems very happy to be alive. He has four children, volunteers with his son's Boy Scout troop, and even helped someone get through a similar rehab program by providing inspiration and encouragement.

Oliver Stone's film *World Trade Center* revolved around John McLoughlin's experiences on September 11. At some point during the filming, McLoughlin called John Busching and asked if he wanted to work on the film. "I told him it's whatever you want. You were the victim. It's your story."

John did go out to Los Angeles for a couple of weeks to give technical advice on how things should look. But when it came time to edit the movie, the role John Busching played saving John McLoughlin's life ended up on the editing room floor. But John has no complaints. "Oliver Stone was really great about the whole thing," he said. "He told me he couldn't be sure how the film would play out, that there were a lot of firemen, medics, and cops and that some scenes might get redundant. I didn't have any problem with that."

John worked twelve-hour days for three solid weeks at Ground Zero. Some days, he says, were better than others. Day after day of searching for their dead colleagues, finding nothing but piece of flesh or a small body part that had to be packaged up and sent to the morgue, took a toll on everyone there.

"When you were at Ground Zero, you had to isolate one task and focus on it," John said. "But if you looked at the whole scene, you could go crazy. There was no way any one individual could do much on their own. You had to focus on small, manageable jobs."

Everyone involved with the tragedy says looking back it was the funerals that prolonged the grief. A total of 409 first responders died, and everyone had a separate funeral. As one officer pointed out, to have gone through an experience like that and be around that much grief was extremely depressing. "You could never get over it," he said.

John said his brother, a firefighter, took it worse than he because of all the funerals. "I guess everyone did the best that they could, but it was really tough. It is a testament to the city that we had very few suicides. I think there was only one EMT who took his own life. That is a quite a tribute to the toughness of New Yorkers."

* * *

John Busching has a favorite expression. When he's delivered a baby, rappelled out of a helicopter, or crawled inside the smoldering wreckage at Ground Zero, his buddies say they often hear him saying, "It's really something."

When you get to know John, you understand that despite the tragedies, the bureaucracy, the paperwork, the endless rules and regulations, and the tragedy of September 11, he still believes that being a cop in New York City is the greatest job in the world. And how many people do you know who after twenty years at the same job are still saying, "It's really something," when they talk about their work?

John, his wife Chris, and their son Joseph enjoying
a vacation in upstate New York, July, 2008.

John rappelling
off the top of
the Brooklyn
Bridge.
Emergency
Service officers
practice these
maneuvers
regularly.

John and his Dad, Warren, on John's graduation day from the NYPD Police Academy, June 25, 1986. Warren served 36 years with the New York City Fire Department.

John Busching on the far left, with fellow officers from the Emergency Service Unit, on assignment protecting the President of the United States when he was visiting New York City.

John Busching (left) with John McLoughlin on June 16, 2004 at Medal Day at NYPD Headquarters. John McLoughlin, a former Port Authority police officer, was the last person to be rescued alive from the rubble at Ground Zero. Busching was one of the people credited with saving McLoughlin's life.

John with his tactical-medical sack. John had to replace the bag he carried with him when he crawled 30 feet down into the wreckage of Ground Zero right after the attacks of September 11 to give Port Authority cop, John McLoughlin, life saving help. The bag, he said, was damaged beyond repair. He replaced it two days later on September 13, 2001.

Chapter Seven

Bobby Johnson: He Follows the Money

"Hell is empty, and all the devils are here."
—William Shakespeare

Bobby Johnson has spent the better part of his twenty-two years with the NYPD chasing drug dealers. He has confiscated every kind of narcotic imaginable. The dollar value of the seizures is up in the hundreds of millions.

Drug trafficking around the world brings in over $400 billion each year to those who control the production, distribution, and sale of illegal narcotics. Gross profit margins can top 300 percent annually. The illegal drug business generates ten to forty times more money than running a restaurant, a retail store, or a small manufacturing firm.

Narcotics trafficking is a violent enterprise that exacts huge costs and inflicts a terrible toll on communities where these well-financed and ruthless businesses flourish. Where there are drugs, there is also crime, lots of it. Addicts rob, steal, and even kill to get money to buy their drugs. The dealer side is rife with extortion, kidnapping, robberies, and murder. Despite the best efforts of law enforcement, to date the war on drugs has had little impact. For every kilo seized, five more make their way to the street. It is a testimony to Bobby's commitment that he is still passionate about his work close to two decades after his first "buy-bust" assignment as a rookie cop.

Since 2009, Bobby has been a Detective Sergeant working as a Group Supervisor with the New York Organized Crime Drug Enforcement Strike Force, a relatively new organization that includes a number of law enforcement agencies including the NYPD, the Drug Enforcement Administration, FBI, IRS, Customs, Immigration, U.S. Marshals, ATF, and the New York State Police. Operating as a single unit, members of the Strike Force share resources, technology, personnel, and ideas in their ongoing efforts to eradicate the menace of illegal drugs.

"I won't lie," Bobby says. "In the beginning, it was a bumpy road for the Strike Force. The lead agency is the Drug Enforcement Administration. It took the FBI a while to get used to the fact that they had to defer to them. In the past they were always the top dog on any multiagency task force."

While there was tension among some members at the outset, Bobby says that everyone was quick to put petty ego trips aside and work together on the common goal. "My team is fantastic," he said. "We've had the same group working together for the past four years. I'm not exaggerating when I say that these are some of the best investigators in the world. You just could not have a better team.

"International drug cartels are well financed and well run," he continues. "They hire chemists who figure out how to soak powdered drugs into fabrics or bake it into bricks or concrete and then transform it back again. They've got travel agents who find the best flights and shipping lanes to streamline their deliveries, and they've got bankers and accountants who are geniuses at turning illicit drug money into legitimate funds."

The United States has taken the lead among all the world's nations in the efforts to suppress the flow of illegal drugs. But experienced narcotics detectives like Bobby Johnson say the huge amounts of money being made, the seemingly insatiable demand—especially in the United States—and the international nature of the business make it impossible for one country to combat the problem alone. You have to go global," Bobby says. "The only way to do that is to develop relationships and gather intelligence in the countries that are involved."

For the Strike Force, going global has meant reaching out to countries in South and Central Asia as well as Latin America, the areas of the world that supply most of the world's illegal drugs. The work also requires developing confidential informants who follow the money, a relatively new approach for U.S. law enforcement, especially for local agencies like the NYPD.

"Ten or fifteen years ago we weren't focusing on the money trail," Bobby explains. "But that's all changed. We've got this huge chart on the wall that lists every priority target in the world with detailed information on the money flow. It's all broken down by geographical region. These organizations are huge."

Bobby's group is hot on the trail of drug smuggling operations in Mexico and Colombia, organizations that today are larger and more organized than anything Pablo Escobar ever dreamed of. "When you compare the amount of drugs sold and money made now to what it was ten or fifteen years ago, there's no comparison," he adds. "In February 2008, Mexican soldiers seized over twenty-three tons of cocaine from one cartel —enough for 200 million lines. It was the largest cocaine bust in history."

Throughout the decade that began in 2000, cartels in Mexico sold between $10 billion and $30 billion of illegal drugs to the U.S. market. When the Mexican government tried to clamp down, retribution was fast and furious. Scores of Mexican police officers were assassinated, and several were beheaded. On February 21, 2009, narcotics traffickers attacked a police headquarters building in coastal Zihuatanejo using hand grenades, grenade launchers, armor-piercing bullets, and antitank rockets. "Drug cartels," Bobby explains, "are engaged in a serious arms race. Their purchases of weapons rival anything bought by rogue states around the world."

In one attack, a group of armed men went into the house of a police officer in Tijuana and shot him at point-blank range before turning their automatic weapons on the officer's wife and nine-year-old daughter. An entire family killed in less than thirty seconds. Armed men have battled police and soldiers in clashes lasting for hours, turning some Mexican residential areas into war zones. The drug trade has meant a virtual plague for many cities and towns whose boarded-up buildings are riddled with bullets and streets are awash in blood.

Observers say the orchestrated attacks show that Mexico's long-standing drug violence has entered a new phase. In the past, rival gangs fought over different smuggling routes into the United States that were used to ship large amounts of cocaine, heroin, and marijuana. "We used to see narcos against narcos. Now we are seeing narcos against cops," Jorge Chabat, a Mexican drug expert, said in early 2009. "The Mexican president, Calderón, is paying the price for taking on the cartels."

CNN correspondent Karl Penhaul spent several weeks in 2009 tracking the gangs of the Mexican underworld, the corrupt officials who support them, and the cops who are trying to halt the violence. In a special report to CNN, Penhaul wrote that the pervasive corruption at all levels of the Mexican government is only adding fuel to the flames. "In the last two decades, hundreds of police, soldiers, and politicians have been convicted of working for the cartels," he said. "Mob assassins are no longer content with efficient execution-style killings. Sinaloa cartel hitmen have been known to place pig masks on the faces of their Juárez cartel victims. And in a grim seasonal touch, in 2008, killers in Juárez decapitated a cop and placed a Father Christmas hat on his severed head."

In early 2009, in just one of hundreds of raids conducted that year, Mexican police officers stormed a middle-class Mexico City home and found thirty guns, twelve grenade launchers, thirty grenades, and more than forty bulletproof jackets with the initials FEDA, the Spanish acronym for "Special Forces of Arturo Beltrán," one of Mexico's violent drug cartels responsible for trafficking hundreds of thousands of kilos to the United States and Europe.

* * *

Despite the overwhelming odds, Bobby believes the Strike Force will eventually bring these criminals to justice. "These cartels are major employers," he observes. "Their business model is brilliant. All the tasks are compartmentalized. At most, each player knows only one or two people in the organization, so they can't rat out one another. Nobody but the guy at the top knows where the money is. They are not afraid of the police. They worry more about their competitors in the drug trade ripping them off, which is one of the reasons they keep their operations so secretive."

Sergeant Johnson's office looks like the bunker where World War II generals planned the invasion of Normandy. Charts and maps cover every blank space on the wall. Drug trafficking and money laundering routes are outlined in painstaking detail, and diagrams of the organizational structures of the world's largest drug cartels are prominently displayed.

In the 1990s, Bobby spent the bulk of his time seizing the drugs himself. He spent years doing drug buys and arresting the dealers. Today his team is more interested in the money. "We've gotten good at following the money through the pickups, drop-offs, and on to the dummy corporations," he explains. "We follow it as far we can. Our goal is to find its ultimate destination. When we hit the end, we rope it back in and arrest everyone who had a hand in cleaning the money. This strategy hurts their operations way more than seizing the drugs."

While disrupting the money flow is more effective, it is also much more complicated. Most of the big international narcotics syndicates are based outside the United States. To legitimize their cash flow, they have to convert the American dollars they receive when they sell the drugs in the United States into their own currency.

Bobby explains that his group focuses on the big targets—organizations that are the largest drug smuggling and money laundering operations in the world. "We've had task forces in the past, but mostly just the FBI, the NYPD, and the State Police were involved," he says. "This is the first time we've had the resources of agencies like the Internal Revenue Service, the U.S. Marshals, and the Drug Enforcement Administration on board. They bring different resources and skill sets to the table, and it's made a big difference in our efforts to identify and arrest the drug dealers as well as the people they're working for."

Bringing together the resources of agencies as diverse as the Internal Revenue Service and the Drug Enforcement Administration has paid off. "People said it couldn't be done," Bobby explains. "We're a tight team, and we work together. If we need to check tax status, we have two IRS agents who can do that work. If we need to know if a group has terrorist ties, the FBI checks that out. Customs plays the most important role, tracking movement in and out of countries. And the DEA is just amazing. Its network of experienced agents and informants is huge."

The Strike Force has contacts in every country of interest, ranging from high-level law enforcement officials to confidential informants on the street. Bobby says the network of undercover operatives working all over the world is impressive. "If we're looking for someone in Mexico, we've got many people we can reach out to. It's the same for Colombia. These operations are top secret. Our success depends on our confidential sources providing us with accurate information, and we work hard to keep their identities secret. If people find out they're working with us, they probably will end up dead."

In early 2009, Bobby and his team turned their attention toward a group in Queens. For several months, Strike Force investigators tapped their phones and followed them twenty-four hours a day, seven days a week. Finally, the days and months of listening in on what seemed like meaningless conversations paid off. Something was about to happen in a parking lot behind a warehouse in a remote area of Queens. When the dealers met up and switched the bag of money from one car to another, the cops were waiting.

"We chased them," Bobby said. "Once we got them in cuffs, we searched the car. We found a million and a half dollars, and that was just in one bundle. There were at least three other bags in that car. The amounts of money involved are phenomenal."

By the time the money was seized in the parking lot in Queens, it had traveled a long circuitous path from its starting point in Medellín, Colombia. That's where the cocaine was purchased by men representing a Colombian drug cartel. Payment was made in pesos and represented a small fraction of the money that would be made on the next transaction.

The cartel knows the cocaine they just purchased will bring in around $20 million on the street in New York. A cartel representative now goes to the peso dealer in his own country and says he has $20 million worth of cocaine about to hit the street in New York. In a typical deal, the broker for the black market peso exchange will give the drug cartel 80 percent of the value. In this case, the drug cartel takes $1.6 million in pesos from the peso dealer, and they're out of the game.

Now the money laundering begins. The peso broker now has claim to $20 million of U.S. currency that's in the possession of drug dealers back in New York City. The peso broker reaches out to his contacts in New York and tells them to go pick up the money.

"Money laundering is the most complex and dangerous part of the operation," Bobby explains. "Mostly, they launder it by buying manufactured items like cars, appliances, and high-priced electronic equipment and shipping it back to Colombia, where it gets sold legitimately. People in Colombia have no way of knowing whether their new washing machine, car, or flat screen television was part of an elaborate operation cleaning up dirty money made by selling illegal narcotics on the streets of a foreign country."

The Strike Force works with hundreds of informants in New York City and other places around the world. Without their information, the investigations would come to a halt. "Some of the informants we work with are very wealthy," according to Bobby. "And the motives for working with us differ. Some are working for cash. Others have developed a passion for getting the bad guys. Some want revenge. Whatever is driving them to work with us, we're happy to have their help.

"We once had an informant flying in from another country. We were responsible for getting him a hotel room. That weekend it seemed like every room in New York was booked. We finally found a place for him to stay. We all thought it was pretty decent, but, of course, we're cops.

"He called at seven the next morning. You could tell over the phone he was upset. We drove over and picked him up. He was very well dressed, the kind of guy who probably gets a manicure every week. When we got to the office, he opened up his laptop. He typed in a couple of things and then spun the machine around so we could see the screen. The screen showed a mansion overlooking the ocean. 'That's my house,' he says. Then he types a few more words and spins the screen around again. Now we see six very expensive cars. 'This is how I live,' he tells us. 'This is my house, and these are my cars. Don't ever put me in a hotel like that again.'"

* * *

By any standards, the Task Force has had impressive seizures of money and drugs.

"Before we go in, we spend hours on the tactical plan," Bobby explains. "The operation is extremely well organized because the threat is so serious. These people are always heavily armed."

Tactical plans outline the operation down to the last detail. A detailed description of the location to be searched is the first item of business as well as information on all the players involved. There is a synopsis of the evidence that convinced a judge to grant the warrant, as well as a complete breakdown of what to expect inside, paying special attention to whether dogs, children, or innocent people might be encountered. Specific assignments for the officers on the team are spelled out, including who is to lead the entry team, what equipment is needed, who is to provide roof and rear security, and the whereabouts of a "hospital car" in case someone is injured and needs fast medical care.

"One time we planned to hit an apartment in Queens that had $12 million in drug money," Bobby recalled. "NYPD detectives, some of whom worked undercover for a long time, had collected enough evidence to get a warrant, and we were ready to go in and make the arrests. Cops who go undercover are in extremely dangerous situations. I've always believed they are the unsung heroes of law enforcement.

"After we make entry, we arrest them and seize everything inside that is considered illegal or that we need for our investigation, including cocaine, heroin, computers, phones, money, and guns. But they are still innocent until proven guilty, and we have to return their personal property unless we can prove it was purchased with drug money and a jury finds them guilty in court. Whether it's an apartment, a storefront, or a house, when you go in, you get overwhelmed at what you see. It looks like the whole world is awash in guns, drugs, and dirty money."

* * *

Bobby's first stint working the drug problem was in 1992. He was an undercover officer, and the tactic was simple. He would approach a dealer to make a score. As soon as the dealer took the money and passed over the drugs, he'd find himself under arrest. It was a classic buy-bust operation.

"I wasn't too concerned," he said. "I didn't have a family to worry about, and I never worried they would follow me home. But I was aware that I am white and there were only two reasons I would be in a Hispanic or black neighborhood. I was either looking to buy drugs, or I was a police officer looking to lock someone up for selling drugs."

One time Bobby and his partner were making a buy in the Bronx. His job that day was to play the ghost, the undercover who watches the other undercover, and he was dressed like a construction worker. He had found the perfect place to fit in, a building under construction.

"Unfortunately for me, I had been there only a short time when a bus pulled up and several big guys with baseball bats jumped out. I learned later that they were members of a gang called the Coalition. Carrying guns and baseball bats, they would drive around to construction sites. When they saw that there were none of their people on the job, they would threaten the site managers and demand they hire five or six right on the spot. Lots of fights would break out.

"On this particular day, because I had dressed up like a construction worker, they thought I was the foreman. I was supposed to be protecting the undercover, and I wanted to avoid trouble, but they surrounded me. There were probably twelve guys, but it seemed like fifty. Thank God, the undercover noticed what was going on. He ran to a nearby backup car and told them I was in trouble. I heard the brakes screeching and saw all the cops jump out just as they were just getting their hands on me. Any police officer will tell you when you are about to get beaten or even killed by an angry mob and you hear the cars pull up, the doors shut, and the voices of a bunch of angry cops, there is no greater feeling in the world. I knew I was going to be okay."

Bobby got out of that jam in the nick of time, but there were a few other times when his colleagues never knew he needed help. "One time when I was on a buy-bust assignment in the Bronx," he recalled. "I went up to a woman on the street who we knew was selling drugs. I told her I was looking for cocaine. She said she had the drugs and asked me for the money. I handed her the cash before I got the drugs, which was a big mistake. The minute I did it, I knew I'd screwed up. She put the money in her pants pocket and told me to come with her.

"I asked for the money back, but there was no way that was going to happen. We walked around to the projects on 138th Street. She told me, 'If you try anything, my friends will kill you.' I followed her into a building. When she told me to wait in the lobby while she went upstairs to get my drugs, I grabbed the pocket of her pants, ripped it off, and took the cash. She screamed, and my ghost was there within seconds. I didn't want to expose myself as a cop, but things were getting out of hand. Three of her friends came running down the street. One was waving a baseball bat. The other cop and I started to run, but our instincts told us it was too late. We were going to have to take this group down by ourselves. We pulled our guns and tackled them. I am sure it occurred to both of us as we were wrestling on the ground that the odds were bad: there were four of them and two of us. That day we were lucky. We blew our cover but got out safe.

"The big operations I work on now are much different. Everything is planned out to the last detail. You can't plan out a buy-bust, which makes them dangerous. You'd better be on the top of your game to do this work, otherwise someone is going to get hurt. Never again did I front the money before I got the drugs."

* * *

Bobby Johnson, like all his colleagues working on international drug and money laundering investigations, had a long apprenticeship before the Department felt he was ready to handle this complicated work. "What helped me is that prior to this assignment, I was on a task force with the Westchester County District Attorney's office," he said. "The group was composed of law enforcement people from Westchester County, the NYPD, and the New York State Police."

Bobby feels he did some of his best work during those years. "I learned a tremendous amount. The culture was different from the NYPD, and I had to adapt. I began to understand why it's important to listen to the people you're working with so you can understand what they need and give it to them. I learned how to work on a team."

During a three-year stretch, the Westchester County team seized a lot of drugs and guns and removed many criminals from the street. This was the time heroin was making a big comeback. Users, afraid of getting AIDS, had stopped shooting the drug into their arms. To avoid using contaminated needles, they were sniffing the drug, a turn of events that was good news for drug dealers. Heroin prepared for sniffing, as opposed to injecting, is a lot less pure, which meant more money flowing into their pockets.

One of Bobby's high points with the Westchester task force was an investigation into an operation that was putting hundreds of pounds of high-grade marijuana on the street. It was so potent, each pound was selling for close to $6,000. One day a call came in from an informant. Growers were about to harvest a huge crop in the basement of their home. Along with the pot, the caller said, they would find a lot of guns.

There were actually two homes involved. Both were set several acres back from the road, which made regular surveillance, usually done from the street or a nearby building, difficult. The suspects also lived in the homes, which made things even more complicated. "It was impossible to stake out the houses or get them under surveillance," Bobby remembered. "All we had was the informant's information and an electric bill that was high enough to confirm something unusual was going on."

With little more than a tip from someone they didn't know, the task force investigators went to work. First they had to convince a judge to give them a search warrant based on nothing but an electric bill and a call from an informant. That was not going to be easy. If they were successful in getting the warrant, they'd make their tactical plan, which would include a detailed map of the area and a list of all the resources they would need, including K-9s, air units, a SWAT team, uniformed officers, and technological support.

The judge issued the warrant.

"It was a great hit," Bobby recalled. "Each house had a huge basement, and they were filled with marijuana plants. They had heat lamps on tracks, an automatic fertilizer system, and the whole system was hydroponic. The plants were three to four feet high. We seized a lot of guns as well. The informant had been right on every count. If we had waited another week, we might have missed it. That crop could have been cut, dried, and on its way to the street."

While Bobby and the team were proud of their work, they were worried about prosecuting the case. "Successfully prosecuting people arrested for any sort of marijuana offense is difficult, but we were hopeful it might have a good result because the strength of the drug was very strong. If the drug is so potent that it will lead to serious health problems for the user, there was a good chance we could win."

Bobby's fears were unfounded. The case never got to court. Everyone they arrested pled guilty.

While the work on the Westchester task force was productive, it was also dangerous. Along with the risk of facing down heavily armed criminal suspects, there was also the risk of exposure to toxic chemicals. Methamphetamine production, for example, is a highly explosive process that releases dangerous chemicals like phosphine, hydrochloric acid, and vaporized methamphetamine into the air. Officers raiding meth labs are routinely exposed to these dangerous toxins, which have contaminated all the internal surfaces, the ventilation system, and the waste drains of the lab where the deadly brew is cooked up. For each pound of meth, there are five pounds of hazardous waste. Other threats include contracting AIDS after being punctured with a dirty syringe and exposure to hepatitis C as well as the deadly MRSA virus.

Bobby knows firsthand about the risks officers take when they go in to clean up these drug dens. His best friend and fellow officer, Stu Cohen, died after a raid on a heroin mill in Westchester County. Doctors still don't know what caused this healthy young man to get sick and die. "Stu was my best friend," Bobby said. "To this day I feel he was the best person I ever met. People always thought we were brothers. His strong work ethic was the reason we did so well in Westchester County."

The cops had raided a house in early December 2006. By Easter Sunday 2007, thirty-eight-year-old Stu Cohen, a holder of a sixth-degree black belt in the prime of his life, was dead.

The cops executed the search warrant after an informant told them heroin was getting cut and packaged for sale there. The moment they entered the house, they knew they were in the right place. The tools were spread out on a table—spoons, grinders, and packaging bags. Nearby were the chemicals used to cut the heroin. Ten kilos were all packaged up and ready to go. When the informant called the next day to say they had missed several kilos hidden in the walls of the house, the team went back and found the rest of the stash.

That evening on his drive back home, Stu Cohen, who had been on both raids, called his supervisor to tell him his wrists were aching. The sergeant told Stu to go to the hospital and get checked out, but Stu decided to stop at home and to see his family first. By the time he pulled into his driveway, he had a strange pain radiating in his stomach. He drove himself to a small hospital near his home in Dobbs Ferry. The doctor on call checked him over, gave him some antacid tablets, and sent him home.

As the night progressed, the pain in his stomach and wrists got progressively worse. The antacids weren't helping. Sure that something was seriously wrong, Stu went back to the hospital, but the doctors still couldn't figure it out. They transported him to a larger facility in Bronxville. Within a few hours, his condition deteriorated further, and he slipped into a coma. Nobody had a clue what was wrong with him. At some point, doctors recommended that Stu be moved to a New York City hospital, Columbia Presbyterian.

Bobby said one of the saddest things about Stu's illness was that his doctors were afraid to expose his kids, so they weren't allowed to visit. "Stu was close to Sydney and Haley. They were only six and eight years old, and they weren't allowed to see him. From the time he got sick right before Christmas, those kids never saw their dad again."

Bobby has stayed close to Stu's wife, Gina. He calls her twice a week to see how she's doing. "She's become a sister to me," he said. "I would do anything for her. She had more tragedy in a year than most people have in a lifetime. Several months before Stu got sick, her mother died. How you cope with all that, I have no idea. She moved out of the house they lived in together and bought another place in the same town but a different neighborhood. She goes day by day."

Bobby wears a black bracelet. Stu's shield number, 510, is on one side in red. On the opposite side are six red stripes, signifying his sixth-degree black belt achievement. Bobby says he will never take it off.

Seeing the toll illegal drugs take on the people who use them has made Bobby leery. "The people who mix this stuff up are not chemists, and these are not drugs from Pfizer," he says. "Every one of them will hurt you in one way or the other, and they all have an impact on the brain. These hard-core heroin users are a mess. Most of them have lost all their teeth. Heroin has to be laced with something. If you took it straight, it would kill you. A lot of dealers mix the heroin with laxatives. They're cheap and easy to get. When we're up on a rooftop and we see a lot of human feces, it is a sure sign someone's been there shooting up."

Bobby is especially concerned about drug use among young people. "I'd like to show them a video clip of people in a filthy basement concocting the lethal mix they just spent good money on. I think if these kids could see the actual person who had their hands on the drugs they were about to take, they might have second thoughts."

* * *

Bobby Johnson wanted to be a cop for as long as he can remember. "My dad was a fireman in New York. He was always talking about taking the civil service test. He wanted us to go to college, but he also kept pushing us to take those tests."

Bobby must have broken a record when he took the civil service test to become a New York City police officer a few months after his sixteenth birthday. He did well, and unaware of his young age, the Department called him. "They took one look at me and said come back in four years and stay out of trouble."

He remembers that first trip to NYPD headquarters as thrilling. "I was just a kid, but I looked around, and I knew this was the place I wanted to be. I turned twenty in May. By July I was in the Academy. I couldn't go into a bar and have a drink, but there I was training to become a New York City cop."

Looking back, Bobby says he's not exactly sure why he was drawn to police work. "I know I loved the SWAT stuff, making tactical plans, arresting the bad guys. But over the years, my interests have changed. I've come to enjoy more strategic work, like figuring out the problem and making a plan to solve it.

"I also enjoy interrogations. It's a skill that takes a lot of practice. I learned a lot about how to be successful with both interviews and interrogations when I attended the thirteen-week FBI National Academy in Quantico, Virginia. They used actors for role-playing exercises, and everything was videotaped.

"You learn you've got to be honest, and you can't scream or threaten. Coming across as a person who is very authoritative does not work. You already have them under arrest, so your job is to convince them you want them as your friend and partner. I tell them, 'Hey, we're going to become friends and partners. I won't lie to you, but don't you lie to me.' You keep your word unless they cross the line. Then it's over."

Bobby says even his worst experiences during his two decades on the force never caused him to second-guess his decision to become a law enforcement officer. On December 2, 1991, he was working the four to twelve shift. The first few hours had been fairly quiet. Then a call came in to go to a plaza off the Bruckner Boulevard and check out a disturbance. "We got to the plaza, and you could see a McDonald's at the end of the parking lot," Bobby said. "As we got closer, we saw a man standing there frantically waving his hands. He told us the McDonald's was being robbed and the men had guns."

Bobby jumped out of the car and ran over to the window. "I could see that everyone in there was lying on the ground," he said. "As I started to put it over the radio, I saw three men leap over the counter. I ran to the front, but they escaped out the side door."

Bobby took off after them. He's not certain when it happened, but at some point, one of the men turned around, looked him in the eye, and started shooting. "I saw the muzzle flash and heard the pop of gunfire. Then I heard a bullet whiz by my ear. He was only twenty feet away. It was incredible."

With no place to take cover, Bobby pulled his weapon and fired back. In 1992 New York cops were still using revolvers. After six rounds, he had to reload.

When the second suspect started shooting, Bobby's odds for survival dropped by half.

In between shots, he called it in on his radio—robbery with shots fired, officer in trouble. Then he needed to reload. Running toward the suspect, he pulled his speed loader, but in a freak accident, his knee smashed into it. The speed loader went sailing through the air. He had no idea how many rounds he had left, maybe one, maybe two. He couldn't be sure.

Bobby kept up the chase. He was gaining, but suddenly another gunman fired two more shots. Two more officers pulled up, and they started shooting. Bobby was able to get one more round off. "I knew right away I'd hit him," he said. "But he didn't go down. There's no way to describe what you're going through in a situation like this. There's so much adrenaline in your system. Everything is distorted. I tried to get another shot off, but I was out of ammunition. The good news was, the shooter was out as well. There was no ammo left in either of our guns."

Bobby finally caught up with the man who tried to kill him. "At this point, commands were useless," he explains. "I hit him with my gun, then I dove on top of him."

Within minutes, the parking lot was swarming with cops, and a sergeant took control of the scene. When Bobby stood up, there was blood everywhere. He learned later that he had punctured his hand and broken his thumb. "What I'll never forget is that adrenaline rush. It was off the charts. My chest had expanded so much that my body armor felt like it was going to split down the middle. One of the officers was yelling, 'I'm hit, I'm hit.' He didn't seem to know where. We tore his clothes off, but there was no wound. The adrenaline in his system was so bad, he thought he'd been shot."

Over the years many people have asked Bobby why he kept running after an armed man in an open parking lot where there was no cover and the person was shooting at him. "I've asked myself the same question," he said. "The only explanation I can come up with is anger. I was in a rage that this guy was trying to kill me. I got into a mind-set that I wasn't going to let that happen. Everyone says take cover, conceal yourself. I was in a wide open parking lot. There were no cars and no place to go. Even after I'd lost my speed loader, I'm looking at the guy and thinking I didn't want to lose him, so I just kept going. He could have shot people back at the McDonald's, and I was going to catch him."

Despite the fact that his courage under fire earned him a "Police Officer of the Year" award for the Bronx, several months later Bobby was sued by the gunman's family. The lawsuit, demanding millions of dollars, claimed Officer Johnson had tackled the gunman, pulled his service weapon, and shot him without provocation. The case was eventually thrown out by a grand jury.

Immediately after every officer-involved shooting, the NYPD launches its own investigation. "It's pretty intense," Bobby says. "They take you off the street until they make their inquiry. I was reassigned to the Command Center for the Bronx. After I got out of the hospital, I had to give a detailed statement to the Internal Affairs investigators. They cross-check your testimony against evidence found at the crime scene. If there are any inconsistencies, it does not bode well for the officer. The Department's shooting team launches a separate inquiry. They go over every detail to make sure the use of force is in compliance with our rules and regulations and to be sure that you did nothing wrong."

* * *

Looking back, Bobby says it's hard to pick out one incident that captures the drama and pathos of working as a cop. But after a few minutes, he says there is one experience he still thinks about. It happened right before Christmas 1995.

"I was in Emergency Service assigned to the Apprehension Team. It was snowing heavily, and we were on our way to a tactical meeting to plan the details of how we were going to execute a warrant for the arrest of a man wanted for a homicide. I remember we were in one of our unmarked trucks. It looked like a delivery truck for a bakery, but inside we had all our heavy weapons, ropes, and hydraulic tools.

"We were coming up the Bronx River Parkway when an officer's panicked voice came in over the radio. You couldn't make out what he was saying—something about a highway officer involved in a shooting on Pelham Parkway and Boston Road. He was yelling 10-13, 10-13, which means a cop is in trouble. We were close, and we sped to the scene."

The drama had begun when a woman ran into the street and started screaming that a man was shooting people inside the Little Chester's shoe store. Officer Leonel Quiñones was across the street, and he called it in. As Quiñones took cover behind a dark blue Volvo, the gunman came running out of the store. He was shooting everywhere, a witness said, just like in the movies.

When Officer Quiñones stood up from his position behind the Volvo and ordered the man to drop his weapon, the gunman aimed and fired at the cop. He grabbed a hostage to use as a human shield, but the person broke free and ran. The shooter was now exposed, and Officer Quinones fired off a round. It hit the man in the groin, but he didn't go down. As he ran north on White Plains Road, two officers eating at a Chinese restaurant joined the chase. As the shooter rounded a corner, another cop who was off duty saw the commotion and joined the pursuit. Just as the off-duty officer was about to tackle him, the gunman collapsed on the sidewalk.

Bobby and his team of five officers and a sergeant arrived at Little Chester's minutes after the gunman had gone down on the sidewalk several blocks away. They pulled their weapons and ran into the store. They were not prepared for what they saw. Five people including two young children, their mother, and the wife of the store's owner, who was celebrating her second wedding anniversary, lay dead on the floor. Three more people were critically wounded.

"I will never forget it as long as I live," he said. "The bodies looked like mannequins. And to see that mom and her two kids lying there. What can you say? I didn't have children of my own then, but for the cops who did have kids, I just can't imagine it."

Later a witness told detectives that Michael Vernon, age twenty-two, asked for a particular kind of sneaker. When the girl behind the counter told him they didn't carry it, he pulled a 9 mm semiautomatic and shot her in the face. As he turned his weapon on the other customers in the store, he yelled out, "You should have given me those sneakers."

* * *

While Bobby was assigned to the Emergency Service Unit, he passed the sergeant's exam, received his promotion, and was transferred back to the 43rd Precinct. The first time he reported for duty, proudly wearing his sergeant's stripes, was a midnight tour. He would supervise thirty patrol officers working that shift.

In most law enforcement agencies, sergeants coordinate the resources deployed at each incident. "You listen to all the calls coming in over the radio, then you make decisions about which jobs need your attention," Bobby notes.

"The sergeant's got to know when to call in more people. You decide if it's a Level One right up to Level Three or Four. The higher the level, the greater potential for violence which determines the amount of resources you call for. Understanding what you're dealing with is key. The sergeant is 100 percent accountable for everything that goes on. It was a new job for me, and I was nervous."

Even before roll call, Bobby realized his first shift working as a sergeant was going to be challenging. The dispatcher was holding a lot of jobs from the previous shift, several patrol cars weren't working, and a car they did need was stuck in Queens.

Bobby and the officer who was driving him had been out for an hour when Bobby suggested they get a cup of coffee. "I told the officer to go to Ellie's," he said. "It was a hot Saturday night in the fall, and there were a lot of people on the street. For some reason, the driver decided to make a quick U-turn so he could pull right up to the coffee shop. In a freak accident, he missed the brake, hit the gas, and ran into a girl crossing the road. She bounced up on the hood of our police car and rolled up on the windshield before she fell back onto the street."

Bobby jumped out of the car. "She was trying to get up, but I encouraged her to lie back down while I called for an ambulance. Thankfully, the ambulance and the EMTs showed up in a couple of minutes. Just as they pulled away, a group of Highway Investigation detectives arrived on the scene. They spent hours making diagrams and charts and interviewing witnesses. Then the Captain of the precinct showed up. He was angry. I can still hear him tearing us up. I was worried sick about the girl we hit. When I called the hospital, I found out she had a broken hip, which made me feel worse. That's a pretty serious injury. Six hours later we were still there."

By six the next morning, Bobby was exhausted. It was his first shift working as a sergeant, and he felt like a total failure. When the paperwork was finished and all the interviews completed, he got a car and went to get a sandwich and coffee. He hadn't eaten for twelve hours.

"I'm almost at the sandwich place when I get a call to go back to the station. I couldn't believe it. When I got back, someone tells me to go see the Commanding Officer. The other sergeant standing there wouldn't look at me. When I got into the CO's office, someone from Inspections and Investigations was slumped in a chair. When he sees me come into the room, he jumps up and says, 'I have some bad news for you. You have to make an arrest.' Then he tells me it's another cop I have to bring in—a police officer whose wife claims he hit her. I said, no way. That's a mistake. Internal Affairs has to do that. They told me to check the Patrol Guide. If a police officer in the precinct has to be arrested, the sergeant on duty has to do it. Then they tell me the District Attorney wants the wife to come in and make a statement. After I arrest the officer, I should go pick up his wife and bring her to the DA's office, even though they know she doesn't want to go. They're pretty clear about it. I have to bring her in anyway.

"I'm twelve hours into my first shift as a sergeant. An innocent girl is in the hospital with a broken hip, and I have to arrest another officer. I tried, without luck, to convince the officer's wife to come with me to see the DA. When I called to say she would not come, an assistant district attorney got on the phone and accused me of not doing enough to protect a vulnerable woman from her abusive husband.

"I'm a sergeant. It's my first day. I've gone from running someone over, to arresting a police officer, to getting into a scene with his wife. I was wondering if this was a typical day for a sergeant."

* * *

By the time Bobby had been on the job for almost twenty years, he'd had only minor injuries—a pulled muscle, broken thumb, or a sprain. "Then my luck ran out," he said.

It was October 2007. Bobby and his partners were doing an undercover buy. "We were on the trail of a guy we believed had $500,000 in drug money," he said. "We were told he'd have the money in the car. When we saw his car approaching, we put on our lights and pulled him over. We got out and walked over, but as we got close, he threw his car into gear and took off. We chased him. It was only a minute or so before he spun out on the road. He jumped out of his car, which was still running, and took off. I got out of my car and chased him. As he cut back and I turned to follow him, I ran right into a scaffolding pole." Bobby broke his elbow and his collarbone and ruptured three discs in his neck. He has had to accept the fact that his discs will never be back to normal.

The cops had no trouble finding the money. The dealer had left all the cash in the car. Hundreds of heat-sealed packages of $50 and $100 bills were piled up on the backseat.

The only other time Bobby was seriously injured was when he was still assigned to the Emergency Service Unit. The call came in the afternoon. A tractor trailer had smashed into an overpass and was wedged up into the cement underpinnings of the bridge. Bobby was using a Hurst tool, spreading it to get the back of the truck disengaged from the overpass, when it collapsed. A piece of metal from the truck came crashing down and pinned his hand to the Hurst tool. For all practical purposes, Bobby Johnson was impaled on his own equipment. "They had to use another Hurst tool to get the metal out of my hand," Bobby said. "All my tendons were severed."

Bobby credits his doctor for a remarkable recovery. "Once they got me free of the metal sheet, there was a helicopter waiting to take me to the hospital, where a team of hand specialists was waiting. The Department was absolutely great. Everything was coordinated. They even went and picked up my wife and flew her to the hospital. It was the NYPD at their best."

* * *

After two decades of working for the New York City Police Department, Bobby says he still feels as lucky as he did on his first day in the Police Academy. "There are so many different ways you can go in this Department. You can make whatever you want out of it. People say you have to know someone to get the interesting work, but that's not true. I never knew anyone, and I've had great assignments the whole time."

As he approaches retirement, Bobby has started to think about the next phase of his life. "There are times I think I'd like to do more in this Department, but I'd also like to take all my experiences here and go to a smaller Department and make it better. I think they could benefit from learning how we do things in New York City. The NYPD is a great law enforcement agency—maybe the best. We have a lot to share."

Things were pretty calm for Bobby Johnson and his wife, Jeannine, until their twin boys, Hunter and Tanner, arrived on the scene. Fortunately their older sister Giana (pictured below) has been great with the new babies. "She was only eight when they were born, but she's very maternal," Bobby says. "She's the best."

Bobby with his colleagues at the Westchester District Attorney's Office. The group was about to execute a search warrant in the Bronx. Bobby is the first one in the front row, kneeling, on the left.

Bobby Johnson gets promoted to detective-sergeant. The certificate of promotion is being presented by Assistant Chief Anthony Izzo, February 29, 2008.

Above, members of the Drug Enforcement Strike Group Z-12 celebrate the conclusion of a successful investigation. Bobby is second from left in rear.

Bobby Johnson (right) and his partner Billy Neice in 1991 at the 43rd Precinct after an arrest for money, guns and drugs. Bobby and Billy worked together for five years and are still good friends.

Officers raided the heroin mill on December 15, 2006. By the following Easter Sunday, Bobby's best friend, Stu Cohen, pictured above with his wife, Gina, and children, Sydney and Haley, was dead. Doctors never would say what killed him, but the cops were sure it was a toxic substance in the heroin mill that made him sick.

Bobby and his parents, Ann and Bob Johnson, Sr., at Yankee Stadium Awards Night where he was presented the Public Service Award for Heroism.

Chapter Eight

Steve Bonano: It's Not a Job, It's a Calling

*"Saints have no moderation, nor do poets,
just exuberance." —Anne Sexton*

Steve Bonano was twenty when he graduated from the Academy. His first assignment was in the 42nd Precinct in the Bronx. It was the summer of 1982, and large parts of the borough were still burned out from the fires that had devastated the area a decade earlier. Most of the streets resembled bombed-out war zones. Life in the 41st Precinct to the east was the subject of the 1981 film, *Fort Apache the Bronx*, and the 4-2 was where President Jimmy Carter announced a program of massive federal aid in 1977. "We're going to change all this," the President said, as he drove a shovel into the scorched ground in one of the many vacant lots that littered the bleak landscape. Off-duty officers who worked in the Bronx wore T-shirts emblazoned with slogans like "Warriors of the Wasteland" and "What you call hell, we call home." When Steve Bonano reported for his first day of work in August 1982, the 4-2 was the only precinct in the city without a single restaurant or coffee shop. It was a grim place.

Sometime during that first year, Steve got the call all police officers respond to sooner or later: a situation that forces them to confront the reality that the profession they've chosen could get them killed. It was a little after four in the afternoon at the beginning of the shift when the dreaded words came in over the radio. A 10-13 in the 4-4. The 44th Precinct was only a couple of blocks away, and a 10-13 meant an officer was in trouble. Steve and his partner sped to the scene. When they pulled up, squad cars with doors open and red lights flashing were everywhere.

Two cops had chased a man into a building. The suspect took cover in a corner of the hallway, pulled a gun, and started shooting. In the hail of gunfire, one of the officers had been hit. They knew he was down and trapped in the hall, but no one knew the extent of his injuries. His partner had managed to get himself out of the line of fire. Somehow, the wounded officer was able to get some shots off. When he ran out of ammunition, his partner tossed his own gun over so he could keep firing. Finally, a round hit the target, and the gunman went down.

Steve watched as the EMTs and paramedics anxiously waited for the shooting to end. They could not help the injured officer while there was gunfire. Later they learned the wounded cop might have bled to death if the gun battle had gone on much longer.

After that night Steve never looked at the job in quite the same way. "I had been pretty naive about being a police officer," he said. "I had this cocky attitude, 'Hey, look at me. I'm a cop.' I'd even told my friends I couldn't believe I was getting paid money to go out and have so much fun. But after seeing that wounded officer carried away in an ambulance, I said to myself, 'This job isn't a joke.' I never bragged again about getting a paycheck for having a good time."

He realized something else that day as well. He had taken a solemn oath to run toward a threat no matter what the danger or risk and to do whatever he could to stop it.

* * *

Steve had an abundance of enthusiasm, but he was still new on the job, and he lacked experience. Law enforcement officers learn the nuances and subtleties of police work the hard way. They adjust their tactics after making mistakes and observing more experienced officers do the work.

It was a warm summer day when Steve got his lesson on the tactics of patrol. They had just finished roll call when the sergeant called him over. A nearby street had filled up with unlicensed street peddlers. The local merchants, who were renting their stores and doing business legitimately, had called the police to get them removed. The sergeant didn't give Steve advice or tips. All the rookie knew was that his sergeant expected him to get the job done.

He walked briskly to the location, found the peddlers, and told them they had to leave. Everyone complied except one man. Steve remembers him as a large and intimidating man who was selling an assortment of trinkets and jewelry on a flimsy, makeshift tray. He flat-out refused to move.

"I decided to be calm and polite," Steve recalled. "I said, 'Excuse me, sir. You can't sell that jewelry here.'" Steve thought as a New York City cop, that was all it would take. He was confident the confrontation was over. He walked into a deli to buy something to eat. When he came out, the peddler was still there.

"I tried to be more assertive. 'Sir,' I told him, 'you can't peddle here without a license. It's against the law. You can't do this.' I can't believe I was so naive. I even tried to make him feel sorry for me. I told him I would get in trouble with my sergeant if he didn't move."

Any cop with a few years on the job could predict what happened next. "The guy totally blew me off," Steve said. "He looked at me like I was annoying him. He said, 'Hey, look, I'm getting tired of you. You're the one who needs to leave.'"

Now Steve was angry, which is never a good thing for a police officer. "Even though I had never hit someone, I pulled my stick out. The peddler put his tray down and came at me. We ended up on the ground wrestling." Fortunately, officers from the neighboring 46th Precinct showed up. "When I called it in, I couldn't remember the right code," Steve said. "They teach you how to do this in the Academy, but out on the street, wrestling with this large man, I forgot everything. All I could think of to say was I needed a unit and I was in front of Woolworth's."

It must have been obvious to everyone who heard the call that Steve was new on the job. He began to hear the squealing of approaching sirens before he even finished his message. While the cops from the 4-6 got the cuffs on the peddler and put him in the back of their police car, Steve stood there feeling foolish. "It seemed like nothing to the other officers, but I felt I'd started a lot of trouble, and I was embarrassed."

Developing skills to work the street takes a lot of experience as well as the ability to learn from your mistakes. It's a complicated process of knowing when to negotiate, when to sympathize, when to protect, and when to exert authority. Determining which persona to take on requires intense powers of observation. You need the ability to read people and figure out what they are up to. But that's not all. The officer also has to have the confidence and experience to make a decision, often in a split second, about what to do next. Being able to read people and take action quickly are among the most important skills a police officer needs.

What Steve didn't understand when he first approached the street peddler, but began to learn by the time his shift was ending, was that showing up in a uniform with a firearm and handcuffs is not enough to exert control. He was learning that enforcing the law is a power struggle. It's a battle of sorts that always has to be won by the officer, hopefully without using force.

Four years later, Steve was working in plainclothes in the Anti-Crime Unit. Unless the precinct was really shorthanded, Anti-Crime cops did not answer 911 calls. They were free to be proactive and look for trouble before it started. One night when they were shorthanded, Steve's sergeant asked him if he would mind putting on a uniform and going up to Fordham Road in the Bronx. Once again complaints were coming in from shop owners that peddlers were back on the street taking away their business.

"I got down there and saw one of the peddlers," Steve recalled. "I walked up and told him I'd give him a few minutes to leave the area. When the time was up, there was no sign he was leaving. I went over and put my face very close to his. I looked him in the eye and said, 'I thought I told you to leave.' He just stared back at me, almost daring me to try and make him go. I pointed at his tray of trinkets and told him if he didn't clear out, I'd dump them on the ground, then I'd lock him up for peddling without a license. That was it. He took off."

Steve Bonano had learned the art of patrol. Many years later he said, "It probably took me close to those whole four years, but over that time, I learned how to be a cop."

* * *

Active police officers, the ones who are the most passionate about doing the job, don't like to wait for the dispatcher to call something in over the radio. They are already out there hustling and stalking the bad guys. Back when Steve was assigned to the 4-2, the precinct wasn't busy enough for cops who liked to work. The neighborhood was still filled with burned-out buildings, and most people had moved out years ago. "It was frustrating for us," he recalled. "We didn't get many calls in the 4-2. The 46th Precinct just to the north in the Bronx was a different story. The calls there never stopped."

Steve says he can still hear the dispatcher's voice. "'Time is now 1911 hours. KOP-911 radio zone 7A. No jobs in the 4-2, two in the 4-8, 36 calls for service in the 4-6.' Calls in the 4-6 usually included 'shots fired,' 'man with a gun,' or 'armed robbery in progress.' Almost every call for service was some sort of serious crime. All I wanted to do was get transferred there."

When Steve worked in the 4-2, Mike Coleman was often his partner. Mike also dreamed about moving to a busier precinct. The two would sit in their police car and brainstorm about ways they could leave their own precinct, go to 4-6, and not get in trouble with their bosses. One day they came up with a plan. They'd take the dispatcher's phone number when they were out on patrol. When they heard her say she was holding jobs in the 4-6, they'd go to the nearest pay phone so their supervisors couldn't hear what they were doing. They would call her up and ask if she would reassign them out of their precinct. NYPD cops are supposed to stay within the confines of their assigned sector, and Steve and Mike knew the dispatcher might be hesitant to go against the rules. But every time they called, they would hear her voice as soon as they got back to the car. "4-2 Adam, are you available to respond to the 4-6?"

"We'd answer in the affirmative and ask her what she had," Steve recalled. "We were like little kids, we were so happy."

Their scheme worked. Every time they made the call, Steve and Mike were sent to the 4-6. Their workload doubled.

* * *

It wasn't long before Officer Bonano's bosses began to notice that he was unusually observant and especially good at figuring out who had an illegal firearm. "I grew up in a bad neighborhood," Steve said. "I wasn't a bad kid, but there were a lot of kids who were, and I knew how they acted. If you're doing something illegal, you don't feel comfortable around cops. Once I became a police officer, I picked up immediately if someone was nervous when I was around."

One night Steve was working with Dave Erosa, his best friend since kindergarten at the Holy Cross Grammar School in the Bronx. It was a Wednesday evening, and they were working the four to midnight shift in the 46th Precinct.

They had just gone out on patrol when they saw a car ahead of them go through a stop sign. The officers pulled the vehicle over and kept their hands over their holsters as they approached. "I went to talk to the driver in the front seat, and Dave opened the back door of the car on the passenger's side," Steve remembered. "Within seconds, Dave and the guy in the back seat were fighting. Dave yelled, 'He has a gun.'" A simple stop for not heeding a stop sign had escalated.

"I grabbed the driver in the front seat by the collar and pulled him out of the car, all the while keeping my weapon aimed at the passenger. I called for backup. I knew they could tell by my voice we were in trouble. All I had to say was, '6-Adam, 182 and Creston,' and help was on its way. I barely got the words out of my mouth before I heard the sirens. When you're in trouble, there is no greater sound than that one. The cavalry was on its way."

Dave Erosa explained that although he and Steve were childhood friends and Steve had been best man at his wedding, Steve had already been on the job a couple of years when Dave entered the Academy. After graduation, when Dave's first assignment was the 46th Precinct, Steve became his mentor.

"You couldn't have a better experience than working with Steve," Dave said. "He's a great leader and really good at getting guns off the street. He is a great cop with a big heart."

* * *

One night when Steve was on patrol with Tommy Crowe, they heard a barrage of gunfire. They headed in the direction of the shots. Tommy was driving. He made a left turn, and both officers saw a man standing on the corner, randomly shooting a firearm.

"Another cruiser pulled up at the same time, and we almost ran into each other," Steve said. "Once we got closer, we could see the man was shot up pretty bad, but he still had a gun in his hand."

The cops pulled their weapons and ordered him to drop the gun. The suspect was incoherent. The police could tell he could not hear them. One of the officers, Joe Zallo, tackled the man and got him face down on the street. Steve said despite the fact he was riddled with bullets, but the man put up a fight to keep hold of his gun. "A few seconds passed before Joe was able to get hold of the weapon and put the cuffs on," Steve recalled. "When Joe stood up, he was covered with blood."

When someone who's had little or no contact with criminals witnesses a police officer acting aggressively toward someone on the street, they often get the impression that cops are violent people who enjoy preying on victims. But the reality is just the opposite. Bystanders at the scene, unaware the man was armed, must have wondered why it was necessary for a police officer to tackle someone who was so badly wounded.

As Steve was reporting the incident over his radio, several people ran up and pointed to a Jeep that was stuck in traffic. "The people in that Jeep shot this guy," they said, pointing to the man who was still lying in the street in a rapidly growing pool of blood. If they were right, Steve knew the people inside the Jeep would be heavily armed.

Zallo and his partner stayed with the handcuffed suspect while Tommy and Steve ran toward the Jeep. Three men were inside. The cops ordered them out of the car and told them to keep their hands high in the air. When they searched the vehicle, they found two machine guns, an AR-15, and a semiautomatic handgun. These were heavily armed criminal suspects even by New York City standards. They were only two-and-a-half hours into their shift, and they had four suspects, two machine guns, and a semiautomatic.

* * *

On another occasion, Tommy and Steve were working a midnight to eight shift in the Bronx. Steve had been promoted to sergeant and was assigned to the 5-2, another very busy precinct. The pair grabbed coffees and headed out on patrol. A few minutes later, Tommy saw a cab go through a stop sign. There was something about the cab that made him suspicious. He signaled to Steve and flipped on the lights.

"Once we got closer, you could tell there was something up with the passenger in the back," Steve recalled. "He was acting nervous. Then we saw him reach down. That's almost always the sign they've got a gun."

The cops didn't say a word to each other. They didn't have to. Their instincts told them something was wrong. Pulling their Smith & Wesson 38s, they approached the cab from the rear.

"The cab had dark, tinted windows," Steve recalled. "Someone rolled them up as we approached. Tommy approached the man sitting in the backseat on the passenger side. When I opened the back door on the driver's side, Tommy had the guy on the other side in a headlock. With his other hand, he was trying to prevent the man from firing his gun, which was pointed directly at my chest. The suspect was struggling, trying to pull the trigger, but Tommy was able to keep his right hand on the gun's top strap, which was preventing it from firing. The two of us wrestled the gunman out of the car. Finally we were able to subdue him."

When they searched the cab, Steve and Tommy found property belonging to a garage in Manhattan. "We called them and found out the garage had been robbed earlier that evening," Steve said. "When the Manhattan Robbery Squad detectives heard the details, they were pretty sure we had caught someone who had committed over fifty robberies at gunpoint.

"His MO was pretty much the same for each armed robbery," Steve explained. "He'd go into a parking garage and rob the attendant. When people came to get their cars, he would rob them, too. Sometimes he'd hail a cab and rob the cabdriver at gunpoint. After a few months, he sought more thrills. He tied up his terrified victims and left them in the garage, where they waited, bound and gagged, until someone found them."

It was phenomenal police work. From nothing more than a cab going through a stop sign, Tommy and Steve had taken a violent criminal off the street, and fifty armed robberies and assaults were cleared. The man was found guilty and sentenced to life in prison. "This guy," Steve said later, "was a real badass."

* * *

Tommy Crowe has known Steve Bonano for more than twenty years. The two men were partners for much of that time. "If I had to describe Steve," Crowe says, " I would say the quality that impresses everyone the most is his intelligence. He's extremely smart and can quickly size up a situation."

Tommy had a distinguished career with the NYPD as well. His last assignment was with the Organized Crime Control Bureau, where he was the one who arrested Vincent (Vinny Gorgeous) Basciano, the head of the Bonanno crime family. As for Steve, Tommy says he is the type of person who inspires confidence.

"One time a cop in a neighboring precinct was shot," Tommy said. "They rushed him to the hospital, and Steve and I were the first people there. Most people would be surprised at the chaos that goes on at a hospital when the doctors are operating on a high-profile shooting victim. Reporters and photographers are everywhere. They'll barge right into the operating room if they can in order to get their story. When Inspector Louis Anemone showed up and saw Steve, he asked him to take control of the scene.

"When Steve was put in charge, a reporter tried to push his way past him to get into the ER," Tommy continued. "Steve stood there with his arms folded, blocking the reporter's way. He told the reporter he didn't care what credentials he had. There was a police officer in there, and most likely he was dying. There was no way a reporter was going to get by him. When he has to be, Steve is very intimidating."

* * *

In law enforcement, lots of things go wrong. One of those times for Steve happened when he was working a four to twelve shift. Tommy was driving.

"We had just pulled someone over," Steve said. "Tommy approached the driver to check his license and registration when an unmarked police car pulled in behind us. I heard the door slam, and I could see a man in a suit coming toward us."

It was Inspector Louis Anemone. Anemone had a reputation as a fair guy, a cop's cop. But he could be tough if you weren't following the rules and regulations.

"He was all business," Bonano said. "He said, 'Sergeant, why is that officer out of uniform?' It was over 90° that day, and Tommy had loosened his tie. Other than that, I couldn't see anything else. I yelled over, 'Hey, Tommy, fix your tie.' But that wasn't enough for Anemone. 'Put him in the minor violations book for not wearing a proper uniform,' he told me. 'And put yourself in for failure to supervise.'"

When Steve got back to the station, he told an older lieutenant the story.

He hoped the older cop might tell him to ignore the whole thing. But the lieutenant was quick with his response. "Anemone is tough, and he'll send someone to check," he said. "You better do what he said."

Sergeant Bonano was happy he followed the lieutenant's advice. Early the next morning, a sergeant at the borough called to make sure both disciplinary reports were written up, the facts were accurate, and the paperwork filed in the appropriate places.

"Another day Tommy and I arrested a man for possessing an illegal firearm," Steve said. "Tommy was still a patrol officer, and I was a sergeant. The officer is responsible for the paperwork. I knew it was going to take a couple of hours, so I decided to go back out on patrol by myself. All of a sudden, I see four guys in a car. Something about them made me suspicious. I started to follow them. When they made an illegal U-turn, I pulled them over. I was questioning the driver when I see an unmarked police car pull up. I couldn't believe it. It was Anemone again. The Department does not like one officer to stop a car by themselves, especially one with four passengers. Those are bad odds, and tactically it is not the wisest thing to do. He caught me. I knew I was in trouble now for sure."

Steve is still amazed at what happened next. "Anemone jumps out of his car, runs over to the passenger side, and helps me remove a gun from one of the passengers. There were still three passengers to be searched, and he jumped right into it. He starts interrogating the passenger in the front seat. Seconds later, he's pulled his gun, and he's telling the man to get out of the car with his hands up. It turns out that that guy had a gun, too."

Later Anemone told Bonano he'd decided to stop when he saw a sergeant working alone stopping a car with four people in it. When he got out of his vehicle, he'd noticed the guy in the passenger seat in the front reach down like he was trying to hide a weapon.

"We both were nominated for an award," Steve said, "but Anemone intercepted the recommendation and removed his name. I did get a note from him a few days after the incident. It was brief and to the point. 'Sergeant Bonano: Don't make car stops by yourself.'"

*   *   *

In the late 1980s active cops in the Bronx were averaging several arrests each year for possessing illegal firearms. Known in the NYPD as "gun collars," Steve Bonano was making several every month. People started to call him the Gun Man.

One night Steve was working with Jimmy Gildae, a newly promoted sergeant who had just been assigned to the precinct. Like Steve, Jimmy had been very active in the 4-6, and the men shared a strong work ethic. Steve said Jimmy was a cop who was first on the scene and first through the door. "He was the guy you could count on to watch your back," he said.

It was the start of their shift. Steve and Jimmy were sitting in the car, sipping coffees, and watching the street when they heard shots. Seconds later a limousine with shaded windows drove by. "We knew right away there was something wrong with that limo," Steve said.

They turned on the lights and pulled the limousine over. Contrary to what most people believe, when the cops approach a vehicle, they do not unholster their firearms. "We approach cautiously with our hands on the grips in case we need to pull our weapons," Steve explained. "In most situations like this, you never pull your firearm. There's always the chance you'll end up wrestling with the suspect, and that can be bad if you have your gun out of its holster."

This time they were lucky. The suspects, young kids in their early twenties, followed orders. They got out of the car with their hands in the air. Once they were cuffed, Steve watched the suspects while Jimmy used his flashlight to search the vehicle. That's when they found the guns—an Uzi machine gun, a Tech-9, and a semiautomatic.

When people outside of law enforcement ask cops like Steve and Jimmy how they have the courage to run toward a car whose occupants are heavily armed or shooting, they shrug. "I am not sure," Steve says. "Maybe you don't get scared because it's all happening so fast. And thank God most people are good people and will not shoot a cop. I've always believed that I am not going to get shot."

A few days after Steve and Tommy made the arrests and seized the weapons, Bonano was scheduled to work a four to twelve. When he got to the station to report for his shift, the desk sergeant looked worried. He told Steve that along with their own Commanding Officer, two inspectors were waiting to see him. "I was scared," Bonano remembered. "Three high-ranking officers waiting to see someone was unusual. I had no idea what they wanted, but I knew it couldn't be anything good."

He took a deep breath and made his way to CO's office. The three commanders were sitting there, starched white shirts standing out against the dark navy uniforms, chests covered with medals. No one was saying a word.

"Along with my own Commander, I recognized Louis Anemone," Bonano said. "He was the first to speak. He asked me if I knew why they were there. I said I knew I must be in some sort of trouble. I asked if I had done something wrong."

Bonano was surprised at what happened next. Inspector Anemone smiled, walked over, and shook his hand. "We were going over the arrest stats. We couldn't believe your precinct was making so many gun arrests," Anemone said. "You've had a very short tenure here, and you've gotten a lot of guns off the street. We want you to know we appreciate what you're doing."

* * *

The dictionary defines a "glass ceiling" as an unacknowledged discriminatory barrier that prevents minorities and women from rising to positions of power. While Steve readily acknowledges there has never been a door yet that shut on him because he's Hispanic, he has not been immune from wisecracks about his ethnic background.

"To some guys, I know I'll always be the 'quota sergeant' even though affirmative action had nothing to do with my promotions. It doesn't matter how well I do. A few people will always believe I moved ahead because the NYPD was being forced to promote minorities. During the 1980s an antidiscrimination lawsuit forced the Department to hire a percentage of minorities for every nonminority who was promoted. If you were black or Hispanic or a woman and you took a promotional exam, you had an advantage over a white male candidate. As a result of the lawsuit, minorities who got promotions were stigmatized. It caused problems for people like me who passed the exam and got promoted without the benefit of a quota system. I remember this one guy who kept getting in my face after I was promoted to lieutenant. He'd say, 'I know you, you're the quota sergeant.' It didn't matter to him that I had gotten one of the highest marks on the lieutenant's exam and had made over three hundred arrests before I even made sergeant. I knew that no matter what I did, to him I'd always be the quota guy. When I became a police officer, I was naive about how some white guys would feel about me, but I don't worry about it any more. I've learned to accept that there's a small group who will always think I got where I did because I'm a minority."

* * *

If there is a glass ceiling in the NYPD, Bonano rocketed right up through it. He scored high on the sergeant's and lieutenant's tests. Several years later he decided to take on the captain's exam, a test considered by many as being more difficult than the New York State bar exam. Steve took six weeks off to study, and he worked at it twelve hours every day. When the marks got posted, he was crushed: He'd barely passed. Even after taking a one-year leave to earn a master's degree at Harvard University in 2009, he still says the captain's exam was the most challenging test he ever took.

The doors kept opening for Steve, and he kept marching through them. He became the first Hispanic officer in the history of the NYPD to command one of the agency's most elite divisions, the Emergency Service Unit. "Ever since I joined the Department, I always felt I was the poster child for all the possibilities available to anyone who joins the New York City Police Department."

After two years in the 4-2 Precinct, followed by another two in the 4-6, Steve went to the Vice Unit in 1986. Working as an undercover investigator, he spent almost four years investigating prostitutes, people running illegal gambling operations, and employees of social clubs, after-hours bars with no operating licenses and a lot of crime. Steve is still amazed that his friends outside law enforcement were envious about the fun they imagined he was having on the prostitution detail.

"People have no idea what these women were like," he said. "Every arrest requires the arresting officer to inventory and voucher the contents of their purses. You can't imagine how disgusting it was to have to do that. They had bottles of creams and lotions for sexually transmitted diseases. Everything was filthy, and it smelled really bad. I'd tell my friends, there's no way anyone would want to have sex with these women. You didn't even want to touch them."

While dealing with the prostitutes was unpleasant, shutting down social clubs was dangerous. "These places are really bad," Steve said. "They sell liquor without a license, which on the face of it doesn't sound dangerous, but there are usually a lot of drugs and guns being bought and sold, and they attract a serious criminal element. It's extremely dangerous for the undercover cops to go in and get enough evidence to make the arrests and shut the places down."

Once Steve was sent into a club in a particularly bad section of the Bronx. He had a small gun hidden in his crotch. "If they didn't know you, you'd get searched before they let you in," he said. "I had been searched hundreds of times before, and no one had ever discovered the gun. I never thought they'd find it, but they did."

The bouncers quickly surrounded him. Steve knew he had to talk fast. "I told them, 'Look, this neighborhood is rough, and I have a gun to protect myself.' I figured they would beat me or maybe something worse, but they decided to just physically throw me out."

Back on the street, his relief soon gave way to frustration. The way Steve saw it, he had a job to do, and he had been interrupted. He returned to his lieutenant at a predetermined location and told him what happened. Steve gave the lieutenant his gun and told him he was going back inside. The lieutenant looked stunned as Steve walked back toward the club.

When he got to the front door, Steve told the bouncer he'd gotten rid of his gun. "I told the guy I didn't want any trouble. I just wanted to have a drink and hang out."

They let him in. After sitting at the bar for two hours posing as a regular patron, Bonano established a rapport. From that night on, he was able to come and go when he pleased. Eventually he witnessed enough criminal activity to get a search warrant. When Vice detectives and uniformed cops from the precinct raided the club, Bonano was handcuffed and removed from the scene along with the other patrons and employees. The arresting officers read them their rights and put them under arrest, and the club was closed.

From Vice, Steve Bonano was transferred to the 52nd Precinct. From there it was on to the Aviation Unit. Not many people knew he had been flying since his dad took him up in an airplane for a surprise ride on his tenth birthday. He'd had a passion for it ever since. Soon after he was promoted to sergeant, a memo went out that the Department was looking for pilots. Steve decided to do everything he could to become a pilot for the New York City Police Department.

As he began to talk to people about getting a transfer, he got some negative feedback. "I was surprised that some people were not impressed with Aviation," he said. "I knew that helicopters are great at certain kinds of patrol.

They've got infrared equipment and can light up a really large area. If officers on the ground are chasing someone on foot and lose their suspect, the helicopter can light up the neighborhood, pinpoint a criminal suspect, and pass his location on to the cops."

Not everyone saw it that way. When Steve approached one inspector about transferring to the unit, his reaction was hostile. "He told me that in his opinion, a helicopter is like a flying radio car that can't make stops. In his view, for law enforcement, aircraft are pretty much worthless. He seemed to think the Aviation Unit was just a bunch of good old boys up in the air screwing around. He told me I belonged on the street, that if I went to Aviation, I would be wasting my training and my talents."

In New York City, where most of the cityscape is dense and decidedly vertical, helicopters don't play as significant a role as they do, say, in Southern California, with its endless freeways and one- and two-story structures spread over a vast area. Air support units in the Big Apple can't follow fleeing suspects like they can in other areas because of the tall buildings and narrow streets.

Still, Steve believed helicopters were effective tools in the law enforcement arsenal, and he was determined to achieve his goal. To apply, he found out that he needed a commercial pilot's license, which required a major investment of time and money. When the flight school told him the cost for the training, he almost gave up. There was no way he had that amount of cash. But when Steve's father learned his son had put his plans on hold, he made the decision to help him out.

Four years into his eight-year stint with Aviation, Steve Bonano made history. He and his copilot, Matt Rowley, had been up for over an hour when the dispatcher's voice came blaring. A highway unit had attempted to stop a stolen vehicle, and a chase ensued.

"Matt and I picked up the chase," Steve said. "We followed the cars with the helicopter. The vehicles finally came to a stop in a shopping center. The next thing we knew, the officer was fighting with the driver. The suspect managed to break free and run toward the supermarket. The officer took off after him. I think that's when the adrenaline kicked in, and we made the decision to land."

As they brought the helicopter down in the shopping center parking lot, they could see they had a problem. An elderly woman sitting in her car was right in the middle of the only space big enough for them to land. The officers signaled her to move. "She was staring at the chopper," Steve remembered. "She looked frozen with fear. Finally she got her car going and drove it out of the way."

Steve jumped out, and Matt stayed with the bird. "When I got into the store, I saw the officer chasing the guy through the aisles," he said. "They were coming right toward me." Steve ran toward the suspect and tackled him. He pulled the suspect's arms behind his back, forced his wrists together, and got the handcuffs on. It was only at that moment that it hit him that landing the helicopter might have been a very bad idea.

After making sure the officer who began the chase was okay, Steve raced back to the chopper, desperately trying to tuck his shirt back into his trousers as he ran. He was completely out of breath when he got back to the helicopter. Matt was ready to go, and they lifted off.

They were feeling pretty good. The cop was okay, and they had nabbed a bad guy. They took a moment to enjoy the calm before the storm. The moment turned out to be a short one. Just a few seconds after they lifted off, a call came in on the radio.

"I can still hear it now," Steve said. "'Base to number six.' Matt and I looked at each other. It was the Commanding Officer of the Aviation Unit. I knew the same thing was going through Matt's mind. He's never on the radio, and we know why he's calling."

"Did you just land a helicopter in a shopping center and engage in a foot pursuit?"

Steve thought for a quick minute about lying but decided that would probably be his second bad idea that day. It was clear the boss knew something. "That's affirmative, Sir."

"I've got the Mayor's office on the phone," the commander bellowed into the radio. "They called to tell me someone from Aviation landed a Department helicopter in a shopping center parking lot."

The Commander told them to land the chopper and call him immediately from a landline. He wanted the conversation out of earshot of the police scanners. Matt and Steve knew that whatever the boss had to say, he wasn't interested in having anyone hear it.

Matt, who would be facing the wrath of the boss as well, had an idea. "No sense both of us getting transferred,' he joked. "Why don't you say you ordered me to do it? Tell them all I was doing was following your orders."

In the end, Steve and Matt never faced disciplinary action, and the people who had doubted that Aviation had a legitimate role in law enforcement were impressed. Chief Anemone, now the Chief of Patrol, said, "That's what they should be doing up there—apprehending criminals."

The commanders who disparaged Steve's ambition to go to the Aviation Unit realized it didn't matter where a guy like Steve works or on what assignment. He's a street cop, whether he's flying a helicopter or walking a beat. If he sees an officer in need of assistance, that's it.

* * *

Steve Bonano grew up in a middle-class Catholic family. His dad, Tony, was born in Puerto Rico and was six years old when he immigrated to the U.S. Tony Bonano held advanced degrees in physics, electrical engineering, mathematics, and education. He worked most of his career as a physicist at the Brooklyn Navy Yard. Steve's mother, Vivian, was an executive secretary at the United Nations. She was born just a year after her family moved to New York from the Dominican Republic. All three Bonano children went to parochial schools, and it was expected that Steve, his brother, and his sister would all go on to college.

When Steve was born, his family lived on Hunts Point Avenue in the 41st Precinct, home to the famous Fort Apache. When Steve was five years old, his mom and dad moved the family to the Soundview section of the Bronx in the heart of the 43rd Precinct, a tough neighborhood that frequently led the city in homicides. His friends and neighbors all spoke Spanish, and until Steve started school, his parents only spoke Spanish at home. When six-year-old Steve started school, he didn't know a word of English. Just after the holidays, Steve's teacher asked to meet with his mother. She was told there was a good chance her son might be held back.

Looking back, Steve says that that meeting must have alarmed his parents. He was too young to remember the details, but it was obvious they'd made a pact. From that day forward, they only spoke English at home. The irony is, today, Steve speaks only English. He regrets he never learned his parents' native language. "Everyone knows I'm Hispanic," he says, "and sometimes people start speaking to me in Spanish. They just assume I understand them, so it's embarrassing when I tell them they have to talk to me in English."

While his younger brother and sister were doing well in the classroom, Steve was excelling at athletics. At Cardinal Hayes High School, he played football and basketball and was a member of the swim team. His academic career was less impressive. The low point occurred in high school when he was forced to take physics.

When Steve brought home a failing grade, Tony sat his elder son down and told him that he would work with him every day for as long as it took until he got his physics grade up. And there would be no swimming, no basketball, no football. In short, there would be no fun.

There wasn't much time to turn things around, but Steve's father was giving him no choice about improving his grade. "Every day he taught me physics," Steve said. "I had my own private tutor."

When the school year ended, Steve received the highest grade in his class on the final exam. It was such a phenomenal turnaround that the teacher accused him of cheating, which infuriated Steve's father. "I wasn't too happy when he called the school and told them if they thought I was cheating, they should give me another test."

When Steve entered City College of New York, all he cared about was taking enough credits so he could be eligible for the swim team. He barely studied, and his grades still hovered in the low Cs. By the time he dropped out to join the Police Department, he had only sixty credits under his belt, and he had never earned anything higher than a C.

* * *

For Steve Bonano, pursuing a career in law enforcement was a long shot. No one in his family had been a cop, and he had never had much personal exposure to the police. But when he turned fifteen and got a summer job as a lifeguard at a public pool in the Bronx, an older cop, Al Vazquez, took an interest in Steve. Vazquez and another officer, Harry Gonzalez, were both assigned to the pool for the summer. They enjoyed telling the young lifeguard stories about their adventures working as cops. They encouraged him to think about joining the force.

"One experience I had at the pool made a big impression," Steve said. "It was hot and sunny, and the pool was filled with young kids and lots of teenagers. It was around one in the afternoon when I heard a strange noise. It was like a rattling, rumbling sound. All of a sudden I see this huge number of guys, bigger and older than me, climbing over the fence that surrounded the pool. It seemed like there were hundreds of them. I knew by the colors of their clothing that they were all in the same gang, the Savage Skulls. We had a lot of gangs in the Bronx in those days, and the Savage Skulls was one of the worst. Within seconds, they circled the pool. They started chanting at the swimmers. I was the only lifeguard on duty, I was fifteen years old, and I was scared. I was afraid to turn my back on them, so I backed up slowly toward the pool house. I was praying they wouldn't notice me. I found Officer Vazquez in the locker room. I told him the Savage Skulls had circled the pool and I was worried what they were going to do to the kids. I'll never forget what happened then. Vazquez jumped out of his chair and pulled his gun belt off of a hook on the wall. I remember his face turned beet red. He looked furious. He growled, 'What in the hell are they doing here?' On his way out to the pool, he called it in on his radio. Vazquez knew that with one cop against dozens of gang members, he might need help."

When the officer got out to the pool, he looked around and sized up the scene. He yelled out, "Which one of you is the leader? Step forward."

"I thought you could probably hear his voice from miles away. He was clutching his nightstick, holding it low on one side. When one of the gang members stepped forward and announced he was the leader, Vazquez grabbed his arm and did some kind of jujitsu move. The next thing I see is the so-called leader down on the ground and scared to death, just like that. By the time Officer Vazquez got him in cuffs, everyone else had scattered. I looked around. I couldn't believe they were all gone. We found out later that there were probably forty of them, not the hundreds I'd thought at the beginning. Yet that one cop took on all those tough guys by himself. A couple of minutes after he called it in, the first police car showed up. By then Vazquez had everything under control. The gang was gone, and the kids went back to swimming. To me he seemed like Superman. I decided right then that when I grew up, I wanted to be just like him. Al Vazquez and Harry Gonzalez made me want to be a police officer."

* * *

Over his three decades with the NYPD, everywhere Steve was assigned, morale went up. Within months, most cops under his command found they had new enthusiasm for the job. They took on more work and did it with pride. He was especially good at advising rookies about the crucial sets of skills they had to master before they would be effective street cops. "I tell them, 'You've got to be nosy, you've got to engage people, and you've got to shake things up if you want to find something. Go out and ask them what they're doing. Find out if there's anything going on. Don't be shy.' Nine times out of ten, it's nothing. When there is something, I tell them that's when they have to be ready for things to escalate. I warn them over and over. Be ready for the unexpected. When it happens, you will have only a second to react."

A lieutenant who worked under Steve in Emergency Service recalls one incident in which the ESU cops were serving a warrant in the 23rd Precinct. "These were serious drug dealers," the lieutenant recalled, "and our information indicated that along with the drugs, they had a lot of guns. When Steve and I went to meet with the Commanding Officer of the precinct to make a plan to take this group down, the Commander was a wreck. He felt that these type of jobs were risky and might end his career.

"Steve had such a different take on things," the lieutenant continued. "He always thought we were going to be successful. I remember him telling the Commander, 'No, that's not how it's going to be.' He told him this could be the biggest drug bust in history and we would all be on the front page of the newspaper for doing such a great job. That's the difference between Steve and so many other people. He's upbeat, even positive. That's rare in our world. He believes in the mission and in himself, and he's confident his people will do the job right."

* * *

While he may be upbeat, Steve knows that enforcing the laws and protecting innocent people from harm is hard work. A lot of police officers burn out. "I never stop trying to motivate the burned-out cops whose views have become negative," he says, "but I like to give more attention to the ones who are still into the job. I like to focus on those who, with a little encouragement, will get out there and try their best to be great law enforcement officers despite the enormous frustrations of the job."

There was one time that Steve let his emotions get the better of him, which is usually a bad idea for anyone doing law enforcement work. He was the Executive Officer, the second person in command of the precinct, when an incident occurred that he botched badly. "There was a neighborhood association for this one block in Manhattan," he said. "It was a middle-class enclave in the center of a poor neighborhood. It was the one block in the entire neighborhood that didn't have a lot of crime.

"One day I was in my office, and my phone rang. When I picked it up, a man instructed me to stand by for Miss So-and-So. I didn't say anything directly, but I was upset somebody would call and then put me on hold."

Steve hung up. Within a minute, the phone rang again. The same male voice was on the other end of the line. He asked Steve to stand by. "I was indignant. 'Stand by?' I told the guy. 'You've got to be kidding. Why don't you stand by?'

"The next time, Miss So-and-So called me herself. Right away she started yelling into the phone. 'Who am I speaking too?' I informed her that I was the Executive Officer of the precinct, the second in command. She started screaming. 'You're not in charge. Give me the person in charge. I know it can't be you.' Finally she realized I was the one she needed to talk to. Then she started in with her demands. First she wanted surveillance cameras placed up and down her block. She wanted lots of them. I knew later I should have had my boss take the call, but by that time, it was too late. I told her, 'Why should we give you cameras? You had one murder on your street in a decade. The rest of the neighborhood needs our attention more than your one block. They don't have cameras, why should you? Even if we had the luxury of putting cameras everywhere, I would not put them on a block with no crime.'"

Steve had broken a cardinal rule of police work: He let his temper get the best of him. People in law enforcement, from the cop on the beat up to the Chief in the corner office, know they always have to be polite. No matter how rude, demanding, inappropriate, or insulting someone may be, cops are trained and expected to respond with courtesy and respect. Steve knew the minute it was over, that despite her rudeness and the fact that her group had fewer than ten members and didn't care about their less fortunate neighbors, he had behaved badly. That did not reflect well on the Department. He promised himself he would never do it again.

People who go into law enforcement must work hard to overcome burnout. The signs are unmistakable. Everyone and everything becomes aggravating. Negativity and cynicism seem to overwhelm everything. The tendency to isolate oneself from friends and neighbors who are not in law enforcement accelerates. With burnout, the jokes that have always been the police officer's best defense mechanism against the constant exposure to rage, violence, and man's inhumanity to man don't seem funny anymore. In Steve's case, after close to three decades on the job, he is relieved that his sense of humor is still intact.

Humor is a double-edged sword for law enforcement. The sick jokes, pranks, and endless hazing that go on between cops are their best defense against the brutal world they are thrust into. It is part of life in every police station in the United States. Law enforcement officers try to keep laughing so they can tolerate the horror they witness, from abused children to car wrecks and all manner of violence and death. But what most police officers find hilarious, civilians find strange. While their jokes help officers stay sane, they are also a wedge between cops and the rest of the world, which has trouble understanding how normal people can joke about events that are tragic.

While Steve may be able to able to joke about sad things he sees on the street, he admits that the constant exposure to rapists, muggers, drug dealers, prostitutes, thieves, and all the other unsavory people police deal with daily can change one's own view of human beings. "A lot of these people you encounter are really horrible," he says. "If you let it get to you, you can lose your faith in the human race."

* * *

It's a long way from that day at the pool in the Bronx when fifteen-year-old Steve Bonano witnessed an older cop take on forty gang members to his life today serving as a One Star Chief in the nation's largest law enforcement agency. It has been a career with so many accomplishments that it is a bit of a surprise when Steve talks about what he still feels is the most memorable moment in his career.

"A call came in for shots fired with the possibility of multiple victims," Steve remembered. He had just turned twenty-one and had only been on the job for a year.

"You could tell this was going to be a bad one," he said. "As we drove to the location, you could see a caravan of red police lights. Every one of the officers was rushing toward the unknown. While they raced toward danger, not one of them was thinking about the risk to themselves or the possibility of a bad outcome. Looking at all those police cars and those brave cops, I began to understand that law enforcement is not a job, it's a calling. It's a profession where we take an oath to protect the innocent and apprehend those who hurt them. It made me so proud to be a police officer. That was my first year on the job. Thirty years later I still feel the same way."

Above, Steve and his parents Vivian and Tony, on the day Steve was promoted to captain in October 1998. "I could not have had more supportive parents," Steve said. "Without their help it would have been hard for me to get my commerical pilot's license, a requirement to become a pilot with the New York City Police Department."

At right, Sergeant Steve Bonano, 1990 in the 52nd Precinct after getting several high powered firearms off the street. Steve had only been a cop for a few years when they started to call him "the gun man." He had an uncanny ability to identify people who had an illegal firearm and was able to make over three hundred gun collars before he was promoted to sergeant.

Inspector Steve Bonano on top of the Verrazano Narrows Bridge, 2004. When this photo was taken, Steve was commander of the NYPD's Emergency Service Unit.

When Steve was 15 years old he worked as a lifeguard at Orchard Beach in the Bronx. The following summer Steve met two NYPD veteran cops – Al Vazquez and Harry Gonzalez who patrolled a pool he worked at. They enjoyed telling Steve about their adventures working for the New York City Police Department and encouraged him to join the force.

At right, Steve and Louis Anemone who would rise up through the ranks to become the highest ranking uniformed member of the New York City Police Department. Steve and Anemone's paths kept crossing; the encounters weren't always positive.

Steve Bonano loved flying since the time his father took him for a
ride on his 10th birthday. Determined to get assigned to the NYPD's
prestigious Aviation Unit, he invested $18,000 to get his commercial
pilot's license, a requirement for entry into the unit. Steve served eight
years in Aviation. People in the department still talk about the time Steve
and his co-pilot, Matt Rowley, landed a helicopter in a shopping center
parking lot to provide backup to another officer who was engaged in a
foot pursuit with a criminal suspect and had lost his radio.

A man who kept a 400-pound Bengal tiger and a three-foot alligator in his Harlem apartment was arrested after emergency room doctors called 911 to report they treated a man with unusual scratches. With Inspector Steve Bonano in charge of the scene, Officer Martin Duffy, armed with a tranquilizer gun and an M-4 rifle, rappelled out of an apartment on the seventh floor. When he tapped on the window to get the tiger's attention, the tiger lunged. Duffy fired one dart to sedate the tiger. The animal was found unconscious on top of a pile of furniture. The alligator was nearby.

Above, Officer Brendan Gallagan, Officer Matt Rowley, UN Secretary-General Kofi Annan and Steve Bonano after flying Annan to an emergency meeting in upstate New York. At right, Steve and Brigadier General Chuck Yaeger. Yaeger was the first pilot to fly faster than the speed of sound.

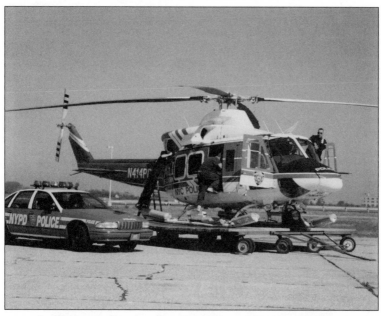

Getting ready for take off at Floyd Bennett Field in Brooklyn.

Seized – one Lugar, one M-16

Chapter Nine

Kai Wong: Man Without Fear

*"Altruism—the eradication of self-centered
desire and a life devoted to the good of others."*
—Auguste Comte (1798–1857)

The cops could hear the tension in the dispatcher's voice. "10-52 with possible weapon." It was a clear, sunny June morning 1998 in New York City.

Roll call had just ended, and Officer Kai Wong was about to drive out of the precinct parking lot. He radioed back. "Seven Charlie. We'll take it."

Kai's partner that day was a rookie. He knew the younger cop was nervous. Wong told him to turn the car around and head toward Boston Road. When they pulled up, the house was just as the dispatcher described it, an older, single-family home divided into separate apartments.

Kai ran up the stairs with the rookie following close behind. Like he had done hundreds of times before, Kai knocked on the door and yelled, "Police."

A woman opened the door. Kai guessed she was in her late twenties. Whatever her age, she was extremely agitated. Shaking with rage, she pointed to a large rock lying just outside the apartment in the hallway. She told the officers her husband had thrown the boulder and hit her in the head. Wong's partner was inexperienced and probably fell for the story, but Kai knew she was lying.

"Her husband was huge," Kai said. "I'd guess he was six feet four and 260 pounds. If he'd hit her with that rock, she'd be dead. I told her right to her face there was no way I believed that her husband had done that."

Every cop in the United States has responded to calls for help from someone who claims they are being harassed, threatened, or injured by an angry spouse, friend, or family member. Along with enforcing motor vehicle laws, quelling domestic disputes is one of the most common responsibilities for law enforcement. It is also one of the most dangerous. Thousands of police officers have been shot, stabbed, beaten, and even lit on fire responding to this type of violence. And all officers have had the experience of arresting a suspected abuser only to have the aggrieved party change the story and refuse to testify when it comes time to make a sworn statement.

In police academies across the country, training for domestic violence calls is extensive. Officers are taught to be extremely cautious while doing everything possible to diffuse the situation. Instructors require extensive roleplaying so recruits will hit the streets armed with the skills to get the warring parties calmed down so a reasonable conversation can take place. Depending on the level of rage, sometimes the only way to accomplish this is to physically separate one party from the other. On this day, the more experienced Wong knew he had to pursue that route to get this couple calmed down.

He asked the man to go outside so they could have a talk. "My first goal was to get him away from the tools in the kitchen that he could use as weapons," he said. "Knives are especially bad. I didn't want to lock him up when I knew his wife was lying. I hoped if I could get him outside, she might calm down and then worry he might be going to jail. Maybe then she would tell me what really happened."

There was just one problem with Kai's plan. The man was not warming up to the idea of leaving his apartment, going outside, and having a talk with Officer Wong. "Come on," Kai pleaded. "Let's just you and me go out and sit on the steps. We can talk out there."

The man stood his ground. Either he didn't understand or he didn't care that his wife was making serious accusations against him. He left Kai no choice. He had to give the woman the benefit of the doubt, and that meant arresting her husband.

As he pulled the handcuffs off his gun belt, the man took a swing, barely missing the left side of Kai's face. An expert in the Chinese martial art of kung fu, Kai easily deflected the punch. In a split second, with the internal power of a great fighter, Kai moved in quickly on his opponent, unleashing a barrage of punches. He hit the man hard, three times on both sides of his face. For a moment the man looked dazed and began to tumble back, but he regained his balance, came forward, and heaved his massive body on top of Kai.

Kai was now pinned on the ground by a violent man who was twice his size. Despite the odds against it happening, he was able to land several fast, powerful punches into his opponent's midsection. As the man gasped for air, Kai got himself out from under the huge body. As he began to stand up, the man grabbed Wong's legs and pulled him back down on the floor. They were on the second floor of the two-story apartment, very near a steep staircase, and within seconds, the two men were rolling down the stairs, one on top of the other.

"When we hit the bottom of the stairs, the man had his arms around me," Kai recalled. "The next thing I knew, he tried to pull me up off the ground and toss me across the room. But I held on to him, and we both went crashing through a glass table. Shards of glass were flying everywhere."

The only other time Kai had experienced anything like this no-holds-barred brawl was early in his career when he broke his leg after he'd tackled a drug dealer in a kitchen near the stairs to a cellar. The two men tumbled down the full flight, landing with an incredible crash on the cement floor of the basement. Kai's leg broke in three places.

Kai now had two problems. He had to get the man under control, but he also wanted to avoid getting cut up by the glass that was scattered everywhere. He was in a desperate struggle to force the man's hands behind his back, get his wrists together, and snap the handcuffs on.

"I'm not sure how I did it, but I finally got one cuff on him," Kai remembered. "He was really strong, and he yanked me toward him. We stumbled back, and now we were down on the floor again. I was trying hard, but I just couldn't get a grip on his other wrist. I'm not sure when it happened, but at some point, this guy's wife, the person who placed the call to 911 that her husband was trying to kill her, leapt from the second-floor landing, sailed through the air, and landed on top of both of us."

Now three people were down on the floor clawing and swinging at one another. The shattered glass was like a thousand knives, and everyone was cut and bleeding. Kai knew he was hurt. His neck was throbbing with pain, but he was not going to give up. "I still had the guy in one cuff," he said. "I grabbed the woman by her hair."

One can only imagine what was going through the rookie's mind as he watched these events unfold. His partner was now under attack by the same woman who had called them for help. As soon as Kai and the man rolled down the stairs, the startled rookie called for backup. It only took a few minutes before a swarm of officers arrived in their police cars. Within no time the unruly couple were handcuffed, read their rights, and were on the way to Central Booking.

As Kai completed the reams of paperwork back at the station, the pain in his neck had spread to his back. When his shift was over, he drove to the hospital, where doctors quickly determined he had five ruptured discs, two in his neck, three in his back. Opting against surgery, Kai went for physical therapy treatments every week for a year and a half. Years later the intense aching still comes and goes, and Kai has accepted the reality that he will always have pain, especially when the barometer drops before it rains.

A couple of days later, Wong responded to a similar call. A desperate woman dialed 911 and screamed into the phone that her boyfriend was trying to kill her. When Kai got to the location, he realized it was the house right next door to the apartment where he had ruptured his disks. When he finished up, he walked over to the house. What he found there shocked him.

"There were lots of young children," he said. "Their diapers were filthy." Kai remembers several of them crying. "It was a terrible to see those kids like that. I was disgusted."

He went back to the precinct and contacted officials from New York City's Children's Services Agency. "It turns out that the couple was collecting money from the city for watching young kids during the week," he explained. "But the kids were dressed in dirty clothes, and they were hungry. It was a child care scam." Kai's call started the ball rolling. Within a couple of days, the children were moved to another facility, and the operation was shut down for good.

* * *

From the time he was a young boy growing up in the Bronx, it was easy to imagine that Kai Wong was headed for a career in law enforcement. He had the right profile—an intense dislike of bullies coupled with the belief that it was up to him to protect the smaller, weaker kids. He grew up in a tough neighborhood where survival for children, especially boys, meant you knew how to fight. Kai studied martial arts, learned to box, and excelled at football.

Kai's parents had immigrated to New York City from Hong Kong several years before he was born. Kai, along with his brother, Joey, and sister, Jean, grew up in an apartment in the Bronx behind the Chinese laundry their parents ran. When Kai was nine years old, two men waving metal pipes barged through the door of the store. When one of the men took his pipe and cracked it over his dad's head, Kai got his baseball bat. "I smashed the bat as hard as I could against the back of the legs of the man who hit my father," he said. "He went down on the floor."

When he went to hit the other guy, the would-be assailant was running down the street. His mother was crying. "I wasn't going to stand there and let those men hurt Daddy," he told her. It was a harbinger of things to come.

Kai was twenty-four when he graduated from the NYPD Police Academy. It was 1984. He wanted the 46th Precinct. "It's what we call a 'heavy house,'" he explained. "Precincts with lots of crime, lots of calls for service, and a lot of people who need the cops out there protecting them."

He didn't get the 4-6, but his first assignment was the next best thing, the 47th Precinct in the heart of the Bronx. "They put me in a car with a partner," Kai remembered. "We were backed up all night going from call to call. Sometimes we had more than eighty calls in one eight-hour shift. Some of them were serious, but a lot were not. People would call because their cat was stuck, their stove wouldn't go on, or their faucet was leaking. I'd trained to be a cop, and it was frustrating to deal with people who needed a plumber, an electrician, or the animal control officer. The paperwork was endless. I hated it."

Kai's third day on patrol, the sergeant assigned him to work with a thirty-two-year veteran. It was a time when law enforcement agencies were taking serious steps to make the job more professional, but young Officer Wong's partner that day was old school. He didn't buy into the notion of a professional law enforcement officer. "I'd only been in the 4-7 for three days, so I didn't know this guy was a bad cop," Kai said. "One shift was all it took."

After roll call, they headed out. The custom is for the junior officer to drive, and Kai was behind the wheel. As they left the precinct parking lot, the older officer told him to stop at a coffee shop. He went in and ordered seven sandwiches to go. While he couldn't have sworn to it in court, Kai got the impression money never changed hands. The older officer put the bag of food on the front seat between them and told Kai to drive to a car repair shop.

"He went in and handed out a couple of sandwiches," Kai recalled. "It was only my third day on the job, but it didn't seem right. I had a feeling what he was doing was wrong."

When there was one sandwich left, Kai was told to drive to a used-car dealership. It was obvious the senior cop did not know the business was owned by Kai's wife and her brother. "It was so brazen," he said. "He went in, gave them a sandwich, and came out with a battery and a couple of tires."

Witnessing this veteran officer ripping off local merchants who struggled to make a living was shocking to this rookie who believed in the integrity of police officers and the work they do. The fact that his wife's business was involved made it even more infuriating.

The older officer had thirty-two years on the job, but Kai was determined to confront him anyway. "I told him if he took anything else without paying for it, I would turn him into Internal Affairs." Then he added a more explicit warning. "If you ever steal batteries or tires or anything else from my wife's store again, you are going to have more to worry about than detectives from IAB." The rookie's threats were lost on the old-timer, who might have reacted differently had he seen nine-year-old Kai take on the men who were trying to hurt his father.

A week later Kai's wife told him the same cop had come back. He left a sandwich before grabbing another tire. The next day Kai and the older cop were working the same shift. When the veteran officer arrived at the precinct, Kai was waiting. There were at least fifty incredulous cops in the room watching as Officer Wong, with less than a week on the job, lambasted his older colleague for stealing tires from his wife's store.

The older cop did not react well to Kai's threats. "He was a huge guy," Kai said. "I'm only five foot eight. My guess was he had to be six foot five. He picked me up with one hand and pushed me up against the lockers. I think my feet were dangling in the air. I told him if he didn't put me down, he was going to regret it." The older cop let go of Kai, and the standoff was over. "I think he looked at me and understood he was going to be sorry if he didn't put me back down on the floor."

Cornelius O'Keefe supervised Kai back when O'Keefe was a Captain in the 47th Precinct. O'Keefe didn't know about the confrontation between Kai and his partner, but he was not surprised to hear that the older cop backed down. "Kai is a tough guy," O'Keefe said. "There was something about him. You just knew he was never going to back down."

O'Keefe says it's hard to explain why Kai is so intimidating. "Maybe it's his expertise in martial arts," he said. "Maybe it's the big snake he has tattooed on his arm. Maybe it's because he'll go right up to these mopes on the street, get in their faces, and say, 'Hey, it's just you and me.' Whatever it is, everyone knows he means business."

* * *

Kai was pretty discouraged after his first week on patrol. His first partner was a corrupt, burnt-out cop who was stealing sandwiches and tires from local merchants. This was not exactly what he had expected when he was sworn in by the Commissioner the week before. He decided to have a sit-down with the sergeant.

"I never ratted on the guy. I didn't want to do something like that my first week. I did tell the sarge I wanted to walk a beat and I wanted to do it alone. I told him if he let me work midnights by myself up on White Plains Road, I'd drive his arrest stats up. I promised I would make him look good."

It's hard to imagine what went through that sergeant's mind. It's highly unusual for a rookie with less than a week on the job to ask for a different assignment, especially a foot post without a partner. He told Kai he would give him a chance but warned him as well. He would be watching closely. One slipup and he'd be back in a car with a partner.

It was a strange request. When you ask New York City cops if they know anyone who wants to walk a beat alone in the middle of the night in one of the most crime-ridden areas of the city, they look at you like you're crazy. But this sergeant was about to take the lieutenant's exam, and more arrests would help him get a promotion. He agreed to give it a try.

Kai staked out the Boston Road section of White Plains Road as his own. Located in the northeast corner of the Bronx, it was a neighborhood rife with drugs, prostitution, guns, car thefts, larcenies, assaults, and armed robberies. Outnumbered and outgunned, Kai patrolled by himself during the most dangerous part of the night.

If a crime occurred on his watch, he took it personally. Within a week, arrests were up. Wong was bringing them in for dealing drugs, stealing cars, robbing people with a firearm or knife, and carrying a gun without a permit. He was alone, and he was mobile. He set up his own surveillance posts. Other cops assigned to the 4-7 during those years remember the familiar sight of Kai Wong crouched up on a rooftop watching the street below. From his perch on the roof, he kept his eye out for trouble. He had a special passion for arresting drug dealers and getting them off the street. "Where there's drugs, there's guns," he said.

He spent thousands of hours patiently waiting for a customer to show up. "Those were great arrests," he recalled proudly. "I'd get the guy for possession and the sale. A lot of times there was a gun."

The people in the neighborhood loved Kai. They began to call him Topak 12, a reference to a heavy crime area on Boston Road that Kai had adopted as his own.

Cornelius O'Keefe said when he arrived at Kai's precinct as a captain, Wong was well established. "It wasn't long before he approached me. He told me, 'Captain, if you need someone to clean up an area, set me loose.'"

O'Keefe admits this strange offer took him aback, but all he needed to convince himself that Kai was doing great police work was to attend a few community meetings. "The people in the neighborhoods where he patrolled loved him," O'Keefe said. "They'd tell me over and over again what a great job he was doing."

That was enough for Captain O'Keefe. Kai would continue to patrol on foot and alone in one of the most crime-ridden areas of the Bronx. It was "hot spot" policing before anyone used the term.

Kai rarely called for backup. "I was a Bronx boy," he said. "I grew up in a tough neighborhood. There were a lot of bad kids, and I learned to hold my own with them. They didn't scare me."

He had keen powers of observation and a sixth sense about what was going on in the street. When a child was the victim, he took special offense.

One time he saw a dealer selling drugs to an eleven-year-old boy. "That dealer saw me coming, and he took off," Kai said. "He was fast. I chased him for a couple of blocks before I caught him. I remember thinking, 'I hope this creep resists arrest, then I can give him what he deserves.'"

The suspect took a swing at Kai, barely missing his face. Football and martial arts had made Kai strong, and his reflexes were fast. It took him only seconds to get the handcuffs on and arrest the man for selling drugs to a child and an attempted assault on a New York City police officer. The suspect ended up pleading guilty to a lesser charge. Within a day he was back out on the street, but the word was out. Officer Wong had arrested one of the neighborhood's most powerful drug dealers. His reputation as a tough cop who could get drugs off the street was growing.

A few days later, Kai was walking his beat. It had been a quiet shift, but within a few seconds, that was all about to end. As he came around the corner, he confronted a horrific scene. An old man, curled in a fetal position, lying in a parking lot, was being brutally beaten by a man in his late twenties. In a faint voice he was murmuring, "Help. Police. Help."

"I went over and grabbed the guy, but he broke away and started running," Kai recalled. "I chased him around all through the cars in that parking lot. I finally wrestled him to the ground and got the cuffs on. Then I shook him. I was so angry. I got right up in his face. I was screaming, 'That was an eighty-year-old man. Why would you hurt him?'

"Who knows why someone would do that? It's not good to get emotional when you're a cop, and shaking him was wrong. But when you see a young, strong guy beating up an old man, it's hard to control yourself. I don't know if the older man recovered, but even if he did, he'll never be the same. He'll always be afraid it's going to happen again."

* * *

Every law enforcement officer in the United States could write volumes about the cruel and abusive treatment that innocent people have suffered at the hands of violent criminals. Working in the Bronx, Kai Wong has seen more than most.

One of his most vivid memories was the time someone pistol-whipped a nun at a school for the blind. "You have to be pretty sick to beat a nun who works at a school for the blind," he said. "When we arrived on the scene, they were taking her away in the ambulance, and the Commander was organizing a search of the school. After a half-hour the officers came back down. They had completed the search. The suspect was gone."

Kai didn't buy it. The school was divided into two big buildings, and thirty minutes was not enough time to search them both. He guessed they probably skipped the laundry room, the kitchen, the boiler room, and all the other places the man might find to hide. He approached the lieutenant who was supervising the scene and told him he wanted to go back in. The lieutenant grabbed two detectives. He told one to cover the front door. The other one he instructed to go with Kai.

Wong began his search at the farthest corner of the top floor of the first building. Methodically, he opened every door and searched inside. When he got to the last closet on the third floor and opened the door, staring back at him was the man who had assaulted the nun.

"When I saw him, my heart started racing," Kai said. "He'd beaten the nun with a 9 mm. The chances were good he still had the gun."

He shoved the man back in the closet and slammed the door. "The adrenaline was going, and I was scared. I pulled my gun, opened the door, and tackled him in the closet. I remember the place was filled with books and papers and old clothes. We were rolling around in all that stuff."

* * *

If you talk to officers who worked with Kai Wong, they agree he appears to have a supernatural fearlessness. He is the only one anyone can remember who could persuade other cops to break down a door with heavily armed suspects inside when the wait for the Emergency Service cops was taking too long.

His confidence and courage was contagious. Ray Flood has been a cop in New York City since 1992. He was a rookie just out of the Academy when he met Kai. "My first assignment was the 47th Precinct," Flood said. "Kai made a big impression on us younger cops. He was very friendly and went out of his way to make us feel welcome at the precinct."

It didn't take long before Ray began to hear Kai Wong stories about the tough street cop who never backed down, even when it was one against ten and all the suspects were armed.

"Kai was amazing," Ray said. "He took walking posts no one wanted, and the bad guys respected that. When I talked to them on the street, the first thing they wanted to know was, 'Where is Wong?' They never knew when he was going to pop up, and that scared them. I think they thought he might be hiding in the mailbox. They knew not to mess with him. Kai always did the right thing. He was the kind of cop you wanted to emulate."

One officer who worked with Kai for many years noted that his heart was always in the right place. "He never did anything for personal gain," he said.

* * *

Cops like Kai Wong are never off duty. For them, being a police officer is more of a calling as opposed to a job with a set of specific expectations and confined hours of work. They take seriously their responsibilities to keep people safe, and it's an obligation that extends beyond the hours they are officially on the job.

One summer afternoon Kai was meeting his friend Kevin. Both officers had the day off, and they decided to have lunch out on City Island. They were eating salads and drinking Cokes when a fistfight broke out in the restaurant across the street. It was a hot day, and all the doors were open.

"Two black guys were fighting with a Hispanic man," Kai remembered. "The Hispanic guy's girlfriend was trying to hold him back. She jumped on his back and had her arms around his neck. He was screaming, 'Let me at them. Let me at them.'"

Kevin had been on the job longer than Kai. Both officers had seen a lot, but they were shocked at what happened next. "The three men took off their belts and started whipping each other," Kai said. "The belts are flying, and all of a sudden one of the black guys coldcocks the Hispanic man. He went stumbling back toward the restaurant parking lot. Then nine more Hispanic guys appear out of nowhere. One of the biggest ones in the group calmly walks over and punches the black guy in the stomach. Then he pulls a gun and shoots him at point-blank range. By this time, everyone from both restaurants was out on the street. I bet there were a hundred people standing there watching."

Without saying a word, Kevin and Kai leaped over the table. Their salads went flying. When the men looked over and saw Kevin and Kai, guns out,

running toward them, they split up and ran in opposite directions. Kai signaled to Kevin he would pursue the shooter. Kevin made a 90° turn and went
after the others.

The cops were in a vulnerable position. They were off duty and were not
carrying police radios. On top of that, cell phone reception on City Island
was poor. It was going to be hard to call for help. Their only hope was that
a bystander aware of what was happening would find a phone and call 911.
Kai was gaining on the shooter, but the adrenaline rush was so intense, he
had an extreme case of tunnel vision. "I could only focus on that one guy," he
remembered. "It was like he and I were the only people in the world. I had to
actually turn my head to see if anyone was coming up on my side."

There were only eight feet between Kai and the man who'd just shot someone in broad daylight in the middle of the street. "If he turned around, I had to
be ready to shoot," Kai explained. "But I got lucky. He ran toward a car with
three people inside. He jumped in on the passenger side."

Kai's situation was extremely precarious. Chances were high that all four
people in the car were armed, and he was in street clothes, so they wouldn't
know he was a cop. At least the suspect was confined. That helped.

Kai ran up to the car. He held his gun up high so there was no way they
could miss it. "I knocked on the window and told them I was a cop. I said,
'Shut the engine off, and put your hands on your head.' I told them I assumed
they were armed, and if anyone's hands came down, I'd light every one of
them up." Kai was confident that as long as they kept their fingers locked
with their hands on their heads, he could control the situation until the police
arrived.

Less than a minute passed when his eye caught something strange. Something was wrong with the dashboard. He looked closer and realized it was a
hidden compartment that was slightly opened. With his gun pointed at the
shooter's head, he ordered him to take one hand down slowly and open the
drawer. Inside was the gun that was used to shoot the black man in front of
the restaurant.

A block away, Kevin was dealing with his own set of problems. He'd tackled one of the three people, but the two others jumped into a car. "Kevin
had one suspect down on the street," Kai said. "He had his foot on top of his
throat. He had his firearm pointed at the other two who were crouching down
in the car."

Now the waiting began. They held them at bay for forty minutes, a situation Kai said later was incredibly tense. Finally the cops showed up, and all seven were put under arrest.

The end result was frustrating. "The District Attorney gave the shooter bail, and he promptly took off to the Dominican Republic," Kai noted. "The good news was when he tried to come back after a year, Customs agents arrested him at the airport."

* * *

Historically, most police work responds to crime, its perpetrators, and its victims after something has happened. During the last two decades of the twentieth century and the early years of the twenty-first, that started to change. Innovative programs like Compstat, which made commanders accountable for the crime in their districts and then put pressure on them to stop or at least reduce the problems, allowed the law enforcement profession to make great strides to become more proactive. But even before the Compstat revolution, there were always aggressive, committed officers who knew the area and its players well enough to stop a crime before it happened rather than just arrest someone after the fact. Kai Wong made it his business to know everyone in the neighborhoods he patrolled, and that stopped a lot of crime. "He knew everyone," Cornelius O'Keefe said.

One time a younger officer working with Kai got the full dose of Wong's proactive approach to law enforcement. It was the mid-1990s. They were up on Boston Road, and the younger cop was driving. "We were in the left hand lane, and all of a sudden a car passed us on the right," Kai remembered. "I wasn't sure he was speeding, but I had a gut feeling we should stop him. I told the rookie to put on the lights and go."

As they got closer, Kai recognized the driver, He was a man in his twenties who terrorized people in the neighborhood, especially the elderly. There was a rumor he'd killed one person during a robbery and someone else who ripped him off during a drug deal. Ironically, a decade before, Kai had helped him get a job in a local grocery store just after he turned sixteen. He'd kept the job a month. When Kai asked him why he quit, he said he could make more money in an hour selling crack than he could in a week at the grocery store.

"We forced him to the side of the road, and I flew out of the car," Kai said.

"At this point, I wasn't in fear, but I kept my hand on my gun just in case. The suspect was standing in the middle of the road with his hands on his hips. I remember he yelled over, 'Hey, Wong, you want a piece of me? Well, come and get it.' Then he ripped his shirt off."

Kai intentionally let the man take the first punch. That way he could arrest him for assaulting a police officer and resisting arrest. It only took two subsequent moves from the agile Wong to knock his opponent to the ground. As Kai got the cuffs on, other officers began to arrive.

Later, when the detectives assigned to the case checked the numbers on the man's cell phone, they discovered he had been paying off a clerk at the Bronx Criminal Court to make certain files disappear. The investigation resulted in the arrest of fourteen people on a variety of charges, including racketeering, sale and distribution of narcotics, assault with a deadly weapon, and possession of illegal firearms. The young man Kai had helped years ago was sentenced to nine years in prison.

* * *

Along with drugs, robbery, extortion, and murder, after-hours clubs are another blight on poor neighborhoods of the city. The owners, employees, and patrons of these clubs are almost always heavily armed, which poses a serious risk to undercover cops who do the investigations and ESU officers who execute the warrants.

When an after-hours club gets raided and the owners are fined or arrested, in most cases that action follows an investigation by the NYPD's Vice Unit. The raid is usually preceded by weeks of undercover work, mostly by officers working in pairs. Their mission is to gather enough evidence so a judge will issue a warrant.

That process was too slow for Kai. He liked to put these clubs out of business his own way. "I didn't make a big deal out of it," he said. "I never had trouble getting in. They were open when the city said they should be shut. I didn't need a warrant because their doors were open and they were doing business."

He cited them for as many infractions as he could, including serving minors, staying open after hours, having no cabaret license, and disturbing the peace. "I banged out the summonses, wrote up the reports, and left them on the lieutenant's desk along with my phone number so he would see them first thing the next day," he said. "The fines ranged from $100 to $1,500. That was a lot of money for some of these places. Some would close because they couldn't pay the fines." Kai is proud that over the course of his career, mostly alone, he was able to shut down eight after-hours clubs in the toughest neighborhoods of the Bronx.

After over two decades working in some of New York City's most crime-ridden areas, Kai has an unshakeable conviction that stopping the sale of illegal drugs is one of the most crucial missions for law enforcement.

"When you grow up in a neighborhood like I did, you see firsthand how bad drugs are. I lost a lot of friends to drugs, and it broke my heart to see people I cared about losing their homes, their marriages, and even their lives. I am so against drugs that today that I don't even take aspirin. In my view, most crime results from people who need to get money for drugs. I believe the recession is only going to make the problem worse. People involved in the narcotics trade will get more violent. You can already see that happening."

Kai adds that the brains behind the drug organizations who were active in the 1980s and 1990s are either dead or in prison. "The people who deal drugs these days are punks," he says. "They're more like gangbangers. They're young and stupid, and it's much easier now for a cop to get shot than it was in the past. The older guys knew there were consequences for killing a police officer, and they avoided that. These younger kids don't care. They just pull the trigger."

* * *

When Kai began to have success getting some of the top people in the drug business off the streets of the Bronx, he started to get death threats. When he received five separate messages from one drug gang that his family was going to be killed, the Department put two officers in a marked car in front of his house twenty-four hours a day. They insisted he take home a police radio in case he needed to call for help.

Wong wanted none of it. "If you lost your radio, it meant five days' pay," he explained. "Putting a marked car in front of my home was an even worse idea. I told them, 'Now you're telling these guys where I live. How smart is that?'"

Finally the Department agreed to take the radio back and remove the marked car. Luckily for Kai and the NYPD, nothing happened to him or his family.

* * *

The public has long been fascinated with law enforcement work. Perhaps it's the crazy, violent people the police come in contact with that's of interest. Whatever the reason, movies and television programs have used the goings-on in the law enforcement profession as their story lines so often that the public believes they understand what police do. But there's so much about the work that doesn't make for exciting drama or good comedy, and that's the part people never see and don't know about.

No one producing films like *Police Academy II* or *The French Connection* or television dramas like *Law and Order* or *NYPD Blue* shows the enormous amount of time and effort it takes to gain a working knowledge of the hundreds, if not thousands, of laws the police are charged with enforcing. It's a staggering body of information, covering everything from operating a motor vehicle to ordinances on loud noise. The reality is, law enforcement officers must master mountains of written information and learn a myriad of tactical skills in order to become good cops and investigators. It's difficult, painstaking work, and it doesn't make good drama.

"When I came on the job, all the training officers were detectives," Kai said. "They had a lot of experience, and they were great teachers. That system really worked well. I'm a believer that you learn a lot at the Academy and you learn a lot from the street, but you have to have good teachers, too. The part of our training when we rode around listening and talking with those older, more experienced detectives was like getting a PhD in law enforcement.

"One training officer I'll never forget was Tito Sleuter. He was German, and you would never know he was a cop. He looked more like a biker or a hippy. He knew a lot, and he liked to share the information. He taught me to recognize certain behaviors that meant something illegal might be going on, like hand-to-hand sales and money passing hands.

"Another person who trained me was Mike Garvey. He was phenomenal. He treated all the younger cops like we were his own kids. He'd organize barbecues for the people at the precinct, and everyone went. You knew he cared about you, and he was always fair. I learned from Mike how important it is to treat your subordinates well. If your supervisor cares, it makes you want to do your best. Mike Garvey was an important role model for me."

In the first years of the twentieth-first century, the NYPD experienced a wave of retirements, and Kai is worried there aren't enough seasoned officers to break in the new people. "These days a lot of the kids who enter the Academy come from the suburbs," he observes. "If you grew up in Upstate New York, you are not used to diversity. That's not the best background for being a police officer in New York City."

There's another issue he worries about. "A lot of these younger cops have never been in a fight. I don't care where you work. At some point this job gets physical, and you end up taking a punch from someone resisting arrest or wrestling with a drunk who's harassing people in a bar. If you've never been in a fight, it can be quite a shock the first time it happens. The most serious downside is it's easy for the criminal to get the upper hand in the confrontation with the officer."

Kai says some younger cops he knows are under the mistaken impression that the uniform, a gun, and a shield are all they need for respect. In Kai's view, it's not that easy. He tells a story about two young cops to make his point.

"Two officers responded to a disturbance call from a restaurant in the 45th Precinct. They'd been on the job about a year. When they arrived at the scene, they found seven known drug dealers milling around in front of the restaurant. They were harassing the customers and blocking the sidewalk, so people had to go into the street to get around them. The two officers pulled up in a marked police car and got out. When one of the dealers threatened to beat them up if they moved closer, the officers turned around, went back to their car, and left.

"The story spread around the Department like wildfire," Kai continued. "The older cops were horrified. They never should have backed down. When you're in uniform, you're in charge. You've always got to let them know who's boss. You never retreat like that. They made the problem worse. What they did was going to make it much harder for the next group of officers who would eventually be sent to deal with them."

* * *

Several longtime NYPD veterans said Kai Wong is the best cop they'd known. A lieutenant who supervised Kai called him an army unto himself. "Mentally," the lieutenant said, "the guy was focused."

Sometimes his extraordinary work would filter through to headquarters and he would end up with a medal, whether he wanted it or not. One of those times happened in the first minutes of 2000. His courage under fire earned him the prestigious Medal of Valor.

It was a minute after midnight when a call came in for a man threatening to slit his own throat with the large sharp knife that he was holding up against his neck. Kai and his partner took the call. "We rushed to the address," he said. "I told my partner to approach him from the front and talk to him. That would give me time to sneak up from behind and tackle him."

There's a rule that cops are supposed to stay at least twenty-one feet if someone has a knife. Any closer and they can kill you. Kai thought his plan would work, but when a contingent of ESU cops arrived on the scene, a sergeant ordered Kai to stand back. At that exact time, there was the unmistakable sound of gunfire. Pow. Pow. Pow.

"It sounded like the shots were coming from 228th Street and White Plains Road," Kai said. "Three of us jumped into a car, drove around the corner, and pulled in close to the curb so we wouldn't block traffic. We thought there were just three suspects. We hadn't seen the fourth one hiding behind a pole. When the three of us got out of the car, the man behind the pole started shooting. I think he fired three rounds in all." Kai's partners dove down behind the car, but from where Kai was positioned, there was no cover.

"That night I was in uniform," he said. "I hadn't put it on in months. Nothing fit. My vest was like a bib." Kai tried to get his gun out of its holster, but it was brand new. When the gun wouldn't budge, Kai tore it out of its holster. He was now eight feet away from the shooter. The man turned around and fired at Kai. The round came close but didn't hit him. Kai shot back. He missed. "I chased him, but he got away," Kai said. "The good news was he dropped his gun, and I recovered it."

Kai identified the suspect from a book of mug shots. The man had a serious criminal record. "They caught him three days later," Kai said. "The worst part was that one year before, a Bronx jury had acquitted him for a homicide."

Most of Kai's acknowledgments for a job well done didn't come at the Department's annual awards ceremony but from the people he served. One time he even got a standing ovation.

Kai and his wife were out for dinner in a restaurant in Chinatown. They were just about to dig into their lobster Cantonese when the unmistakable sound of gunfire rang out from across the street. Kai looked out the window from his table on the second floor. He saw one man running in one direction and two others fleeing the opposite way. Two is always better than one, so it wasn't hard for Kai to decide which way to go. He raced down the stairs out to the street. When only one foot separated him from the two suspects, he leapt through the air and tackled both gunmen. Someone in the neighborhood must have called it in because scores of officers were on the scene within minutes.

When he got back to the restaurant, his wife was patiently waiting. The lobster Cantonese had gone cold. As he climbed the stairs and went back to their table, the diners stood and applauded. His wife told him that when he ran out to the street, everyone jumped up and ran over to the window to see what was going on. Kai learned later the men he tackled were professional assassins who had been hired to kill three people on the first floor in the restaurant. They'd had the wrong descriptions, however, and three innocent diners were gunned down instead.

* * *

Despite the fact that crime plummeted when Kai was on patrol and the people in the neighborhood loved him, his unorthodox style made a few of his supervisors nervous.

"Mostly I had the good fortune to work for great bosses," Kai said. "The best ones made you feel good about yourself and your work. They knew how to motivate people, and they knew who the active cops were."

Kai still doesn't know what he did to get on the bad side of one lieutenant. Whatever it was, the lieutenant seemed determined to make Kai's life miserable. Things got out of hand when the lieutenant accused Kai of corruption. When Kai asked what he had done wrong, the lieutenant fired back that he knew Kai had taken a free cup of coffee. Considering that Kai does not drink coffee and that his wife's nearby used-car business had free coffee available all day, the charge was ludicrous.

"I told the lieutenant that if I had wanted a free coffee, I would have gone to my wife's shop. The whole thing was ridiculous, but he was determined to get me on corruption charges. I actually had a hearing in the NYPD's trial board room. They made a union lawyer go with me. The attorney from the Police Benevolent Association wanted me to take the two-week suspension and not fight it, but I said no way. I'm innocent. I will never agree to the suspension." At the end of the proceeding, which lasted the better part of a full day, the panel of judges ruled in Kai's favor. He was exonerated.

A few years later, Kai had a captain who gave him trouble. "He didn't like me," Kai said. "He decided to take me off the street. He told me I was the precinct's new fleet maintenance guy. 'I hope you like figuring out which cars need attention,' he told me, 'because that's your new job.'" The captain must have known that for someone like Kai, the worst thing you could do was make him work at a desk.

He had a few other detractors as well. There was a district attorney looking to move ahead by prosecuting an aggressive cop, a few supervisors who resented the freedom he had to make his own hours, bad guys who never knew when he would show up, and the people he arrested who saw an opportunity to claim he used excessive force and sue the city.

There was one constant. Whatever the reason, every time the Department took him off the streets of the Bronx, the residents would be up in arms. Within a day, neighborhood activists would circulate petitions, and hundreds of people lined up to sign them.

"I was always amazed how much the community appreciated Kai Wong," Cornelius O'Keefe said. "There was no one who didn't believe he was doing a great job getting criminals off the street and keeping the neighborhood safe."

It's a given of police work that aggressive cops like Kai Wong, who are masters at intimidating criminals and suppressing crime, will accumulate complaints. And there are many people who know that filing a claim of police brutality and suing the city is an easy way to make a quick buck. "When I retired, I had a lot of civilian complaints," Kai noted. "Most of the time the city would pay them off. They gave a lot of people $70,000 just to go away. That had a bad impact on my morale. These people were making more suing the police than we were being the police."

* * *

Over the course of his career with the NYPD, Kai Wong rarely used his firearm, and only once was he forced to take a life to save his own. "If I hadn't killed him, he would have killed me," he said.

"It was right after my discs were injured rolling down the stairs with that huge guy and getting tackled by his wife. The doctors didn't think I was ready to go back on the street, so I was still working in Central Booking up on 161st Street. It was my daughter's birthday. After work I went to my friend Joey Papapalo's store to buy some soda and cake for her party. It was broad daylight in the middle of the summer.

"I wore a fanny pack, but I never put my gun in there. I kept my gun in the waist of my pants in case I needed to get it out in a hurry. I paid for my stuff and was talking to Joey when two men came in. One guy pulls out a metal pipe, goes over to Joey, and hits him hard on his head. He went down. He was knocked out cold. The other man grabbed me and stuck a gun in my ear. They told me to give them the money in the register, or they would kill me. I told him, 'Hey, I'm a customer. I don't have money. Whatever I had is on the counter.' The guy with the gun was over six feet and looked like he weighed at least 240 pounds. My reflexes are usually fast, but the whole thing took me off guard, and I was slow to react. It was broad daylight, and there were kids in the street. I kept thinking, 'How did this happen? How did I let him get so close?'"

Everyone who has spent time with cops can't help but notice that some seem nervous, even paranoid. "Never let anyone get too close," they tell you. They are always checking out escape routes and trying to see who has a weapon or determining what's around that could be used as one. That day Kai had been complacent. It turned out to be a bad lapse for this hypervigilant cop.

Kai had $1,500 in his pocket, but he was determined to keep it there. The man who owned the store was out cold on the floor. The attacker was going through Joey's pockets.

Looking back, Kai says there are two things that probably saved his life that day. First was an expertise in hand-to-hand combat. Second was the rage many cops feel when they're about to become victims. With a gun pointed at his head, Kai reached up, grabbed the weapon, and pushed it away. He never let go of the firearm. He knew if he did, the man would be able to take a step back and shoot him. Even with his hand clutching the gun, Kai's opponent was doing his best to pull the trigger.

"I got a hold of his finger and bent it back," he continued. "When I heard the bone break, I thought, that's good. I broke the guy's finger." Wincing in pain, the man was momentarily distracted. Those few seconds gave Kai the upper hand. "I punched him fast, three times. Then I reached into my pants, pulled my gun, and shot him."

But this was real life, not the movies. Even after he was shot, the man kept struggling for Kai's gun. "I grabbed him by his hair, but he kept on fighting. I wondered if I had hit him. I thought about shooting him again, but thank God I didn't. The autopsy would have shown I shot him a second time after I had fatally wounded him. If I had taken that last shot, the NYPD would have suspended me and started a criminal investigation. My career could have been be over."

Joey Papapalo was just coming to when he heard the sound of gunfire. Believing Kai was shot, he collapsed on the floor and started crying.

It was only minutes before an army of police officers arrived, including a contingent of bosses from the precinct and detectives from the Internal Affairs Bureau. Despite the fact that eleven witnesses all told the same story, IAB investigators were not taking anyone's word for what happened. They pursued their own investigation. Many years later Kai said the facts were clear. He had shot a man who was trying to kill him. Even so, a few Internal Affairs investigators treated him like he was the criminal. Eventually the shooting was ruled justified. Officer Wong had acted in accordance with his training and the expectations of his job as a New York City police officer.

When law enforcement officers are forced to take a life, the way they cope with the aftermath is as varied as the individuals involved. Studies of officer-involved shootings show that about one-third have no problems whatsoever. One-third have minor but manageable symptoms of post-traumatic stress disorder. The last one-third are not so lucky. These are the people who will never be the same after taking a life, no matter how necessary or warranted. They may live the traumatic moments over and over again in dreams, flashbacks, or just random thoughts. Most of people in this group will leave their careers in law enforcement. For a tragic few, life becomes unbearable, and they take their own lives.

Kai never had a flashback or a bad dream. "I slept fine," he said. "He was the one who was trying to kill me. The way I saw it, I still had a job to do. The man who'd bashed Joey with the pipe had gotten away."

Two weeks later Kai was in the precinct finishing up some paperwork when something unexpected happened. "Another cop came running in and told me the wife of the man I'd shot in my friend's store was downstairs looking for some paperwork." Kai almost knocked his chair over as he jumped up and ran down the stairs to the front desk.

He approached the woman. "I told her that her husband's friend was a bum. He left him there on the floor of that store to die. I asked if she would help me find him." She told Kai she would help him. "She said her husband and his buddy had started robbing people to make extra money. She wasn't sure where he lived, but she did know one place where he spent a lot of time

Kai found the two detectives assigned to the case. The three cops drove to the location and waited. Every day for two weeks, they sat in the car and waited and watched. The suspect never showed up. But on day fifteen of the surveillance, he was there, sitting in the middle of a group of people.

Kai ran toward the group. "His eye caught mine, and it seemed like he recognized me," Kai said. "He turned around and started to run, but he ran right into one of the detectives. The case against him was rock solid. The indictment stated he was responsible for forcing me to shoot his friend, and he was charged with robbery and reckless endangerment. He did seven years in jail."

* * *

Like most police officers, Kai is haunted by the criminals he knew were guilty but got away. "I'm still bothered by this one drug dealer," he said. "Dealers come in all shapes and sizes, and this one was a real bad guy. The word on the street was that he'd killed his grandmother and stuffed her in a closet. He had no problem shooting at cops. One time he went into a gas station and asked the guy who worked there if he believed in God. When the man said yes, he told him he had better start praying. Then he tried to shoot his leg off with an AK-47. It still bothers me that we never got enough evidence to arrest him."

When it comes to injuries, Kai believes he had it pretty good, although stories about his opting for root canals without novocaine are legendary. There is even a persistent rumor that Kai talked a doctor into performing a hernia operation without an anesthetic because he didn't want to be groggy and have to call in sick.

Along with the ruptured discs in his neck and back and his broken leg, the only other serious injury he recalls happened nine days after the planes hit the Twin Towers on September 11, 2001. When the first plane hit the North

Tower, another cop called Kai and told him to turn on his television. "It was hard to know what it was," he said, "but I knew I had to get down there. My wife didn't want me to go, but we both listened to the reporter on television telling public safety personnel to respond to our commands. I told her I had no choice. I was going down."

That first week after the attacks, Kai worked seven days straight, sometimes getting only two or three hours of sleep, mostly on cardboard boxes on the street in the midst of the rubble. A couple of times he crawled into the backseat of an empty police car to take a short nap. "We slept only as long as it took to get some energy back," he said.

On the third day, climbing through the rubble, frantically trying to find survivors, Kai got cold. "I was standing in a pool of water," he remembered. "It was cold, and my feet had been soaked for hours. I had started to shake when this old woman walked up and asked me if I needed anything. I told her I didn't feel very well. I was cold, and I needed was some dry shoes and socks. A half hour later she came back. She had a pair of boots and some heavy socks. To this day, that was the nicest thing anyone has ever done for me. It made me so happy. I told her, 'Lady, I could kiss you.' I pulled my wet socks and shoes off and put on the dry ones. That woman had gone out of her way to find socks and boots for someone she didn't even know. That's the spirit of New Yorkers. It made me proud to be one."

Six days later Kai was at the precinct taking a nap. "When I woke up, I tried to tie my shoelaces, but I couldn't do it. I felt like I was going to pass out. I went to the sergeant and told him I couldn't get my shoes on. I think he thought I was kidding, but then he took a look at me, and he panicked."

The next thing Kai remembers is two cops helping him into the back of the police car and driving fast to the nearest hospital. As Kai laid on a stretcher, three doctors began arguing about whether his disc problems were causing the pain. Fortunately, a neurosurgeon happened to walk by and recognized instantly that Kai was having a stroke. "There was a clot the size of a pea in my brain," he said. "They put me on Coumadin and kept me in the hospital for six weeks."

When the doctors were sure he was stabilized, they laid out his options. First, he could stay on blood thinners the rest of his life. That was an option he promptly dismissed. He told the doctors, "No way. I'm not doing that. I'm a cop. If I get cut or shot, I'll bleed out." Second, they could surgically repair a defect in his heart that enabled the clot to pass straight to his brain. This option required open heart surgery with an eight-month recovery period. Kai was not enthused about that plan either.

The doctors were frustrated. They told him if he didn't do something, chances were good that he would have another stroke, and that one would be more serious. "I'll take my chances," he said.

Then he discovered there was an outpatient procedure. When Kai learned he would be in and out on the same day, his dilemma was over. "I had it done at Mt. Sinai," he remembered. "Two days later I felt fine. The Department doctors wanted me to stay on light duty, but I was ready to go back to work." Three days after the procedure, Kai Wong was back on the street when a call came in for a man with a gun. "I looked up the street, and there he was," Kai said. "I chased him for a block and a half, and I caught him. I was a little winded, but other than that, I felt pretty good."

* * *

Kai has two daughters, Justine and Madison, and a son, Nikko. He met his wife, Maria, during his first year on the job at a used-car lot she owned with her brother on Boston Road. When they fell in love, Maria put Kai's picture up on the wall of her business.

"All the drug dealers knew her," Kai said. "Some of them bought their cars from her. I had to break it to her that I had a lot of enemies, and they knew my face. I told her the photo of me was not going to be good for business. She took it down."

Kai's not sure why his marriage fell apart, but after thirteen years, Maria left him. "We had a beautiful home. Our kids went to Catholic schools, and I made enough money so that my wife didn't have to work unless she wanted to."

Kai said when they met, she knew he worked a lot of hours. "I thought she understood that was my life. But I was also different from a lot of cops, who mentally are always working. When I left the job, I really left it. I never socialized with cops when I was off duty. I don't think any of my neighbors ever knew what I did for a living. I thought it was a good life and that we were okay. I had to face the fact I was wrong."

The divorce was contentious, and Kai is still worried about the impact it had on his older daughter, Justine. "The younger kids are okay," he explained.

"But Justine was different. You could see how angry she was when her mother and I split up. It broke my heart." Things are better now, and Kai is relieved that Justine is turning her life around. "I've always told her it's not too late to fix your life up. She went through a lot, and I'm very proud of her."

Madison and Nikko did not experience the trauma from the divorce the same way as Justine. "Madison is well rounded," Kai says proudly. "She excels in every sport she tries. She loves lacrosse, soccer, and basketball. But what's really great is that her grades are really good. Every term she makes the honor roll."

By the time Nikko turned nine, a speech impediment was getting worse. He was falling behind in school, and his teachers were hoping private tutors might help him get over his disability. It was expensive, but Kai was happy to pay the price. "Those tutors worked one-on-one with him for two years. They saved my son's life. When Nikko started his tutoring, he had fallen behind at least two years. Now he's eleven years old and is tutoring four kids in math. If you'd told me when he was nine that he'd be doing this, I'd have said you were nuts."

Kai admits he became pretty cynical after his divorce. Including another woman in his life was not an option. But when Joan, a friend he'd worked with in a nursing home twenty-five years before, called him out of the blue and asked if they could get together, he agreed.

"That was two years after I was separated," Kai said. "We're still together, and I hope it stays that way. There's no game playing. We don't argue, and we don't scream. We talk things out. We act like adults. We listen to each other, and we enjoy the same things. We love to go to plays, to the movies, and out to dinner. She's absolutely wonderful."

* * *

Kai retired in 2004 but he still misses the job. "I had such a great time," he says. "I was so lucky to have a career in law enforcement, especially with the New York City Police Department. The job taught me so much. I learned how to talk to people, to negotiate, to mediate. I loved getting to know the merchants and business owners and talking to them about their problems. Sometimes you could come up with an idea that would help them. That was really great."

But what Kai remembers most is the wonderful people he met all those years he patrolled in the Bronx. He'll never forget the afternoon he was fighting with a drug dealer. A woman who owned a store that sold nurses' uniforms came running out to help him. "She tried to join the fight," Kai said. "I told her, 'You can't do this. Get back in your store.' She wouldn't go back in. She kept saying, 'I need to help you.'"

He's also become friends with the doctor who diagnosed the stroke. "I found out his father was a cop," Kai said. Every once in a while, they meet for lunch and talk. The doctor even volunteered to be a character witness for Kai during his divorce proceeding.

As soon as he announced he was retiring, the offers poured in. After agonizing over the decision, Kai opted to run the security operation for a family that owns three hundred apartment buildings in the city. One of the buildings, with 2,600 apartments, had the moniker *New Jack City.* But that was before Kai Wong arrived on the scene. It took him a few months, but crime has plummeted, the drug dealers are gone, and there's no loud noise at night. Just like the folks up on Boston Road in the Bronx, the people who live here love him.

In July 2007, Kai Wong was the recipient of the New York City Police Department's Medal of Valor Award. His two youngest children, Madison and Niko, attended the ceremony. Despite a career filled with heroic acts, Kai wasn't interested in receiving awards or medals. "The work was enough of a reward for me," he says.

Kai standing in front of his parents' Chinese laundry on University Avenue in the Bronx in 1964. A few years later Kai would take his baseball bat and attack two men who assaulted his father with a pipe while he was working in the laundry. His mother made the suit he's wearing.

From left to right: Kai's Uncle, Dad and Mom. Kai is seated with middle daughter Madison on his lap. Son Nikko is on the right; daughter Justine is in the front.

On vacation in Virginia. Kai and his son Nikko take a fighting stance. Kai hopes his son will pick up his Dad's interest in the martial arts.

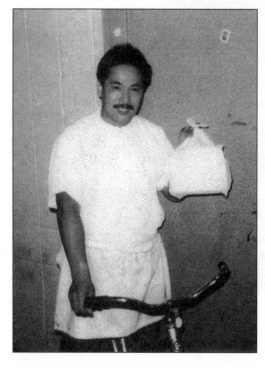

Chinese delivery boys are a common target for armed robbers and Kai went undercover several times with the hope that they would rob him. He was disappointed but no one was suprised when the bad guys stayed away.

Above, Kai's mother worked hard in the family business. She was a devoted wife and mother. Kai said he always admired the way she cared for his Dad during the last years of his life when he was crippled with Alzheimers and dementia. "She never complained," he said.

On January 4, 1984, Kai graduated from the NYPD Academy. Above, Kai with his proud Mom just after Kai was sworn into the largest law enforcement agency in the country.

Kai with his sister Jean and young daughter Justine at Cardinal
Spellman High School the day he received an award from the
Boston Road community in the Bronx for his outstanding police
work on their behalf.

Chapter Ten

Barry Galfano: Dog Day Afternoons

"If one advances confidently in the direction of his dreams, and endeavors to live the life which he has imagined, he will meet with a success unexpected in common hours." —Henry David Thoreau

Barry Galfano is a cop who loves the action. He cannot remember ever hoping for a quiet shift, but on this particular Tuesday night, it was all he longed for. The day before, he had worked the day shift. It was just a couple of weeks before Christmas, the busiest time of year for police officers patrolling Midtown Manhattan. The purse snatchers and muggers were out in force preying on holiday shoppers. The work was nonstop.

When he'd gotten home that night, all he wanted to do was relax, but his wife met him at the door and insisted he sit down with her and make plans for the holidays. When he told her he was tired and asked if they could do it tomorrow, she was upset.

"She told me she was fed up," he said. "She began complaining that all I did was work and study for the sergeant's exam and that planning for the Christmas holiday that was just two weeks away was not unreasonable." Barry said maybe it was because he was so tired, or maybe he was sick of the same old arguments, but the conversation quickly degenerated into name calling and angry accusations.

He went to bed angry and barely slept. The next day he was scheduled to work at night. As he drove into the city from his home on Long Island, all he wanted was a quiet shift patrolling with his German shepherd police dog, Harry.

Unless the dispatcher called him with some impending disaster, his assignment Tuesday night was to patrol Times Square with Harry. Known as America's crossroads to the world, Times Square is a cultural hub of theaters, concert halls, clubs, hotels, and restaurants. Every New Year's Eve, it's the place that millions of people in every country watch as the giant ball drops from a tower. But the area is also a popular gathering place for drunks and derelicts, and lately there had been a surge of robberies and assaults. Nevertheless, Barry was hoping he might get lucky. "I just wanted all the dirtbags and perps to go somewhere else," he said.

But quiet it was not to be. He had only been out on patrol for an hour when he went into the passageway of the subway station and saw three men robbing a woman.

"I held onto to Harry, pulled my gun, and ordered them down on the ground," he said. "Once they were down, I put my gun back in the holster and called for backup on my radio. It was only a second, but before I could get the call through, the dog spun around behind me and lunged up in the air to my left."

The dog's sudden movements distracted Barry. For a split second he took his eyes away from the men on the floor. Barry was now in a vulnerable position. It was three against one, and he had lost eye contact with the suspects. Not realizing what was happening behind him, he yanked on the leash and yelled at the dog to stop. What he did not know, but the dog did, was there was a fourth man in the group. As he struggled to keep control of the three men on the ground, someone else, gripping a large piece of wood, was approaching him from behind. When the dog saw him coming, he flew around to Barry's back, lunged and sank his teeth into the arm of the man wielding the wooden plank.

* * *

Over a law enforcement career of three decades, mostly spent training police dogs for the nation's largest and busiest canine unit, Barry still says Harry was the best police dog he ever worked with.

"He was a very protective animal," he said. "If I gave him the signal, he'd go after anyone. Sometimes I didn't even need to give a signal. Harry had a sixth sense, an amazing ability to know what posed a threat. I've never worked with a dog who was better at regular patrol work. During the ten years we were together, Harry helped me send some very hardened criminals to jail."

Barry still talks about one arrest he made with Harry. "It was a cold winter night in 1985," he explained. "I was patrolling inside a subway station in Queens when a Hispanic man came running up to me. He was completely out of breath and obviously upset. His English wasn't the best, but I was pretty sure he was telling me his wife had just been raped and that the attacker had run out of their apartment when he'd returned home. He'd chased the guy until he disappeared into a nearby bar."

Galfano and Harry followed the man to the bar.

When the bouncer saw Barry was a cop with a dog, he told him he could not go in with the dog. "He tried to shut the door, but Harry managed to wedge his head in just before it slammed. I yelled out that I was the police and we were coming in. The bouncer was a big guy, but when he saw Harry barking, he backed away. As we came through the door, the patrons in the bar started screaming. They were jumping up on top of the bar stools and even on top of the bar itself. Toward the back of the room, I saw a kid jump up and run toward the back door. The husband, who followed in behind me, was gesturing in a way that indicated this was the same person who had raped his wife. In a loud voice, I announced I was going to let Harry loose. That caused even more mayhem. Just before I let him go, I could see the back door of the bar would not open. The suspect was trapped." At that point, with the rapist cornered, there was no reason to let the dog loose.

The suspect looked young, and he was—just a few days over sixteen. Back at the precinct, Barry began writing up the endless reports the Department requires after making a felony arrest, a task that can take up to three hours. He was only one hour into it when the suspect began asking strange questions.

"First he asks me how I know where to put information down on the form," Barry recalled. "Then he starts telling me how amazed he is I know how to write all this stuff down. I told him if he stayed in school, he might learn to read and write, too. I tried to get back to the questions, but then he interrupts again and asks how I learned to shoot. At this point I was getting annoyed. I told him I was the one in charge of asking questions, not him. Then he tells me he's amazed I know how to do all these things when I'm blind and have a Seeing Eye dog. I couldn't believe it. I said, 'Are you really serious? Do you really think I'm blind and go out on patrol with a Seeing Eye dog?' I even called my lieutenant over and asked him to say it again. For some of the stuff that happens on this job, you have to have a witness, otherwise no one would believe you."

* * *

When Barry Galfano was picked to head up the New York City Transit Police K-9 Unit, it was the culmination of his lifelong love affair with dogs. His family had owned dogs from the time he was born, but it wasn't until Barry was ten that they got their first German shepherd. She was pure white, and her name was Snowflake. Barry began to devour books about dogs. He found a manual on the training of police and guard dogs, and it wasn't long before his backyard was transformed into an obstacle course. He taught Snowflake to jump over fences, fetch things, growl at strangers, and attack his arm on command. "I wanted her to be just like Rin Tin Tin," he said.

After Barry graduated from college, he went on to earn a master's degree in urban policy sciences and management. He was hired by the New York City Office of Management and Budget. It was what he had trained to do, and the job had a lot of opportunities for promotion, but the days spent running numbers and making graphs and charts seemed endless. His close friends and family knew he wasn't happy, and his uncle Joe, a veteran New York City cop, started talking to him about joining the Police Department.

Getting a master's degree had taken time and effort, and Barry was reluctant to give up his career. But one night, flipping through the newspaper, he came across a story that got his attention. The New York City Transit Police Department was going to start a K-9 Unit. "I saw that article, and something clicked," he said. "I decided to sign up for the test. My parents and wife weren't too happy about it initially, but as always, they supported my decision in the end."

That was in February 1981. By October he was enrolled in the Police Academy.

Back in the early 1980s, it was very unusual for someone with a college degree to take the police exam. When the instructors at the Police Academy learned he had a master's degree, they must have wondered what was up with this overeducated recruit.

His first months on the job were a mixed bag. He got some bad guys off the street and took the satisfaction all cops get from protecting people from criminals and helping them when they have problems. But there was a lot about the experience he found difficult.

"I was working as a transit cop, which meant most of the time you walked a beat," he said. "There were times I thought I would freeze to death working a midnight shift patrolling alone in a subway station when it was below zero and the wind was blowing. We're talking eight solid hours. The warmer months weren't much better. Most of the stations were brutally hot all summer. Then there was the problem of some older cops who gave new meaning to the word 'negative.'

"In the 70s and 80s, it was rare that patrol officers would become bosses or move up the chain of command," Barry explained. "A lot of those people were stuck doing the same job year after year, and they did nothing but gripe and complain. They were negative about everything, and that really got to me. I had to ask myself if I wanted to do this for the next twenty years and maybe end up like them. That's when I decided to start studying for the sergeant's exam."

* * *

Like all police officers, Barry has many memories he can't leave behind. One occurred in 1984. "The call came in at 1:30 in the afternoon," he said. "Someone called in to report a shooting at the Pacific Street and 4th Avenue subway station. The victim was a fourteen-year-old girl. She was just a young kid, an innocent victim who got stuck in the wrong place at the wrong time."

When he saw the girl collapsed on the street outside the station, Barry called for help on his radio and looked for a place to tie his dog, who was now in an agitated state. The girl, shot inside a coffee shop, had staggered out to the street. Once he got his dog secured, he rushed back and picked the girl up in his arms.

"As I held her, she began talking to me," Barry said. "There was a small hole in her blouse where the bullet had entered. There was very little bleeding, so I thought she would be okay. She started to cry, and I just kept holding her close to me. I told her everything would be fine, but she died in my arms while we were waiting for the ambulance."

When Barry told this story, twenty-five years had passed, but he still had perfect recall of everything that happened and was visibly emotional when he spoke about her death.

* * *

Very few cops who patrol the New York City subways are spared the agony of responding to a call where someone has been run over by a train. "It's a terrible thing to see a human body after it's been crushed by a subway car," Barry says. "Depending on how you fall, the train can hit you and push you up against the platform, wedging you between the platform and the subway car. Everything is okay in the upper torso but from the waist down, the body is crushed. We call it a 'space case.' I remember this one guy who waited until he heard the train coming before he jumped. The train ran over him and pushed his body up against the platform. I called it in on my radio and sat with him, waiting for the Emergency Service cops who are trained to deal with this type of situation. He was conscious the whole time. Once the police arrived, they took one look and must have known his injuries were fatal. They found out he was Catholic and told me we needed to get a priest down there fast. They asked the man if he had any family they could call. I thought it was terrible they were talking to him like he was going to die. I hadn't been through this type of thing before, and I had been telling him he was going to be fine. I had no idea that once that train was jacked up and the pressure came off his body, his insides would flow out and he would bleed out in less than a minute. Even though he was trying to kill himself—and you could tell he wanted to die—it was very traumatic to see someone end his life like that. Those Emergency Service cops were the last people he talked to."

* * *

In 1979, two Transit cops were killed in the line of duty, each with his own gun. Their deaths occurred within weeks of each other, and the stories were on the front pages of the city's newspapers for days. The president of the City Council, Carol Bellamy, was particularly distraught. A debate began about whether it was too dangerous for subway cops to work alone. But it turns out the costs of having officers work with a partner were high so Bellamy and others began to talk about the possibility of having the police patrol with dogs. The pressure to do something to prevent more officer deaths kept building, and after a few months, the Transit Authority and the City of New York approved the funds to launch a two-year pilot program to have Transit officers patrol with police dogs.

Barry followed the political battle closely. When the funds were okayed in 1982 to make the pilot program permanent, he knew this might be his big chance. But he had only been a cop for a year, and he knew the bosses would be looking for veterans with at least eight years under their belts for their expanded K-9 Unit.

"I went to see the sergeant," Barry remembered. "He looked at my paperwork, looked up, and told me he was not going to waste his time. He said he would be the laughingstock of the Department if he recommended me with only one year on the job."

But Barry was not deterred. He found out he needed an interview to get the K-9 assignment, and the only way to do that was to get the sergeant to recommend him. "I told the sergeant he had to approve an interview for me, that the whole reason I wanted to be a cop was to work with dogs. I said, 'Look at me. I'm not the average rookie. I have two kids. I have a master's degree. I'm 28.'"

Barry kept at it. "I met with him again. I asked him to sign the paper so I could get the interview. He said forget about it. We went back and forth. I told him they only way I would stop bugging him was if he'd sign the form."

Everyone who knew Barry Galfano predicted his persistence would be no match for the sergeant. Finally the Sarge did relent. He signed the form. Barry would get his interview.

He was nervous when the big day came. When his name was called, he was escorted into a windowless room with a large conference table in the middle. A captain, two lieutenants, and a sergeant were already seated. Barry was told to take a seat at the head of the table.

The first question was hostile. One of the lieutenants asked if it was true he had a master's degree. When Barry said yes, the lieutenant seemed angry. "He asked me what I was doing there. I told them my dream in life was to be a cop and work with dogs. You could tell they weren't buying it. One sergeant asked me outright if I was lying."

The interview was not going well. But then the captain, who had been quiet up until now, weighed in. He agreed Barry was not an average rookie and said he would be willing to give him a chance. "I'm sticking my neck out here," the captain said. "If you screw up, it's going to come down on me for recommending a guy who doesn't even have two years on the job. So don't screw up." Barry still remembers that moment as one of the happiest of his life.

The captain need not have worried. That decision was the beginning of a stellar career for Barry Galfano, who would go on to become one of the nation's leading experts on the care and training of police dogs.

* * *

At the K-9 Unit, Barry was happier than he could imagine. It took a long time before it sank in that he could do the thing he loved and get paid for it. What he did not know was there were powerful people who were not pleased with the Unit. There was trouble ahead for the dogs.

"I wasn't aware of it, but the K-9 Unit had become a serious political and financial liability," Barry explained. "The first dogs and their handlers were sent to Philadelphia to get trained, but the Philly P.D. was still using training tactics from the 60s, and their dogs were very aggressive. When the decision was made to keep the Unit and train the dogs at the Brooklyn Army Terminal, my class was the first to be trained in New York. They hired the former trainer from Philadelphia to come here to train us. After graduating in July 1983, I was assigned to late-night tours to combat rising subway crime. Working nights was easier because there were fewer people on the system, but I do remember the most stressful time during that period was getting on and off a train with my dog. Because of the way he was trained, the dog saw every person walking by as a potential threat to me. All those dogs wanted to do was bite people."

Homer Green joined the K-9 Unit around the same time as Barry. The two quickly discovered they shared a passion for dogs as well as a concern that they had been trained to be too aggressive. The dogs were great at criminal apprehensions but counterproductive when it came to helping their handlers assist people.

"Barry's dog, Harry, and my dog, Blackie, were probably the most aggressive dogs in the Unit," Green remembered. "They were also the best at apprehending criminals. I know Blackie would run through a hail of gunfire to protect me, and Harry would have done the same for Barry. We talked almost every day about different ways to handle our dogs. You had to be very vigilant to keep them under control."

As the public became aware of some of the incidents in which the dogs had attacked innocent people, the pressure mounted to eliminate the K-9s. By this time Barry had been promoted to lieutenant and put in charge. He was elated to be running the show, but it wasn't that long before he realized his bosses had put him in charge to dismantle the Unit. The dogs had become too much of a liability.

Barry decided he would not let them go without a fight. He knew police dogs were effective in reducing crime. He just had to figure out a way to prove it.

An opportunity presented itself when the new Chief, Bill Bratton from Boston, asked the heads of all the departments to give him a report on their divisions. "The Chief of Patrol had already written his four-page report," Barry remembered. "It was all negative. He argued that the dogs were useless, vet care was too costly, and the dogs had no positive impact on crime. A sergeant in the Chief of Patrol's office who wrote the report told me it was pretty much a done deal. The Unit was going to be disbanded."

Barry asked a lieutenant if he could submit a second report on the dogs that would be more positive. The lieutenant agreed.

He had three weeks to create his presentation. He gathered statistics on the drops in crime that occurred once the dogs were on patrol. He did some research and discovered that Bill Bratton had been a dog handler in Vietnam. He also learned that Bratton loved statistics, charts, and graphs. This was the early 90s, long before Google and PowerPoint. Barry did everything by hand, using large pieces of white paper, colored magic markers, and a ruler. He spent hours laboring over his charts. He wanted them to be perfect.

"My goal was to convince the Chief that everywhere we took the dogs, crime went down. I set out to prove that police dogs are a tremendous deterrent and that with some minor changes, we could save money on their care and with different training, we could reduce liability costs."

By the day of the meeting with Chief Bratton, Barry and his staff had put together a thirty-page document containing charts, graphs, newspaper stories, pictures, and testimonials.

"I had only been talking five minutes when the Chief waved his arm and cut me off," Barry remembered. "He asked why everyone wanted to get rid of the unit. I was annoyed he'd stopped me. I was told I would have at least a half-hour for my report, but I decided to be respectful. I told him everyone thought the dogs were too aggressive. They were biting transit passengers and other innocent people, which meant we weren't able to help anyone who was sick or lost or in some kind of trouble. On top of that, there was the cost of the food and all the vet bills.

"The Chief opened a drawer in his desk, grabbed a bunch of papers, and shoved them across the table at me. He said this was the report the Chief of Patrol had given him, and nowhere could he find a statistic or an impartial comment. He seemed upset that everything in the report was negative and there were no facts to back up the argument. He studied my charts and graphs. When he looked up, he seemed impressed that I had come up with ways to cut costs and change the training so the dogs would be less aggressive. I had only been in there ten minutes when the Chief announced I had convinced him. The dogs were helping. He would keep the K-9 Unit, but he needed ammunition to go before the MTA Board to convince them that the unit was cost-effective and productive."

Once they knew the Unit would survive, Barry and his team went to work. He knew the Chief would be checking the crime statistics to make sure the dogs really did have a positive impact on crime. "We made a list of the subway stations with high rates of crime, and we saturated them with cops and dogs," he said. "We might have had only ten officers with their K-9s on each shift, but we rotated them through these stations every ten minutes or so. It gave the impression of a massive show of force. To a bystander, it looked like we had a hundred dogs on patrol."

It was not just in the subway stations that the dogs had an impact. The K-9 team made a list of eight sites in the city that required more stringent security details, including the United Nations, St. Patrick's Cathedral, Times Square, and Rockefeller Center. The K-9 truck would pull up at all hours of the day and night, and ten cops with dogs would jump out of the truck. It was very intimidating if you were someone with a criminal intent.

"We even started having roll call in the subway station," Barry continued. "We'd stay about a half-hour and then move on to the next location. It was spectacular. Crime went down to nothing, and we had the statistics to prove it. More importantly, the public loved the show. They felt safe in the subways when they saw a K-9 team, which was exactly what we wanted."

By the following year, the New York City Transit Police Department would boast the largest police canine unit in the country, with over fifty well-trained police dogs who could apprehend a violent criminal or help their handler search for a lost child.

* * *

When it comes to training dogs, Barry Galfano is an expert. He cautions that training the handler is much harder than training the dogs. Some people, he says, no matter how long or hard they work, will never cut it. "The one quality that's most important is discipline. You've got to be disciplined about yourself and your dog. A big part of that is being consistent and articulate in terms of communicating. A good handler will also be able to pick up on the dog's behavior. I tell the people I train, you have to be able to read your dog."

The bottom line for a police dog is it must obey the commands of its handler and do it without hesitation. If not, the officer has no way to control the amount of force the dog will use. Barry tells cops who seek his advice about becoming a K-9 officer not to even consider it if they're the kind of person who can't get their dog off the couch or get them to come when they're called.

The basic course for K-9s and their handlers is sixteen weeks. Training the dogs to find dead bodies, narcotics, and other search and rescue tasks takes another twelve weeks, a total of twenty-eight weeks, almost a half a year. The average career span for police K-9s is between eight and nine years, but a few work for ten years and longer.

Homer Green, Barry's colleague on the K-9 Unit, spent twenty of his thirty years on the job with that Unit. Homer explained that Barry's reputation as one of the nation's top police dog trainers took off after a competition in 1986. "Our canines had been competing for six years, and we had never won anything," Green remembered. "Barry and I decided it was time to get serious."

When the Department refused to allow them to train for the competition on agency time, they did it on their own. To prepare, they worked with the dogs for three months, two to three hours every day. "Once Barry makes up his mind to do something," Green says, "you can count on the fact that it will be done."

With the three months of training behind them, Green and Galfano traveled to Philadelphia for the competition. Over thirty dogs were competing, and everything was done off leash. The event is run by the United States Police Canine Association, the certifying agency for police canines in most parts of the country. Things could not have gone better for the two New York City cops. Homer Green and Barry Galfano came home with fifteen trophies, including first prizes for both obedience and criminal apprehension.

*   *   *

If you talk to the people who know Barry, you learn pretty quickly that he is widely admired. Vic Medina, a lieutenant who worked with Galfano for an extended time, said Barry would never ask you to do anything he would not do himself. "And he always thought outside the box," Medina said.

Medina first noticed Barry's creativity when he set out to convince the Department that police dogs were an effective, cost-effective way to reduce crime. "He came up with so many unique ways the dogs could be used in proactively, like having them patrol in the trains. At the time this had never been done. It wasn't just ideas he'd come up with. He understood you had to gather facts and data and analyze the information to prove your point."

"Barry is a straight shooter," Medina continued. "He's honest and fair, and you always know where you stand with him. I think one of the things I admire most is that he never avoided problems. He would meet a challenge head on and deal with it."

Homer Green agrees that Barry has strong leadership abilities. "He's a man of strong principles," Green said. "I told him early on that he would never get above the rank of captain. Once the promotions were based on political skills, he'd be done for. Guys like Barry Galfano cannot play the political game. They're just too honest."

Green says Barry has another trait that's vitally important in gaining the respect and admiration of the people you work with, especially in law enforcement. "Barry is an incredibly gutsy guy," Green said. "If something dangerous is happening out on the street, he is the man you want by your side."

Green said he first noticed Barry's courage when the Department decided to move the K-9 Unit from its central location, split up the dogs, and send them out to the districts. "Once they were moved, Barry discovered one station in which the dogs were tied up with a rope and left in small wooden crates in the middle of a room. When the Department refused to respond to Barry's complaints, he broke one of the cardinal rules of the NYPD: He went to the press. The *New York Post* did a story, and the Mayor's office got bombarded with complaints. The dogs were moved back to the central location with the appropriate facilities within weeks. "It was a move," Green said, "that required enormous courage."

* * *

When his alarm rang on September 11, 2001, Barry was looking forward to his day off. He planned to make a fast trip to the gym to work out, come back home for a quick shower, then go to a nearby beach for a run. He was training for an upcoming race, and it was a perfect day for a long run.

He was just about to turn into his driveway after working out at the gym when his police radio started to crackle. "There was lots of noise—something about a small plane crashing into one of the buildings at the World Trade Center. I remember thinking, wow, how could that happen?"

Experienced law enforcement officers know when something big is happening by the sound of the voices on the radio. When Barry heard the frantic voices of the operators going back and forth trying to get information, he knew there was no way he was going to the beach that day. He ran into the house and turned on the TV just in time to see the second plane hit the South Tower.

After the shortest shower of his life and a couple of swipes with a towel, Barry threw on some clothes and drove to Floyd Bennett Field, headquarters of the Emergency Service Unit. His wife was at work. Two of his four kids were in school. His oldest daughter was still living at home and teaching at a local elementary school. His oldest son was serving in the Navy in the Special Forces. Barry never thought to leave a note.

Barry was a Captain in charge of the NYPD's K-9 Unit, but he was new to the Emergency Service Unit, and he had not gone through search and rescue training. He felt understandably anxious about what awaited him as a high-level supervisor at a major disaster where he knew ESU cops would take the lead.

When Barry got to Floyd Bennett, he changed into his uniform and drove into the city over the Manhattan Bridge. "I've crossed this bridge hundreds of times on my way to the city," he said. "There is one point—around the middle—where there is a clear shot of the two towers at the World Trade Center. Just when I reached that spot, I saw there was just one tower standing. It's hard to explain what that was like. My mind was racing. I knew I'd seen something big, but I didn't understand what it was. The noises coming over my police radio were unlike anything I had ever heard. The dispatchers did an incredible job trying to keep everyone calm. They were trying to collect information, but chiefs were screaming for units, and everyone was cutting off one another. I remember one operator kept asking the same thing over and over. 'The building came down? The building came down?' Listening to that operator, I thought the world might be coming to an end."

Barry was driving down the West Side Highway when the second tower fell. "When I couldn't drive any farther, I ditched my car. I left it in the middle of West Street and started running through the streets toward the Trade Center. I finally found an ESU cop. When I told him I was the new Captain, he just looked at me and said, 'Well, welcome to ESU. Here's some goggles. You're going to need these if you want to see anything.' I put the goggles on and followed him in."

As he got closer, Barry's first impressions were surreal. "I'm a skier, and all I could compare it to was fresh snow on a mountain after a heavy snowstorm. There was over a foot of ash. It came up to my knees."

He tried to focus. "By this time we all knew it was no accident. My training taught me that the first attack is usually a diversion. Once all the resources are tied up at the first incident, they hit you again. The second attack would be much worse. When I looked around, I knew I would not make it home that night, but I decided I would do my part to try and stop whoever did this to us from hitting us again."

Barry took his lead from Mike Curtin, a sergeant with ESU. "Mike was a Marine, and he was very conscious that there might be more attacks. He went tactical with heavy weapons. So did I."

Barry gathered a group of officers together. He told them to keep searching for victims but also be aware that a second wave of attacks could kill even more innocent people. "We were thinking there was a good possibility that whoever was behind this could be heavily armed and ready to attack us as we were looking for victims. I told them to keep searching but keep their eyes open. I fully expected a ground attack with suicide bombers and AK-47s. I was ready to stop them."

Two cops with dogs and three ESU cops armed with Heckler & Koch MP5 submachine guns that fire thirty rounds at a time checked the perimeter of the site to make sure there were no observable threats. After that they began coordinated patrols in hopes their heavy weapons and presence might prevent another attack.

As hours went by, Barry realized they were going to be there a long time.

* * *

The search for bodies went on for nine months. Regular patrol officers worked two consecutive days at Ground Zero and then were rotated out back to their regular assignments. Emergency Service officers were there every day.

The massive cleanup effort eventually involved hundreds of construction workers, ironworkers, and crane operators. "The first couple of days did not go well," Barry said. "It wasn't until the cranes arrived that things started to happen. The crane operators learned quickly that this was a massive crime scene with a lot of victims, and they would not be able to clean it up quickly. It was amazing to watch them lift up a bar of steel and be so careful. They were so respectful once they knew there might be dead bodies there. Anybody who was down there will tell you those crane operators were a godsend."

In the days and weeks after the attacks, hundreds of people came to help. They came from all over the United States and Canada, and scores brought their dogs. Barry would end up in charge of all the canines volunteering at the site. "It was very confusing," he said. "During those first weeks, we had more than one hundred dogs. We had to figure out which ones were trained for search and rescue. We told the people who brought their family pets to leave, but some refused. We learned months later that some of these individuals even had the nerve to file claims for injuries they claimed their dogs had suffered while they were working at the site."

A big part of Barry's job was to determine which dogs had FEMA training. With the exception of the NYPD and the Las Vegas Metropolitan Police
Department, most law enforcement agencies do not send their police dogs
for FEMA training, so they are not experienced at search and rescue missions. The dogs who were trained for rescue work were frustrated when they
searched day after day and were unable to find any survivors. "You could read
it on the dogs' faces and by their body language that they were just as dazed
and confused as we were."

"At the beginning we thought we'd be able to help hundreds if not thousands of people," Barry said. "We climbed into every nook and cranny. But
even with the dogs, we couldn't find anyone. All the dogs were getting were
body parts or small pieces of tissue."

Finally, the grim reality began to set in that there would be no one to rescue. At that point the decision was made to call in the cadaver dogs, and they
began making a lot of hits. They found thousands of body parts—everything
from legs and arms to ears and fingers.

"It's hard to explain how discouraging that was," Barry remembered. "We
had all kinds of emergency vehicles, ambulances, doctors, nurses, and EMTs
lined up for miles waiting to rush victims to the hospital. At the beginning,
when we couldn't find anyone, we were hoping they all got out. It took a long
time for us to accept the fact that all of those innocent people had been incin-
erated or crushed to death."

* * *

Once Barry realized the work would be mostly looking for body parts so
that families and loved ones could have some closure, he felt his job as a captain was to take care of his crew. More than one hundred ESU officers worked
the night shift from six in the evening to six the next morning. There were six
lieutenants, ten sergeants, and eighty cops on Barry's team. They spent nine
long months at their grim chore.

"Every day started off with a meeting with the city's Office of Emergency
Management," Barry said. "They would update us on what had happened the
day before, which mostly was a list of the bodies they had found. Then they
would assign groups of firefighters and cops to work in specific sectors of the
site. The dogs were the heroes of this story. They would come across a small
clump of dirt and start barking, and it would turn out to be a piece of body

tissue. There was no way a human being could have done that. The Medical Examiner took the tissue and identified the person through DNA, which allowed the families to come and retrieve their loved ones' remains."

Of the twenty-three New York City police officers and thirty-seven Port Authority cops who died in the attacks, only seven bodies were found. "If we recovered a firefighter, we would call them to take out the body," Barry said. "They did the same for us. Everyone wanted to carry out their own guys."

Later, as the magnitude of the disaster became better known and forensic scientists began their studies, people learned that the bodies of the people trapped in the towers mostly disintegrated when the concrete and steel from the buildings fell and crushed them.

There was one spot on West Street where the Atrium used to stand with a massive mound of debris. It took Barry and a team of one hundred officers, working twelve-hour shifts, two months to dig their way to the bottom of the forty-foot pile.

"When we got down there," he said, "one of the guys yelled up that his dog had found something. The dog was barking at a sheet of metal that was totally flat. We were sure he had made a mistake. One of the cops got a crowbar and pried the metal up, but all we could see underneath was a piece of paper that looked like it was wet. The dog still seemed agitated, and we kept staring at the paper. It's hard to say how many minutes went by, but at some point someone said they didn't think it was wet paper. It turned out it was a person's arm that had been totally flattened under the metal. It made you realize the human body is not much more than a bag of water."

The day of the attacks, Sergeant Mike Curtin, one of the most respected officers in the Department, and all of his team but two, perished when the second tower fell. Curtin was one of the first officers on the scene when terrorists mounted the first attack on the World Trade Center in 1993. In 1995 he went to Oklahoma City to assist with the recovery efforts after the bombing there left 168 people dead and 800 injured. Until the September 11, 2001, attacks, the bombing of the Oklahoma City Federal Building was the deadliest act of terrorism on U.S. soil.

The day he arrived in Oklahoma City, Curtin was combing through the wreckage when his eye caught a piece of fabric. It was blue with a red stripe on it. He recognized it immediately. It was a piece of a dress blue uniform worn by Marines.

Curtin had found the remains of Captain Randy Guzman, the officer in charge of recruiting at the Oklahoma City Federal Building. He requested permission to recover Guzman's remains. The body was in a dangerous spot, and Mike and four others were given only four hours to bring him out. They made it with only a few minutes to spare. While they were freeing the Marine's remains from the rubble, someone found an American flag, and Curtin draped it over Guzman's body before they carried him out. The heart-wrenching recovery of Captain Guzman was the lead story in news broadcasts around the country. When a reporter asked Mike Curtin why he risked his life to recover the remains of Captain Guzman, he answered simply that Marines don't leave their own behind.

Almost a decade after September 11, 2001, Barry is still emotional when he talks about Mike Curtin. "Several days after the attacks, one of the ESU sergeants with engineering experience figured out how to go back and listen to the audio tapes of the cops' transmissions on September 11. He plotted those transmissions on the blueprints of the World Trade Center and was able to find the place where Mike Curtin and his team were last heard from. Once they pinpointed the spot, the search began.

"I know this is probably hard to understand, but knowing where Mike and his crew might have been during their last moments gave us a lot of hope," Barry said. "We went down layer by layer, day after day. Seven months almost from the day we started, we found Mike Curtin's body. He was still dressed in his NYPD ESU uniform and his MP5 was close by. Mike was a hero to me before 9/11, and it was very important to me that we find him."

Mike Curtin met his wife, Helga, when they were both serving in the Marine Corps. She had come to Ground Zero almost every day while her husband's colleagues searched for their friend. Even though it was the middle of the night, they waited to remove Mike's body until Helga arrived with her daughter. As Mike had done for Captain Guzman in Oklahoma City, someone found an American flag and covered the body bag holding his remains before they carried him out with his wife and daughter at his side. Barry is close to tears when he says that finding Mike Curtain is a memory that will always move him. "Since we didn't recover many of our fallen brothers and sisters, it was very symbolic to at least find one of the most decorated of our heroes. It was also very emotional to see Mike's wife and daughter there to help carry him off the pile and bring him home to rest in peace."

* * *

Seeing death up close is part of the job for every law enforcement officer. Then there's the heartache and suffering they see when they try to help the victim of a violent crime or when someone is killed in a tragic accident. But nothing in their experience prepared the cops to cope with the events of 9/11 and those long months afterward at the site. Barry said the whole thing was like an extended nightmare except you never got to wake up and have it end. The anxiety he felt driving to Ground Zero every day seemed to get worse each day. It was only when he got back to the site and saw the faces of his fellow officers that he began to calm down.

"I thought my job was to keep my guys pumped up, so I gave them a lot of pats on the back and tried to keep them talking," he said. "There was nothing heroic about what we were doing, but it was serious. A lot of guys lost partners, and they came down when they could. Many of the wives were there every day, too. We all got really close."

Barry credits the Police Department for their concern about the mental health of their officers who had the depressing job of looking for the remains of the people who had died. But looking back, he now thinks they sent the counselors in way too soon.

"They had counselors down there two days afterward trying to force people to talk about their feelings. When they showed up, we were still trying to find people we hoped were alive. We weren't about to focus on anything but that until there was no hope we would find them. I told those people up front we weren't ready to talk to them. We had a mission, and we weren't done yet."

As the long sad days turned into weeks and the weeks turned into months, Barry did the best he could to take care of his team. "I tried to keep them talking, but some people just couldn't open up." He learned to recognize when someone was becoming dangerously depressed. "When they withdrew, you knew they were getting into trouble. You'd see them sitting there with a faraway look on their face. When I saw that look, I did everything possible to get them to take a couple of days off. In the beginning all of us looked like that, but most of the cops down there were resilient, and eventually we got caught up in the distraction of the work. But there were others who didn't do so well. Those were the people you worried about."

On June 1, 2002, the city officially shut the site down. Teams of firefighters and cops had worked tirelessly for nine grueling months to find the remains of the close to three thousand innocent victims who had perished.

With his work at Ground Zero over, Barry went back to the Emergency Service Unit, which was unusually busy. As a Captain, along with his regular workload, he shared responsibility for security at the Republican National Convention during the summer of 2004. In addition, his bosses put him in charge of planning the security arrangements for the President during the time he was scheduled to attend the convention. He was also in charge of the FEMA Urban Search and Rescue Team and worked with the FDNY to rebuild the team that had lost so many of their members on 9/11. There was a lot to do, and he did not have the time or energy to focus on the attacks and the nine months he had spent looking for bodies at Ground Zero.

In 2006 Barry retired from the NYPD. It was not long after that before the emotions he thought were buried came flooding back." I was exercising a lot, and my new job as security director for the United Nations Plaza complex was demanding. I was busy. But every time I heard or saw anything about 9/11, I would completely break down. That's when I decided to seek professional help.

"It was during my visits to the counselor that I began to understand what we had all been through," he said. "A sudden death or bad accident or act of violence is one thing. It's usually over in an instant, and you can slowly recover with time. But there were a lot of us who worked at Ground Zero, walking that pile every day, looking for remains of our friends who had died, finding more body parts or even just small pieces of tissue, then calling the Medical Examiner to come and take it away. We had to deal with it over and over again."

Barry's therapist told him that, to her knowledge, there had never been an incident in which first responders had to go back, day after day, week after week, month after month, to the scene of a terrible crime where thousands of people had died. The endless wakes and funerals only added to the extended emotional trauma. Barry attended over forty funeral services for close friends and colleagues in those first months after the attacks. There was no way to escape from the sadness and grief, so he buried it deep inside.

In talking it out with the therapist, Barry began to understand that the stress he was under had taken its toll on his family. His decision to sleep at Floyd Bennett Field so he could be closer to the site meant he did not return home for weeks. He shut out his wife and children by not talking to them about what he was going through. The few times he did go home when he had a day off, things did not go well.

"I remember my first day off," Barry said. "I couldn't sit still. I kept calling my guys, asking them if they'd found anything. My wife kept staring at me while I was on the phone. After a few hours she told me to go back to work. She said it was obvious it was where I wanted to be. So I left and went back to the site. It was my first day off, and I was so restless I could not make it through a whole day at home."

"The bonds we formed over those months working at the site were extremely close, but they worked against us, too," Barry said. "On our days off, we didn't know what to do with ourselves." When he did go home, his wife kept after him to talk to her, but he just couldn't open up. Ultimately, their marriage did not withstand the stress, and Barry and his wife filed for divorce.

"My middle son, Daniel, had just started college in September 2001. He knew we had lost fourteen officers from Emergency Service, and I think he understood how hard that must have been on me." Barry was shocked when Daniel called him and announced he was dropping out of school so he could enlist in the Navy. Barry's older son, Chris, was in the Navy Special Forces, and his younger brother wanted to join him.

Barry is proud of his children. Chris went to the Persian Gulf with the Special Boat Unit, and Dan later served in Iraq as part of the Special Reaction Team. His daughter, Patty, is an elementary school teacher and is married. They have a daughter, Emma, Barry's first grandchild. His youngest child, Matt, works for UPS and is thinking about a career in law enforcement.

* * *

"Looking back I realize the Department should not have kept the same people down there for nine months. They should have sent us home and ordered us to do it. When there was a choice, virtually no one made the decision to leave. Emotions were running strong that we had to find our brothers. I can still hear their voices when I asked them if they wanted some time off. Everyone had a buddy or partner they were searching for. They'd say, 'I'm not leaving until we find Tommy Langone. I'm looking for Vinnie Danz. I'm not going until I bring Mike Curtin home.'"

* * *

Almost a decade after the attacks of September 11, the New York City Police Department has changed dramatically. A substantial portion of its annual budget of $3.7 billion is now devoted to the counterterrorism mission. The Department requires higher-ranking officers to attend lectures and courses on everything from the inner workings of Al Qaeda to how to recognize a potential suicide bomber.

Barry remembers the weeklong course he had to take on bioterrorism. "It was only a month before September 11. One day the professor came into class holding a small vial. He told us to look outside at the clouds and then discussed what a great day it was for a biological attack. He said he could wipe out the whole city with the contents of that one vial and that the clouds would keep it from dispersing. The whole thing seemed crazy."

Two months after that class, Dan Rather received an anthrax-laced letter, and Barry was on the team that went to the offices of CBS to investigate. "To this day, we still don't know who sent that letter," he said.

A few weeks later, when the NYPD needed to establish protocols for police officers responding to calls where biological, chemical, or nuclear materials had been let loose, they put Barry in charge of the project.

* * *

Today the NYPD is a sadder place. The ongoing fallout from the attacks hit many police families hard. Divorce rates are up, and exposure to the toxins at Ground Zero has taken a toll on the people who worked at the site for all those weeks and months. Hundreds of officers assigned to the Emergency Service Unit retired in the first few years after the attacks. Some left the job well before their expected date of retirement. The exodus left ESU with fewer experienced officers to mentor the newer members of the team.

In December 2006 Barry made the difficult decision to retire from the NYPD. He'd received a call from the Chief of Patrol that he was being transferred out of ESU. The Chief told him his experience was needed elsewhere. Barry panicked. Everything he had experienced since being assigned to Emergency Service came rushing back to him: the perp searches, the barricaded EDPs, the bridge rescues, the gang takedowns, the counterterrorism assignments, the President's motorcade details, the New Year's Eve details, the FEMA Urban Search and Rescue Team, the K-9 training, and the nightmares and memories of 9/11. It all came back in waves of emotion.

"I felt like my life would be over if I was transferred out of ESU," he said. "I had been through hell with those men and women, and I could not imagine working anywhere else. I guess I felt a sense of security and a feeling of family working in ESU that I knew could never be replaced. I had suppressed many of the nightmares of 9/11 by working nonstop on counterterrorism assignments. I never had time to unwind. I just kept going at one hundred miles per hour. Now my life was crashing to a stop. It was like hitting a brick wall. They were taking away my family, my friends, my colleagues, many of whom had worked side by side with me at the World Trade Center. They didn't understand what Emergency Service meant to me. I tried to speak with several chiefs about allowing me to retire from ESU, but they didn't seem to understand what it meant to me. They'd never worked in ESU, and they didn't get to experience the things that I did. After speaking with the Chief of the Department and accepting the fact that he wasn't going to keep me in ESU, I went to the pension section and began the process to retire. It would take time to finalize, but my career with the New York City Police Department was over. There is a saying about ESU that makes it so special to those of us who were lucky to wear the uniform. 'When the public needs help, they call the cops. When the cops needs help, they call ESU.' It was a ticket to the greatest show on earth.

"Once I retired, I went back to school to get my degree in homeland security management. It just seemed like the logical choice after my career with the New York City Transit Police and the NYPD and my degrees from the FBI National Academy and Police Management Institute. I also started working as the director of security at the United Nations Plaza. I was recruited for the job by a company that trains and deploys explosive detection dogs, and many of their employees were current or former NYPD K-9 Unit and ESU members. The job is very interesting and I got to meet many dignitaries while working closely with the State Department and Secret Service and protecting several missions to the UN. But the reality for me was, nothing would ever compare to a day in the life of an ESU captain."

* * *

Despite all the trauma from the aftermath of the terrorist attacks and his demanding job with a lot of responsibility supervising forty employees and four bomb dogs at the United Nations Plaza, Barry says there is not a day that goes by when he doesn't miss the NYPD.

"When I was at the UN, someone from Emergency Service stopped in to visit me at least once a week. They filled me in on what was going on. They are great people, and I miss them. And I miss the work. Every day of my life, at least a couple of times a day, I want to be back there."

Barry with his police dog, Harry. "I've worked with many great police dogs over the course of my career, but Harry was the best by far at regular patrol work. He had a sixth sense, an amazing ability to know what posed a threat. That dog helped me send some very hardened criminals to jail."

At right, Barry with the family pet, Harry, during the summer of 2010. Harry was named after Barry's legendary canine partner. Below, ten-year-old Barry with his first Shepherd, Snowflake. "I wanted her to be just like Rin Tin Tin," he said. (*Photo by Dave Fitzpatrick.*)

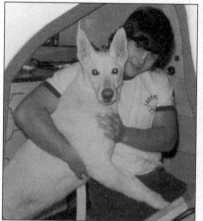

Homer Green (left) and Barry Galfano with their dogs Blackie and Harry. Homer and Barry were celebrating after coming home from a police canine competition in Philadelphia with 15 trophies including first place for both obedience and criminal apprehension.

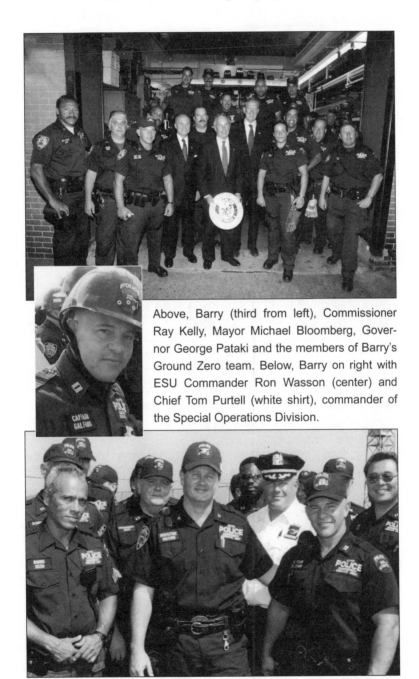

Above, Barry (third from left), Commissioner Ray Kelly, Mayor Michael Bloomberg, Governor George Pataki and the members of Barry's Ground Zero team. Below, Barry on right with ESU Commander Ron Wasson (center) and Chief Tom Purtell (white shirt), commander of the Special Operations Division.

A close knit group – Barry's family. Seated front row, left to right: parents Lenny and Trudy, sons Matt and Chris. Back row, left to right, Jackie Bourne, Barry, sister Patty with her daughter Emma, son Dan. Below, Barry with Emma and Patty. Barry said, "No matter how bad I felt after chemo, all I would need to do is see Emma and I felt much better." (*Photos by Dave Fitzpatrick.*)

When Barry learned he had cancer, his family and friends were a constant source of support. "But no one was there for me more than Jackie," Barry said. "She's a cancer survivor herself and she knew what I was going through. Her love and support never wavered." Jackie Bourne is a lieutenant assigned to the NYPD's 70th Precinct in Brooklyn.

Chapter Eleven

Tony Diaz: The Greatest Job on Earth

*"To love what you do and feel that it matters—
how on Earth could anything be more fun?"*
—Katherine Graham

In 2008, detectives assigned to the NYPD's Major Case Squad had been working from Brooklyn all the way up to the Bronx, chasing a group of thieves who were breaking into scores of high-end jewelry stores and making off with hundreds of thousands of dollars in Rolex watches, diamond rings, and gold necklaces. Their MO was always the same. They would set up shop on the eve of a long weekend in a building next to their target. After the employees locked up and went home for the night, they broke out their high-speed drills and jackhammers. With two or three days without interruption, they took their time boring through to the basement next door. The savvy group had long eluded the NYPD's determined efforts to catch them.

In his five years with the Major Case Squad, Tony Diaz had never been so frustrated. Seasoned detectives will tell you that the pros—the disciplined, smart crooks—come to New York City for one main reason. Opportunity.

"New York is so big," Tony says. "It's a perfect place for criminals to hone their craft. Most of them get a template by trial and error. By the third victim, they usually have it together. Unless they do something violent or mess with the wrong person, they can have a good run. But it only lasts so long. Once we identify their pattern, it's only a matter of time before we take them down."

After a year of dead ends and bogus leads, detectives were feeling anything but formidable. And now that the jewelry store thefts had escalated into bank burglaries, pressure from the Department was mounting to stop them.

They got a break in early November. An informant, someone who'd been connected to the group but was now out for revenge, told the cops his partners in crime were planning a bank robbery on Staten Island. The hit was planned for early Thanksgiving morning.

Tony explains that to pull off this kind of heist, the people behind the operation usually have someone on the inside they are paying to help them. "Along with getting someone to leave the door open and dismantle the alarm, you've got to know the layout of the building and the location of the firewalls, air conditioning ducts, alarms, and surveillance cameras. They understand how the plumbing works and the mechanics of the alarm system. The insiders know how to pace off a floor, find the ventilation ducts, locate the safe, and get it open."

By Wednesday afternoon, to insure everything would be on tape if the case went to trial, detectives with the Technical Assistance Response Unit (TARU) had installed audio and video recording devices throughout the parking lot of the bank. Knowing the suspects could be heavily armed, Emergency Service cops were summoned to breach the door. By four in the afternoon on the day before Thanksgiving, they were ready.

When the burglars arrived on the scene the next morning, TARU cameras caught it all on tape. Four men in a van with shaded windows drove to the parking lot at back of the bank and entered through a back door. A few minutes later another man arrived alone in a car. After watching the surveillance tapes, the cops learned that his job was to reset the alarms as soon as they were tripped. When the timing was right to catch the break-in crew inside the vault, the Emergency Service cops prepared to make their entry.

At two in the morning, body bunkers in position and guns drawn, eight heavily armed police officers entered the bank. After a thorough search, they realized no one was there. They regrouped and entered the Pearle Vision store.

It didn't take long to find the bank robbers. They had crawled up into the space above the entrance to the store. When the officers poked at the ceiling, the four men came tumbling out onto the sidewalk like the contents of a smashed piñata. "That was the first time I saw Emergency Service do an operation of that size," Tony said. "It was awesome. It reminded me of a military operation. I wanted to put the whole thing on film."

The suspects must have been disoriented as they picked themselves up and looked around. Standing by were several armored trucks, police dogs, two NYPD helicopters, and close to a hundred cops, including officers from the Major Case Squad and the Federal Probation Service. They were arraigned later that day on charges of burglary, grand larceny, possession of burglary tools, and criminal mischief. Two of the men were on probation after having served time in federal prison for similar crimes.

* * *

New York City has always had more than its fair share of bank robberies, but late in 2008 the numbers were going up. "Most people say it's because of the economy," Tony said. "I know the recession is bad, but I don't think John Q. Citizen is out there robbing banks because he got laid off or had his hours cut back. My view is that these people would be out there robbing banks with or without the recession."

Most bank robbery crimes are solved by getting a picture of the suspect on television or the Internet. "That's when the tips come in," Tony says. "If you watch a lot of TV, you probably believe forensic evidence like fingerprints and DNA leads us to the person responsible for the crime. But the truth is that only novices touch the counter when they leave a note demanding cash. If they have any idea what they're doing, they never leave prints."

During his five years with the Major Case Squad, Tony Diaz has worked lots of bank robbery investigations.

"I had this one case where a guy robbed seventeen banks over eighteen months. I worked on that case for seven months. It drove me crazy that we couldn't catch him. He'd go out on his lunch hour, find a bank, pass a note to a teller, and leave with a pocket full of cash."

Bank tellers are trained to comply. Every time this man hit a bank, the teller handed over the money and waited until he was gone before calling the police. He was averaging $1,500 to $4,000 each time. When the bank's surveillance cameras filmed the lunch-hour bank robber, the suspect's face was always obscured. All the police could see clearly was a Mets baseball hat. But in what would turn out to be his seventeenth and last robbery, the camera finally got a clear image of the man's face.

The NYPD's Office of Public Information reached out to the city's television stations and newspapers and asked them to air the photo. They got their break the next morning. A woman who managed a small factory on 38th Street called in. There was no doubt in her mind the man she had seen on television was one of her employees.

"She told me she was shocked when she saw his picture, but that she was absolutely positive he was the man we were looking for," Diaz said. "Her only request was that we not arrest him on the work floor. We were sympathetic with that. She told us to come directly to her office. We could arrest him there."

When Tony and his partner showed up at the factory, they entered a big room. "It looked like they were boxing up costume jewelry," Tony recalled. "Everyone was staring at us. Some people were giving us weird looks. Others were nodding their heads like, yeah, he's your guy. We went into the manager's office, and she called him in. The minute he saw us, you could tell we had the right guy. He knew it was over."

Farid Abdul-Ali was cooperative throughout the interrogation and arrest process. A recovering addict with a rap sheet going back to the 1970s, Abdul-Ali admitted to robbing banks in every corner of the city.

The man was in custody, and he had confessed to the crimes. As far as Tony Diaz was concerned, it was on to the next case. But the story caught the attention of local reporters.

"They started dogging me," he said. "After several calls I started to get the feeling they thought we were inept. The phone was ringing off the hook, and their questions were not friendly. They asked me, 'How could you let him rob seventeen banks? Is eighteen a magic number? Why couldn't you get him after three?' They implied we were sitting on our hands doing nothing while this guy ran buck wild around the city.

"I know I can speak for every cop in the country when I say that one of the most frustrating parts of being in law enforcement is that we can't defend ourselves when we're attacked by the media. There are a lot of things we can't say if an investigation is ongoing, and most departments don't allow their officers to speak on the record anyway. After a few years on the job, we all learn it's a really bad idea to get into a discussion with reporters.

"Keeping your mouth shut when people question your professional competence is not easy, but cops have to learn to sit there, be the bigger person, and take it."

* * *

Tony has loved every minute of his time with the Major Case Squad. "The investigations are challenging, and I work harder here than any other assignment I've had," he says. "It never feels like work. It's always something different, it's always interesting, and it's always a challenge. Because our cases take us all around the country, we have to be good at tying information together. We look for patterns and try to incorporate them into a bigger picture.

"You've got to have good crime-solving skills," Tony continues. "You've got be creative, but at the same time you've got to look for a pattern. You've got to have a sense about when people are lying and when they are telling the truth. Along with an understanding of forensic science and computer technology, detectives need good analytical and writing skills to convince a judge or grand jury the case can be successfully prosecuted in court.

"If you're new, you've got to check your ego at the door. Even if you have had a lot of experience doing routine detective work, in a unit like this you have to pay your dues and listen to the guys with more experience."

Detectives in the Major Case Squad are masters at questioning criminal suspects. "You watch and you learn," Tony says. "I learned that some guys you'll never break. They will never talk to you, no matter how good you are. They say, 'I know where you're going with this. I want a lawyer.' Then there's another group—people who don't want to talk but you can sense they are hesitating. You have to find a way to reel them in. It's a subtle process of understanding your adversary and knowing which buttons to push to get the information you need."

The key to a successful interrogation, Tony says, is trust. "I try to be honest with them. I tell them, I don't need you to solve this case. As far as I'm concerned, it's solved. That's why you're here.

"An important part of building trust is being sure you don't make promises you can't keep. Sometimes they'll test you to see if you know what you're talking about. They'll ask for something they know you can't give them. When I get those requests, I tell them there's no way I can do that. They know I'm being straight.

"The goal of any interrogation is to tie up the case, get valuable information about other criminal activity, and hopefully prevent a trial where victims can be further traumatized.

"In the case of the guy who robbed seventeen banks, we had tellers who were afraid of the guy. For them to have to go into court and come face-to-face with someone who could hurt them further is frightening. They've already been through one trauma, and we don't want to put them through another.

"Another objective is to get as much intelligence as possible. We want to find out who they work with and whether they learned their tricks in jail or out on the street. If we discover some jackass in jail is teaching these people how to rob banks, we go up to the jail and work with the corrections officers to put a stop to it. If their mentors are out on the street, we follow up with those people as well."

* * *

At his desk at Police headquarters shortly after eight in the morning, Tony delves into his own cases before perusing the reports labeled "Unusuals," the Department's rundown of all the major crimes that occurred in New York City the day before. If anything catches his eye, he'll make it a point to discuss it with the other detectives in his office. There are only twenty-five investigators assigned to the Major Case Squad, and they cover the entire city. Tony's team of eight investigates major crimes in the borough of Manhattan, including bank robberies, high-end burglaries, kidnappings, and art thefts. They also assist in investigations when a New York City police officer is injured or killed with criminal intent. Each of the squad's eight detectives may be working on as many as ten cases at one time.

"We're on call twenty-four seven," he explains. "Technically my hours are ten in the morning to six in the evening with weekends off. But if something happens on a Saturday or Sunday, they can call you. Unless you're on vacation, detectives with Major Case are always on call. One Sunday my name was up for the next case. I got called in for a kidnapping. It turned out to be a bogus report. Every time this girl has a fight with her parents, she gets herself kidnapped. We started to call her the "serial kidnapped girl." She has one of her friends call her parents and say they're holding her and she won't be released until a ransom is paid. This time they said they were calling from Boston, but we could see it was coming from New York. The whole thing was pathetic."

But for every kidnapping case that's a waste of time, there are dozens that beg for serious action. Most stem from drug deals gone bad—someone who never got their money decides to strike back. "We see it over and over again," Tony says. "Everything's been going along great—sometimes for years—when all of a sudden one guy decides to screw the other."

Hell hath no fury like a drug dealer scorned, and the subsequent acts of revenge are often brutal. Tony remembers one situation where one man almost killed his business partner.

"These two guys had been friends for a long time," he recalled. "They were in business together selling drugs. After what appeared to be a successful collaboration, one guy decided to screw his partner out of $27,000, the going price at that time for a kilo of cocaine. When the other man realized he was out the money, he decided to get a couple of friends, kidnap the friend who ripped him off, and take him to a hotel room in Atlantic City.

"A lot of agencies became involved with this case, including the FBI and the State Police. We used cell phone technology to track their movements. We knew what kind of car they had. Agents with the FBI and troopers with the State Police made the arrest in Atlantic City. They found the kidnapped man lying in the backseat of an SUV. They had worked him over pretty good. He was stabbed multiple times and badly beaten. They put the handcuffs on so tight that two weeks later, he still had bad bruises on his wrist. It looked like his hands were going to fall off."

Cops usually don't feel sympathy for drug dealers, but when Tony saw the way the man had been handcuffed, brutally beaten, and stabbed, it was hard not to empathize. "When I saw the guy, I understood how tough this situation must have been for him. I told him I felt sorry for the torture he went through."

Three men were arrested on federal kidnapping charges. The NYPD then deferred to the FBI, the lead law enforcement agency working the case. "It's important to back off when another agency is in charge," Tony says. "You don't want to duplicate efforts, and if your reports differ even slightly, it's more ammunition for the defense attorney if the case gets to trial."

* * *

Major Case Squad cases frequently end up as the plotlines for novels, films, and television shows. Many stories on the popular television program *Law and Order: Criminal Intent* come straight from the files of the NYPD's Major Case Squad. Tony says he has no idea whether any of his cases have ended up on the show. He rarely has time to watch television, and if he does find a minute to tune in, it's not going to be a cop show.

He has had his brush with the rich and famous, including Marc Anthony and Jennifer Lopez. The NYPD began an investigation when Marc Anthony called the police after his cousin's car was stolen in New Jersey. A laptop computer containing an unedited videotape of Marc and Jennifer's wedding, as well as some events leading up to it, was on the backseat.

"The guy who stole the car called Marc Anthony's manager and demanded a million dollars," Diaz said. "It was a classic extortion case, and the investigation was assigned to the Major Case Squad.

"I decided to call this guy myself, and pretend I was Marc's manager. He was pretty brazen. He told me if we didn't pay him the one million, he was going to go to *US Weekly*, *People* magazine, and all the other tabloids and sell the video to the highest bidder.

"I told him one million was out of the question, that there was nothing controversial on the tape, no naked people, no sex. It was nothing. The video had Marc buying the engagement ring, and there were pictures of Jennifer getting dressed for the wedding, but it was all wholesome and harmless. I told him Lopez and Anthony were willing to pay $50,000 but no more. Marc's manager later complimented me for getting them down from one million to $50,000," Tony said. "He told me if I ever wanted a job negotiating deals, to call him.

"When we were making the arrangements to drop the money off, the guy who had the computer asked me to write out two separate checks for $25,000 each. In a classic case of no honor among thieves, his plan was to split one check between himself and the guy he was working with. He'd pocket the other one. His partner in crime would never know he was getting shafted out of $12,500.

"I arranged to meet him in Lower Manhattan at the Moondance Diner at the corner of 6th Avenue and Grand Street," Tony recalled. "We had plainclothes cops on the street making sure every parking space in front of the diner on 6th Avenue was clear so he could pull right in. The plan was as soon as he parked, the cops waiting on a side street would move in and make the arrest."

Tony arrived at the diner in his suit and tie along with an envelope the suspects would think contained the checks. He found a booth by a window where he could easily be seen from the street. "The television show *Punked* had just come out," Tony said. "When the suspects looked inside the envelope for the money, all they would find was a sheet of paper that said, 'Congratulations. You've just been punked by the Major Case Squad.'"

They thought the plan was flawless. Two unmarked police vehicles followed the extortionists from their starting point in New Jersey all the way up to New York City. Tony had a perfect view of the street, and there were plenty of parking spaces in front of the diner. When the car pulled up, Tony said the driver looked right at him. "I waved the envelope so he would know it was me. But something went wrong. He didn't stop."

Diaz stood in the diner watching helplessly as the car turned the corner and made its way to the street where the NYPD field team was waiting. "I called them on my radio and said, 'Hey guys, he didn't stop. He's coming right toward you.'"

The cops on the street had a split second to respond to the dramatic change of plans. What happened next can be best described as organized chaos. The cops descended on the suspect's car. Three of them jumped on the hood. Another one opened the driver's door and tried to pull the man at the wheel out of the car and handcuff him. Someone else tried to get the car into park, but it just kept rolling. It stopped when it hit another car. "The whole thing went from a surgical operation that was supposed to go down with complete precision to total mayhem," Tony said.

Looking back, Tony said once the car turned the corner, it was all over. "There were so many legal parking places right in front. Who knows why the driver didn't park there?"

The interrogation went badly. "This guy lied, lied, and lied some more," Tony recalled. "Some of these psychos start believing their own stories, and he was one of them. I think he really thought he was a legitimate businessman who had every reason to expect a payment for the stolen laptop."

Fortunately, the cops also arrested the suspect's partner, the one he tried to rip off with the two-check scheme. "We had everything on tape," Tony said. "When he listened to the part where his friend asked us for two checks, that was it. He was furious his partner was going to cheat him out of half his money, and we got his confession."

* * *

Tony Diaz grew up in the Bushwick section of Brooklyn, where both his mother and father's parents had settled after coming to New York City from Puerto Rico in the early 1960s. He became interested in law enforcement work in high school. A lot of his older friends were cops, and Tony was fascinated listening to their stories about locking up bad guys with guns, making arrests, and working on narcotics cases. "They were dynamic, motivated guys, and I looked up to them," he said.

Tony's father worked construction. He went to work at six in the morning no matter the weather. "He'd be so tired when he got home that he sometimes would fall asleep in the bathtub," Tony said. "He always had a nice car and stacks of money, but you could tell his body was shot. He was always telling me his life was too hard, that he wanted something better for me."

Tony decided he didn't want to a job that made him so tired he couldn't eat dinner. He did well in school, seldom getting a grade below A, and the first thing he did after graduating from high school was take the test to become a New York City police officer. He got a perfect score, but he was only seventeen, and the NYPD doesn't accept recruits until they turn twenty. After stints digging holes and planting trees for a landscape company and working as a clerk at an American Express office, jobs he remembers respectively as physically tiring and mentally boring, he enrolled at Pace University to study accounting and finance. But the tuition was expensive, and no one explained how the student loan program worked.

"I saved money for college, which meant I couldn't get a loan," he said. "It was $10,000 a year, and that didn't include the books." Despite strong objections from his mother, he dropped out after a year. Six months later, in

October, Tony Diaz celebrated his twentieth birthday. By February he was enrolled in the New York City Police Academy.

He made his first arrest when he was a rookie. It was the night of his twenty-first birthday. After work he planned to go out with his friends. He was looking forward to his first trip to a bar and legally ordering a drink. He had brought his street clothes to work so he wouldn't have to waste time going home to change.

His shift was almost over and he was making his way back to the precinct when he noticed a young man who looked like he was breaking into a car. "When I was a kid, my own car had been broken into so many times I'd lost count. I did everything I could think of to keep those creeps away from my car. I even left smelly bags of garbage in the back seat, but nothing worked. That crime was always a pet peeve of mine."

Tony pulled his firearm and told the guy to put his hands in the air. The arrest and subsequent paperwork took hours. His friends celebrated Tony's birthday without him.

After twenty years in law enforcement, Tony says he looks at holidays as just another day. "Early on, when I was still on patrol, most of the time we had to work," he said. "We would get swamped with domestic violence calls, especially, on Christmas and Thanksgiving. After those experiences, I think a lot of cops learn to do what I did, which is treat holidays like they're any other day. If you get into the mind-set that it's just another shift, what you're seeing doesn't bother you as much.

"For people outside law enforcement, I think it must be hard for them to understand how tired you get dealing with people who have so many problems. It is difficult not to lash out when people do something that hurts their kids, especially on a holiday. I remember one time when I was working the day shift on Christmas, a call came into 911. A woman was screaming that her husband was beating her.

"When my partner and I got there, it was obvious the man had punched his wife in the face and smashed the television with a hammer. There were two kids crying in the corner. I wanted to tell him, 'It's Christmas Day. Did you really have to smash your TV and punch your wife in the face, leaving me no choice but to lock you up in front of your kids, who have already seen enough?'

"I made a gun arrest one Thanksgiving that cost me that holiday dinner," he continued. "A guy looked suspicious, and something told me he had a gun. My shift was going to end in twenty minutes, and I was planning to have dinner with my family. I knew he was up to something. I chased him into the store and watched him dump a gun into the ice cream freezer. Once that happened, I knew I was never going to make it to dinner."

With the man in cuffs, Tony spent the next eight hours vouchering for the gun, getting a statement from the suspect, collecting fingerprints, and gathering up the information the District Attorney would need to draw up the case. All these tasks had to be completed the same day as the arrest. On holidays this took longer than usual because the DA's office operated with a skeleton crew.

* * *

Before his assignment to the Major Case Squad, Tony worked patrol for ten years, the Gang Division for two, and Narcotics for three. Like almost every newcomer to the NYPD, he had to walk a beat for four years, where he learned to be a keen observer of people and identify which ones might be breaking the law. He did a long stint with his precinct's SNEU team—short for Street Narcotics Enforcement Unit—where he spent months in a battle to keep drugs and drug dealers out of the neighborhood.

It is often said that police work is hours of boredom interspersed with seconds of terror. That's especially true for cops doing street surveillance work. Days can go by before something happens. When it does, the officer has to be ready to go into high gear in a matter of seconds.

When he was assigned to the Narcotics Division, Tony worked in Spanish Harlem. It was the late 90s, and cops were in a perpetual war with well-organized thugs. His team covered a ten-block area from 97th to 125th Street on the East Side of Manhattan.

"These were big gangs," he said. "They were running wild and making a ton of money dealing drugs, selling illegal firearms, and running extortion and bribery schemes. Gang members wore these big gold belt buckles, and they all had the same shirts with their gang logo on them. When we arrested them, they'd deny they were in the gang. We'd say, 'Oh yeah, what about that shirt you have on? Isn't that your logo?'"

The cops learned to recognize the hierarchy of the gang from the type of belt buckle they wore. A belt encrusted with rubies meant they managed the drug sales on a particular street. A belt with diamonds indicated a boss the guys with the rubies reported to.

"These people were enamored with *Scarface*," Tony said. "They'd talk like Al Pacino in the movie when they recorded the messages on their answering machines. 'Hey,' they'd say. 'You've reached the bad guy.'"

Tony says aggressive sweeps of crime-infested neighborhoods can be effective, but they also have limitations. "You can go in and make a lot of arrests, but unless you put a lot of cops in there for a long time, you create turf wars. Opposing gangs see an opening, and they move in. We can take down a drug crew, but if there's no occupying force coming in behind you to keep the ground you gained, another gang will see an opportunity and aggressively move in to take over the territory."

Tony learned this lesson the hard way. "We'd been working on one particularly bad group for a couple of years," he remembered. "We worked hard, and we were successful. We built our case and locked them up. Everyone was found guilty. We were pretty happy with the job we'd done until we realized that we'd created a big void. A real bad guy, Kareem Kilpatrick, moved in and took over. To do that, he went on a shooting spree, and one person was killed."

The New York cops went after Kilpatrick's crew. They rounded up everyone they knew who was connected to him, including street-level managers, crew managers, and runners. "We told them they might be eligible for reduced sentences if they gave us information on Kilpatrick," Tony recalled. "But every one of them was terrified of the guy. In one way or the other, they all said they'd rather do eight years in prison than turn him in. They told us straight out, 'Are you crazy? He'll kill me, then he'll come kill you.'"

All cops have their story about the one who got away, and Kareem Kilpatrick is Tony's. "We never did get him," he said. "Since then he was arrested for weapons possession, but we never were able to get him for the shootings and the homicide."

* * *

"Some people get the idea that everyone in a high-crime neighborhood is bad," Diaz says, "but that's just not true. In the worst neighborhoods, you find the nicest people. As cops, you deal with the worst 5 percent of the population. Most of them don't work. They survive by ripping off all their neighbors, decent people who are working hard to survive.

"When I worked midnights in Harlem, I'd see these security guards coming home at four in the morning. These are the people who become victims. Would anyone choose to work twelve hours a day for $5 an hour? I doubt it. But they're doing the best they can. They're poor. They have no choice where they live, but it's their life, and they make the best of it. Any cop in New York can tell you about a shopkeeper or some elderly person in the neighborhood who wants to help us. They've been there twenty or thirty years. Maybe they own a dry cleaners or some other small business like a grocery store. I've always felt these are the people the police have a special obligation to protect.

"I'll never forget one woman. It was in the 30th Precinct. I was on surveillance on the roof of her apartment building for months. One day I was on my way up, and I met her in the hall. She asked me if I wanted to come in and have a glass of water."

Once Tony was inside her apartment, he could see that the view was much better from her living room window than the roof. "I took a chance and asked her if she would mind if I sat in her window. She never hesitated. She seemed to understand how hard we were working to get these dirtbags who were selling drugs and guns out of her neighborhood."

The woman seemed relieved, even happy, to have Tony's company. She watched her soap operas and knitted as Tony sat in the window with his police radio watching for drug dealers. When it was cold, she made him cocoa. While he could only hear the voices, he found himself getting caught up in a couple of the soaps just from listening to the dialogue.

Three or four months after Tony met her, she died suddenly. Before he heard the news, he went to knock on her door to conduct his regular surveillance, and the entrance to her apartment was all taped up with a sign that read Do Not Enter. "It was sad," Tony said. "She was such a nice, sweet lady. I missed her."

* * *

Every law enforcement agency has experienced the tragic fallout that occurs when one of their officers cannot resist the many temptations the job offers, opportunities that are as numerous as they are lucrative. It can be as simple as accepting a bribe to look the other way when the law is being broken or as bad as flipping over to the bad side and becoming a criminal. Whatever form the bad deed takes, it most always involves the lure of money.

There are almost a million law enforcement officers in the United States. The percentage who disgrace their badge and dishonor their oath is very small. But tales of police officers breaking the law sell newspapers, and the media is drawn to these stories like flies to honey. In New York the number of officers exploiting their positions to do something illegal is less than 1 percent, a remarkably low number when one considers the many opportunities that abound in our nation's largest city. But if you read the newspaper or watch the local TV news, you could easily believe the entire force is riddled with corruption.

Tony's been on the job for twenty years. He says it seems like the big scandals go in cycles. He was assigned to the 30th Precinct in the early 1990s when scores of cops were charged with a variety of crimes including extortion, bribery, selling narcotics, tax evasion, and perjury and brought out of the precinct in handcuffs. That, he says, was a profoundly depressing time.

Tony explains that the temptations for cops in New York City to accept a bribe or do something illegal can be too much for some. "You have to be very well grounded to do this job. You have to be humble and realize that people who are much smarter than you have tried to do things they shouldn't have and gotten caught. I tell the younger kids just starting out, when an opportunity you know is illegal or ethically wrong presents itself, you'd better forget about it. The shame and embarrassment you will bring to yourself and your family is not worth it. And once your integrity is compromised, you are no better than the criminals you arrest."

* * *

In his years as a cop, Tony has so far escaped the injuries that have plagued many of his colleagues. While some cops like Tony are lucky and manage to avoid the injuries and physical pain that often come with a career in law enforcement, there is no way to avoid the emotional distress that's an integral part of police work. One of the most traumatic things that can happen is to be on the scene when a fellow officer gets shot, something that has happened to Tony twice.

In January 1993 three men robbed a supermarket in Washington Heights. Tony and his partner were a block away responding to another call about a possible dead body. When they arrived at the scene, there was no doubt in either officer's mind that it was a homicide. The man, who was lying in a pool of blood in the hallway, had been repeatedly stabbed in the chest. They were just about to call it in on their radios when frantic voices cut them off. "It was crazy," Tony said. "Everyone was yelling at once. We heard, 'Shots fired. Cop down. Cop's been hit. 10-13.' Then we heard the location. We were just one block away."

Tony and his partner responded. "As we pulled up, we saw one of the suspects running down the street. We chased him into the basement of a building and arrested him at gunpoint."

They learned later that after the three men robbed the market, they ran out to the street and jumped into a livery cab. There was a police officer in uniform across the street at a bank. When he heard the commotion, he ran toward the cab and was met with a barrage of gunfire. One round hit him in the upper part of his leg one inch from his genitals.

The officer managed to return fire before he collapsed on the sidewalk. Everyone on the scene thought he was dead, but after a few seconds he stood up and fired off three more rounds. The three men jumped out of the cab and ran.

Tony still remembers the blood. "When we got to the hospital, detectives from the Crime Scene Unit were taking away the officer's clothes. They were soaked. It's hard to describe your feelings when you see something like that. It hits you pretty hard that it could have been you bleeding to death."

On March 10, 1996, it happened again. Four cops and a sergeant from the 30th Precinct were up on 164th Street looking for a car that had been used in an armed robbery. Just as they began to follow a vehicle that fit the description, a crowd of people flagged them down and pointed to a man waving a large black gun. When the cops ordered the man to drop his weapon, he ran. They chased him. At some point during the foot pursuit, the man with the gun turned around, faced the officers, and began firing. Then a barrage of gunfire, which seemed to be coming from the crowd, came at the officers from the other direction. They were being shot at from the front and the back.

Tony and his partner, Santos Gonzalez, were in their car when they heard the shots. "We saw this guy with a gun running toward us. We decided to shoot him before he shot us."

But the rounds didn't find their mark, forcing Tony and his partner to run after the man with the gun. The street was covered with black ice, and Tony went flying on the icy sidewalk and crashed down on his knees. Gonzalez was trying to reload with his speed loader when he too slipped on the ice. Realizing Gonzalez was not only down but out of ammunition as well, the suspect aimed his gun and ran toward him. Diaz was still down on the sidewalk but somehow managed to fire off a few more rounds, one of which hit the target. The man ran one more block before falling facedown on the sidewalk.

If you ask Tony if there was one incident that has had a lasting impact, he says it was the funeral service for Michael Buczek and Christopher Hoban. "They were both killed in the line of duty in separate incidents in Upper Manhattan on October 18, 1988," Tony remembered. "They died within three hours and three miles of each other.

"Mike Buczek was a rookie. He was only twenty-four, and I think he'd only been married a few months. He was shot in Washington Heights by three drug suspects a little before ten in the evening. Mike and his partner had responded to a call on West 161st in the 34th Precinct. After completing the assignment, the officers noticed some suspicious-looking men loitering near the building. When the cops went over to question them, they ran. As the officers followed them, one of the suspects pulled out a gun and shot Mike in the chest. He died a short time later.

"Chris Hoban was twenty-six. He was assigned to Manhattan North Narcotics. He was making an undercover drug buy when the dealers demanded he use some of the cocaine they were selling him. When he refused, they shot and killed him.

"They had a joint funeral for them in this huge cathedral in Brooklyn. There was the longest motorcade I ever saw in my life. Thousands of law enforcement officers, police cars, and motorcycles were there. Someone told me that every city and town in New Jersey sent police officers to show their respect. When I saw this outpouring, I started to cry. I couldn't control it. I had been on the job for a year and kept thinking about my parents, especially my mother. I knew what it would do to her if I were the person they were burying that day."

* * *

Tony had been married for five years when his marriage started to fall apart. When he looks back, he says his job as a cop was a major reason there were so many problems. "When I met my wife, she was in her early twenties, and I was never home," he said. "After my son and daughter were born, I worked midnights, mostly for the overtime. I slept during the day. When she asked me what we were doing on the weekend, I'd tell her I had to work. If she got really upset, I promised her I'd ask for the day off, but the truth is I never did. I realize now she must have been lonely married to a guy who always wanted to be at work. But back then, I was oblivious to her needs."

Now his children are getting older, and Tony would like to spend more time with them. But he is smart enough to know he can't turn back the clock and make up for the time he lost when they were younger and he was working a lot of hours.

"Gabriella is fifteen. She's inquisitive and curious and takes school seriously. My son Anthony is thirteen and a bundle of energy. He's a phenomenal athlete and is especially good at ice skating. He can make anyone laugh but never wants to do his homework. If he had the choice, he would play all day long. I pick him up and take him to school every morning after I've gone to the gym for a workout. I always give him a hug and kiss and remind him not to give his mother a hard time."

Tony's not sure when he'll retire or what's in store for him after he leaves the NYPD. He knows there are a lot of opportunities, especially in the personal security arena. "I could be a chauffeur or bodyguard for a movie star or a big-time athlete or some corporate mogul, but I have to ask myself, do I really want to do that? Would I be just a highly paid babysitter living someone else's life instead of my own? You drive them around, you bring them to parties, you wait outside. You take them to a clubs, then you take them home and tuck them into bed. I'm not sure that's a very fulfilling life."

He's also exploring the possibility of working for a private investigative firm. But the cases don't have the same interest as the ones he works on now, and he would not have the resources of the New York City Police Department at his disposal. "After what I've been doing here, I don't think I'd find that work rewarding or interesting. A lot of it is pretty seedy, like following around someone who's cheating on his wife."

Whether he stays with the NYPD or finds other work, one thing is certain. Tony will stay in New York. "I love New York City," he says. "There's always something going on, and it is always changing."

While many of his colleagues can't wait to get in their cars and leave the city the minute their shifts are over, Tony has a different take. "I go all over the city, and I love every neighborhood. Recently I went to Buddakan, in the Meatpacking District. The bar is as big as Grand Central Station, and it was jammed with people. It looked like a gigantic Chinese mansion. My buddies and I stayed for an hour. We had a great time.

"I like the people you meet when you're out in this city. One night I started talking to a guy who's been in the United States for only a few years. He started out with nothing, then he had a good idea, found a partner, and now he's a millionaire. Where else could that happen but here?"

Standing in front of scores of "Wanted" posters, Lieutenant Christopher Stahly and Tony in the Manhattan office of the NYPD's Major Case Squad. Major Case detectives investigate bank robberies, high-end burglaries, kidnappings and art thefts. They also assist in investigations when a New York City police officer is killed or injured with criminal intent.

Tony with colleagues from the Major Case Squad. Left to right, Detectives Vincent Chirico, Tony Diaz, Mike Dorto, and Sergeant Alfonso DiStefano. This photo was taken the day the team was hard at work searching for a Massachusetts man who had robbed a bank in Manhattan.

Early days on the job. Clockwise from top, Tony and Brian Ranahan at the Academy. July, 1988, Tony and Officer Kobner on Coney Island. Rookie Officers Borofitz, Volas, Diaz and Sanchez. Graduation day with Rich Miller at St. Johns.

Clockwise, starting at top: Police Academy graduation day – (L to R) Dad Leo, Tony, Mom Gladys, friends of family Lucy and Phillipe; Tony with his children Gabriella and Anthony, Puerto Rico Day Parade, 2000; Tony and Gabriella, at her 8th grade graduation; Anthony before his lacrosse game.

Cases from the Major Case Squad files frequently find their way into the plot lines for films, television dramas, and books. The majority of story lines for one of the most popular television programs in history, *Law and Order: Criminal Intent*, came directly from the NYPD's Major Case Squad files. Here Tony (left) and Mike Dorto (second from left) visit the set. The office digs portrayed on the set of *Law and Order*, shown in the photo below, don't bear much resemblance to the real deal at One Police Plaza.

Chapter Twelve

Stefanie Hirschhorn: She Walks the Walk

"Some people come into our lives, ...
leave footprints on our hearts, and we are
never, ever the same." —Flavia Weedn

Stefanie Hirschhorn and Rolando Aleman were finishing up their pasta primavera at Giovanni's, a popular Italian restaurant up on the Grand Concourse in the Bronx. They had decided to eat right after roll call, which, for cops working in the Street Crime Unit, was held at the start of each tour on Randall's Island, situated in the East River. Like all their colleagues, they knew if they waited until they were into their shift, the opportunity to break away and grab a bite might never come.

Stefanie and her partner were assigned to the NYPD's Street Crime Unit, a special squad of about one hundred plainclothes officers working citywide in neighborhoods plagued with violent crime. Street Crime was a coveted assignment. Only officers with stellar records and lots of arrests made the cut.

The two cops paid their bill, got into their unmarked car, and headed over to the 42nd Precinct to pick up the sergeant who would be riding with them that night.

"In Street Crime we drove unmarked cars," Stefanie explained. "Some were better than others. That night we had one of the worst. I think it was a Dodge Spirit. It had power steering, but the turning radius was horrendous. An eighteen-wheeler could make a U-turn in a smaller space than we could."

As they headed down 149th Street, Stefanie and her partner were in deadstop traffic when scores of marked police cars, sirens blaring, red lights ablaze, raced past them on the wrong side of the road.

"The traffic on our side was completely backed up," she remembered. "We wanted to know what was going on. If cops needs help, the instinctive reaction is to go and help them, but we were trapped."

As Stefanie and Rolando frantically scanned the police radio channels to see what was up, two young men stepped down from the curb and crossed the street directly in front of their car. "We could see both their guns," she said. "It looked like they barely noticed us, and it certainly didn't seem like they had a clue who we were. We looked like any other couple out in our Dodge Spirit."

The officers knew they were at a serious disadvantage stuck in traffic in a clunker. The armed suspects were young, which escalated the danger level considerably. If they chased them on foot, they would be out on the street with no cover.

"Once they crossed the street, we made a U-turn," Stefanie said. "The idea was to pull up in their blind spot. But it didn't work. As we pulled up to the curb behind them, they made us. Even though we were in plainclothes in a beat-up car, they knew we were the police.

"Now things happened fast," she continued. "The suspects ran about ten paces and stopped. One of them yells, 'Pull out. Pull out.' The second guy pulls out a gun, turns, and fires at us. Time stood still except for the long, black tunnel pointed right at me with a ball of fire coming out the end."

"When it's life and death, your brain compresses things," Stefanie confided. "The fear, the tunnel vision, it rules your universe even if it's just for a few seconds. Looking back, I'm not sure I was processing what was really going on, but I did know only one of them was shooting.

"The shooter and his friend took off in opposite directions. My partner jumped out of the car. The shooter ran east, but I was facing west. I had to catch him, but now I have serious tunnel vision. I threw my coffee cup out the window, tried another U-turn, and barely made the swing."

Stefanie pulled her Glock and put her foot to the gas. "As I approached the corner where 149th Street intersects Cortland and 3rd Avenues, I see uniformed officers from the 40th Precinct in the middle of the intersection, using the hoods of their cars for cover, drawing down on me. I called in a 10-13. I've got my gun out the window, and I'm driving fast, trying not to lose sight of the perp. They can't see the police shield around my neck and I don't have a free hand to dangle it out the window. I screamed at them. 'I'm a cop, I'm Street Crime. I'm a cop. Get the guy in the red shirt.'"

Hoping they heard her, Stefanie drove her car around the precinct cops. "It's really crowded right there," she said. "There's a subway station, bodegas, fast-food places, a newsstand, and always a lot of people."

Stefanie's histrionics worked. The cops must have been startled to learn she was one of them. The threat to her life, at least from the uniformed officers, was over. One of the worst disasters in law enforcement, wounding or killing one of your own because you don't know they're a cop, had been averted.

As she made a hard left onto Cortland, there he was. "I'm screaming at him and pointing my gun out the window. 'Knees, motherfucker. Down on the ground now. I will shoot you.' He gave it up. I jumped out of the car, ran over, and ordered him down on the sidewalk. Then I pushed him down on the ground. It was obvious he had been through the drill before."

As soon as the uniformed officers began to arrive, Stefanie asked them to bring the perp and her car back around the corner up to the place she last saw her partner.

She raced back up the street and found Rolando standing in the same place where they had been fired on. He was blocking off the perimeter to make sure no one touched or moved anything until the bosses and crime scene investigators arrived to start their painstaking work.

"An off-duty cop who was out shopping saw the second guy dump his gun in a garbage can," Stefanie said. "When that officer saw the guy mingling with the crowd and watching the scene, she alerted a uniformed cop, and the second perp and his gun were snatched up.

"The adrenaline was raging, so my memory is a little foggy, but I remember having this overwhelming urge to touch my partner. I grabbed him to make sure he was still in one piece. I kept asking him if he was okay."

Once the incident was broadcast over the division radios as a 10-13, every available officer in the area raced to the scene. Eventually Stefanie and her partner were taken to the hospital, standard procedure for officers who have been involved in an incident like this. Even though the doctors and nurses told Stefanie and Rolando to breathe deeply and calm down, it took hours before their adrenaline levels were back to normal. Stefanie's blood pressure is normally low, but when the doctors took a reading, it was high.

They learned the person who had shot at them was fourteen years old. Eventually, the case was plea bargained out, and the boy got three to six years.

"I think he served a third of that," Stefanie recalled. "At his sentencing, the judge told the boy he hoped he'd seen the last of him, but somehow he didn't think he had. The other man was over eighteen but the penalty for him was less. He had removed the clip from his gun, so he was only charged with a misdemeanor because his gun wasn't loaded."

Over the course of her career, Stefanie Hirschhorn has been the recipient of many awards and medals. But without hesitation, she says the Exceptional Merit Award she got for arresting the boy who tried to kill her and her partner is the one she is most proud of.

* * *

Nothing in Stefanie's background indicated she was headed for a job with the New York City Police Department. In fact, a career in law enforcement is the last thing anyone would have predicted.

When she was born, her mother and father were living in New York City. Stefanie's mom, Joyce, was one of the first female stockbrokers in the country, but it was the mid-1960s and too big a world with too many adventures to be worrying about stocks and bonds on Wall Street. Just one month after her second birthday, Stefanie, her sister, and her mom and dad drove to California.

It was a wild life for a young girl. In 1969, when Stefanie was in the first grade, she took a busload of hippies staying at her house to the elementary school for show-and-tell. She rode her first horse on the beach in Malibu.

In 1970 Stefanie's parents separated, and Joyce took her daughters and moved to New Mexico. "We stayed briefly at a commune and then moved to a house in the middle of nowhere outside a town called Truchas," Stefanie recalled. "We had no electricity or running water, but we did have a wood burning stove, a well, and an outhouse. The house was at the end of a dirt road that few cars could navigate. Our nearest neighbor was a goat herder. I remember we traded him my mom's chicken soup for milk."

In the summer of 1972, Stefanie's sister went back to California to live with their dad. Joyce packed up, took eight-year-old Stefanie, and flew to Sweden. From there, mom and daughter crisscrossed Europe and the Middle East. Back and forth they went in a Morris Mini, the 1970s predecessor to today's Mini Cooper. They ended up in Kathmandu in Nepal just in time for Christmas.

Three decades later, Stefanie's memories of Kathmandu are vivid. "I remember the bicycle rickshaw taxis. You'd get into this wobbly carriage, and the driver would pedal you where you needed to go. When we arrived, Mom and I took one from the airport to our hotel. It was up at the top of a steep hill. The driver was an old man, and he was pedaling so hard it looked like his intestines were going to fall out. My mother looked at me and said something about having to get out of the rickshaw. She was worried he was going to die. We were trying to help him, but he went bananas. He started screaming at us. We were emasculating him. We believed we were helping him, but in his society, what we did was very insulting. That was my first cultural sensitivity lesson. Things are different in other places, and you have to learn to respect that."

After Kathmandu, mother and daughter traveled back and forth across two continents. As Stefanie approached her tenth birthday, she and her mom were in Iran. It was about that time that Stefanie broke the news to her mother that she wanted to go to school. "I wanted to be around other kids," she said.

For the first time since first grade, Stefanie found herself in a classroom. She loved everything about the experience even though it was hard to catch up. "I went to the United Nations School in Tehran," she remembered. "It was a crash course for me. I had learned the basics at home from my mom. I guess you could call it some semblance of home schooling. But when I got into the classroom, I struggled mightily with all the foundation things—math, science, reading, grammar."

This was also the time that Stefanie rediscovered horses—something that would become a lifelong passion. "When we got to Iran, I made friends with an American-Iranian family," she said. "They bred and raised Caspian ponies, a rare, almost extinct, miniature horse. I started riding every day."

When Joyce got a job offer in Afghanistan, Stefanie thought her world was ending. "I was going to school, and I had my life," she said. "But I knew our days in Tehran were numbered. I begged her to stay. I had a chance to become an Iranian citizen, which meant I could have been the youngest person and first girl to train for their Olympic equestrian team. That was a pretty exciting thought."

But it was not to be. Within a month, Joyce packed up the car, put eleven-year-old Stefanie in the front and their two Afghan hounds in the back, and began the arduous drive from Tehran to Kabul.

Today both mother and daughter say that of all the places they traveled, Afghanistan is still their favorite. "It was so beautiful there then," Stefanie said. "If you respected their culture, the Afghan people treated you like gold. There was never a time I didn't feel safe."

After almost two very happy years, her mother announced she was going back to the United States. It was 1977, and Stefanie was devastated. "I kicked and screamed and did everything I could to convince her to stay in Kabul. But it was no use. We were going back." Mother, daughter, and their dogs—one adult Afghan hound and seven puppies—flew home to New York City.

After graduating from the United Nations International School four years later, Stefanie headed off to college in Maryland for preveterinary studies. The experience was a total disaster. "I hated early morning lab classes," she said. "The whole experience was a shock for me after all the traveling and going to the United Nations School. After a year there I did not want to return, and they didn't want me either."

Stefanie left school and did a series of odd jobs for the next couple of years before she landed a job as a waitress at Phoebe's on 4th Street. She didn't know that Phoebe's, in addition to having the best wings in the city and being a favorite watering hole for actors performing at La MaMa and the Public Theatre, was also a hangout for police officers.

"Years later I still remember so many of those cops I met when I was a waitress at Phoebe's," she said. "Some became lifelong friends. I was taken with the incredible camaraderie. There was a real closeness between them. Beneath all their nonsense and bullshit, there was a family, there was togetherness. You could feel it. They might not like each other individually, but when push came to shove, they would stand shoulder to shoulder and face whatever was coming. That's what I loved about them. To this day I feel fortunate to have had the opportunity to get to know those cops who came on the job in the 60s and 70s."

When Stefanie got the job at Phoebe's, she was in a very rebellious stage of her life. "I wasn't full punk but close," she said. "I had very short, dyed, jet black hair. I shaved these little wavy, design lines right down to my scalp. At first I wasn't sure what the cops who came to the restaurant thought about me. Mostly I think they found me amusing. One night after I got off work, we were sitting on bar stools drinking when one of the guys looked at me and said, "Hey, you're a crazy East Village liberal. You'd make a good cop."

She was taken aback but intrigued at the same time. She knew almost nothing about law enforcement, but she had seen NYPD officers on horses and thought they looked cool.

She signed up to take the police test in 1986. A week after her twenty-fourth birthday, Stefanie Hirschhorn paid the customary twenty-five cents and took the oath to uphold the Constitution and the laws of the State of New York. It was official. She was a New York City police officer.

* * *

Despite her unstructured childhood, Stefanie had no problem adjusting to the paramilitary culture of the NYPD, with its strict rules and codes of behavior. "I had no problem following orders," she said. "When someone of a higher rank told me to jump, I'd say, 'How high?'"

Her first assignment out of the Academy came as a shock. Officer Hirschhorn was told to report to the 25th Precinct in Harlem for her field training. Stefanie had never been to Harlem, and the only time she had ever heard gunfire was at the Academy range. She had just assumed she would be assigned to work in Lower Manhattan with all the cops she knew.

In New York City, during the first six months, rookie cops alternate between walking a foot post and riding with a field training officer in a car. "When you walked a beat, you had a partner who was on the opposite side of the street," she recalled. "Sometimes a small group of us would gather together. Within no time, a supervisor would come by and tell us to separate. No sooner had we split up when another supervisor would come by to sign our memo books. He would say something about safety in numbers and order us to stay together. We laugh about it now. We were like psychotic children."

Every rookie has stories about the cops who take pleasure teaching the new kids about police work. "I'll never forget this one crusty sergeant," Stefanie recalls, her face breaking into a grin. "If you were a woman, you were told you had to keep your hair up. I tried, but my ponytail would fall out. This sergeant had this deep, raspy voice. One time he came up to me and barked, 'Hey, kid, somebody is going to grab that ponytail hanging down out of your hat and swing your little ninety-eight pounds around like a pom-pom.' I remember thinking, 'Oh, shit. He is saying something important.' He created a picture for me—a visual image—and it got the lesson through. It had to be learned, and I learned it."

Rookie blunders are expected. Unfortunately for Stefanie, one of hers was broadcast over the radio to several neighboring precincts. "We were on a foot post, and out of nowhere we heard a sound ripple through the air. It sounded like *ba-ba, ba-ba, ba-ba*. I had seen some kids playing with firecrackers on a side street a short time earlier. When the report came over the radio of shots fired, I went on the air and announced that everyone should be advised no shots had been fired. It was just kids playing with firecrackers. Right after I made the broadcast, a precinct sergeant gets on the air. He's screaming, '10-85, 10-85, 10-85. I've got multiple people shot. Get me some help.' Later, back at the station, he wants to know who said it was just kids with firecrackers. Never one to be shy, I said, 'That would be me, sir,' and I put my hand out to shake his."

Every cop in America knows what happened next. The next day there were hundreds of Chinese firecrackers stuffed in her locker. For months every time she went on the radio, she could count on someone calling back, "What's up, Firecrackers?" If she called something in, someone would always say, "Oh, that must be Firecrackers."

After six months learning the ropes with field training officers, Stefanie got her first assignment. She would be staying in the 2-5 in Harlem. She worked there from 1989 to 1994, five years of hustling from one call to the next. One of her worst memories was the time that she and her partner were handed a blue baby who had stopped breathing.

"We were in a building responding to a 911 call for an emotionally disturbed teen," she recalled. "The elevator opened on the wrong floor. Standing there was a group of totally distraught people. A woman handed us a baby. He was blue and lifeless. I held the infant while my partner got on the radio. We were lucky we had emergency medical personnel with us in the elevator. My partner told the operator to clear the streets and get the hospital ready. We were coming through with a baby who was not breathing."

Their mission was complicated by the fact the police were not looked on favorably in this particular building. Someone heaved a sixty-four-ounce soda bottle from an upper floor of the building, hitting an officer who was trying to clear the street so the fire department with their oxygen tanks could get in. The bottle slammed into his cap device, a metal shield that's pinned to the front of a police officer's hat. The cop was knocked out cold, but miraculously he had no brain damage. His doctors said later they were sure the shield on his hat saved his life.

"That kind of hostility was not unusual," Stefanie explains. "For some people, if you catch them breaking the law, you are stomping on their liberties. They see the police as people who are preventing them from doing what they want to do by issuing them a ticket, arresting them, or whatever, and they get angry. If they are victims, you show up with too little, too late. You didn't help them when they needed you. They are already traumatized, and you weren't there to stop it."

During her time in the 25th Precinct, Stefanie responded to hundreds of calls for domestic disputes, every one of them different and disturbing. One incident came over the radio as a "clothes job"—when someone asks the police to escort them to their former residence so they can remove their personal belongings without being harmed.

"It was winter," she recalled. "We arrived at the apartment building and went into the lobby. The man who called us was waiting there, and he was soaking wet. He was very soft-spoken. We asked him to tell us what happened, but he wasn't talking. He said he just wanted to get some things from the apartment. When we asked him to lift up his shirt, you could see he had been scalded with something very hot. His skin was falling off. He finally admitted that his wife had thrown a pot of boiling water at him."

The cops called for an ambulance, and once the man was on his way to the hospital, Stefanie and her partner paid the wife a visit. They took the elevator to the tenth floor.

"We were surprised when she opened the door," Stefanie said. "She was small, I would guess under 110 pounds. She was pretty forthright about what she had done, which in our opinion was to almost kill her husband. 'I told him to stop screwing around without condoms,' she told us. 'Well, he kept screwing around, and he didn't use condoms, so I boiled a pot of water and threw it on him.'

"There were kids there," Stefanie added. "Fortunately, her sister lived with them, so the children had someone to watch them. We told her to take her off jewelry and put on a pair of shoes. She was coming with us. They had a very nice home. Everything was neat and clean, and she was well dressed. When you're a cop, you learn pretty fast that money has nothing to do with class or people's propensity for violence.

"We took her to jail. Sometime later I got called down to the court after the couple had gone through mediation and counseling. The judge wanted to dismiss the charges against her. It was one of the rare times during my law enforcement career that a judge asked me if I had any objections. I told him no. One of the weird things about being a cop is that you never know what happens to these people. Hopefully they worked it out."

One incident Stefanie remembers was like a scene out of a horror movie. "We got a call to go to an apartment," she recalled. "I can't remember exactly what it was about, some sort of disturbance. An elderly woman let us in. A naked woman was standing at the top of the stairs bleeding like a geyser. The blood is gushing down the stairs to the first floor. Cops never want to come into direct contact with blood. We're paranoid about getting any bodily fluids on us. We found a closet with sheets and towels. We started wrapping her in the sheets, but they were totally soaked in less than a minute. There was so much blood you couldn't tell where the wounds were."

The older woman who had answered the door was the bleeding woman's mother-in-law. Her son was married to the victim. He was serving with the Army in the first Gulf War. The mother-in-law told Stefanie and her partner that she had had a dream. In the dream, her daughter-in-law was betraying her husband by having sexual relations with the older woman's husband. When she woke up, she went into the kitchen, got a meat cleaver, and attacked her while she was sleeping.

"I was calling on the radio for an ambulance," Stefanie recalled. "They told me there would be a long delay. I yelled, 'She's going to die. She is going to die. She is going to die.'"

Once the ambulance arrived and took the bleeding woman to the hospital, they handcuffed the older woman. When they searched the apartment, they found a baby sleeping in a crib. There was blood all over the room, but thankfully the baby was unharmed. The older woman was arrested and sent for a psychiatric evaluation. "I have no idea what happened to her," Stefanie said. "Her daughter-in-law survived, but she was in bad shape. She needed several transfusions and surgeries to repair the damage."

If you ask Stefanie how she copes with horrific events like this, she shrugs. "You go into a zone. You train yourself to keep your distance. Cops know how this works, but it's hard to explain to someone who has never done police work."

* * *

Stefanie was involved in two shooting incidents during her twenty years with the NYPD. The first was the night she was working with Rolando when the fourteen-year-old tried to kill them. She was still assigned to Street Crime the second time the rounds started flying in her direction.

"There were three of us—me, Jimmy Kelly, and Steve Hofmann," Stefanie recalled. "I loved working with those guys. They were fabulous cops. We were sitting in an unmarked car on Amsterdam up in the 30th Precinct in Harlem when a man walked toward our car. There was something about him. All three of us were immediately suspicious. He spoke to us while we were still in the car. When we got out, he pulled a gun out of his waistband, pointed it at us, and ran. We chased him. I pulled my gun out and was running as fast as I could down the middle of the street.

"When shots rang out, I tried to find cover. Jimmy and Steve returned fire. When there was a lull in the shooting, I ran down to the end of the block. There was a young couple in a car there, chatting and kissing. Who knows what they thought when they saw the three us with our firearms out, yelling outside their car. Once our perpetrator was in custody, I start banging on their window asking if they were okay. I didn't think they were shot, but I didn't know if they were okay, either.

"Later, in court, the suspect testified that I kicked him and shot him. The defense attorney asked me, 'Officer Hirschhorn, did you kick him?' 'Yes, I did,' I said. When he asked me why I kicked him, I said it was because he wouldn't bring his hands out from under him, and I had no idea whether or not he still had the gun. He was turned over to authorities in New Jersey, where he had a felony drug charge pending that would keep him in jail longer than the gun possession and menacing charges he was facing in the state of New York."

Stefanie Hirschhorn was fortunate. In her two decades of service, she managed to escape serious injury. Some of her colleagues were not so lucky. "It was March 2001," she said. "I had just been promoted to sergeant when a frantic call came in over the radio. 'Shots fired. 10-13. Shots fired.'"

The location was near the precinct. On their way to that call, another 10-13 came in, and Stefanie knew by the sound of the officer's voice that something was terribly wrong. Every available police car raced to the scene.

"Two officers in my squad got injured racing to that call," Stefanie said. "One of the cops had her arm out the window when the car crashed. The car rolled over on her arm, and it was crushed. When we got there, the police car was upside down, and an emergency medical team was struggling to pull her out. It was a horrible sight. You could see there was nothing left to her arm. It was totally mangled."

"The trip to the hospital was surreal," she continued. "The Major Deegan, Triborough Bridge, and FDR Drive were all closed for the motorcade to get an injured comrade the proper medical care. She went through a tremendous number of surgeries. She had skin grafts and bone grafts. She was in the hospital for weeks. We all knew she wanted to come back to work, but at some point she had to accept the fact that her career as a police officer was over."

* * *

In 1994, Stefanie Hirschhorn was chosen for Street Crime. When she applied, she thought it was a long shot. "The only thing I had in my favor was a good arrest record," she said. "I arrested anybody who was violating the law."

Her first day at Street Crime, a sergeant called a meeting and told the newcomers in the unit that they we were responsible for stopping violent crime in New York City. It was up to them to get guns off the street and stop armed robberies.

In 1997, when a serial rapist robbed and raped twenty-nine women in the

Bronx, Manhattan, and Westchester County, Stefanie was assigned to a Rape Task Force set up to catch the rapist.

"I learned so much working on that case," she said. "Mostly I became familiar with the utterly unglamorous parts of police work. I was fortunate that the detectives on the Task Force were so knowledgeable and that they were willing to teach me. It was totally different work from what I had been doing, and I got to appreciate why it's so important. The background searches were especially tedious. We had to pore over thousands of records looking for possible suspects. That's hard work. Once we determined that an individual had been incarcerated on the dates of any of the attacks, he was eliminated.

"This man raped twenty-nine women. For each victim, we had to check out everyone they were associated with—boyfriends, ex-boyfriends, spouses, ex-spouses, neighbors, family members, coworkers, employers. We'd map out the area around each victim's residence, and then we'd check everyone who lived there to see if they had a record or had been arrested for a sex crime."

Stefanie worked with the Task Force for six months. She will never forget the day they made the hit. "He got his girlfriend to pawn the jewelry he'd stolen from his victims," she remembered. "That's how he got caught in the end. The DNA evidence was irrefutable. They had him."

Before sentencing Isaac Jones to 155 years in prison, the judge, Joseph Fisch, rose up and looked directly at Jones. "Isaac Jones," he said, "you are a vicious, violent, and brutal creature, without remorse, contrition, or regret. You blame everyone but yourself—the police, the press, the district attorney, and you refuse to accept responsibility for your dastardly crimes."

The judge called the assaults "bestial" and described Jones as a relentless stalker who took glee in humiliating women and inflicting pain. "You drove around in the early hours of the morning, in the stealth of darkness as cowards are wont to do, armed with a variety of weapons and disguises. One victim was five months pregnant. You have destroyed lives, uprooted homes, and traumatized an entire community."

It was Stefanie's time with the Rape Task Force that convinced her that having a statute of limitations for a crime like rape is absurd. "I don't care how much time has gone by," she says. "Whether it is twenty years or thirty years, the person who was sexually assaulted deserves to see their assailant caught and punished for their attack. People who think we should forget about a rape because a certain amount of time has passed should read *Un-*

finished Murder. It's a story about one of country's most prolific rapists. You read this book and you understand how horrible the crime of rape really is and the lasting torment it leaves behind."

Many years later, Stefanie still views her time working on that investigation as a peak experience. "I got to work with these incredible people. Watching their patience, perseverance, and attention to detail, I learned what it takes to be a great detective.

* * *

From the Rape Task Force, Stefanie was assigned to the 43rd Precinct's Robbery Apprehension Team. From there it was on to the Bronx Robbery Squad. "In Bronx Robbery, again I had the good fortune to work with great people, and I learned so much. In March 2001 I was promoted to sergeant and went to the 44th Precinct. That place never slows down for a minute. I knew that after a long hiatus off of patrol, I had to relearn everything quickly. The cops there helped me out. They were and are great people. After three years in one of the greatest commands in the NYPD, I went to the Bronx Task Force, where I worked for two years."

When Stefanie was accepted into the Mounted Unit, it gave her a chance to get back to her lifelong passion, horses. It had been years since she had ridden horses regularly, and she missed it. "When I realized I was going to get paid to ride a horse in New York City for the Police Department, I thought I had died and gone to heaven."

By that time Stefanie had married Michael Mount, an officer assigned to the Emergency Service Unit. "It was a big joke among my friends and coworkers that the only reason I got the assignment was because of my last name. People routinely hung up on me when I answered the phone at work, 'Sergeant Mount. Mounted.'

"It was pretty cold work in the winter," she recalled, "If you get into a situation and you can't pull the trigger because your hands are so cold that your fingers can't move, that's bad. But unless it was dangerously cold, our job was to be out there riding our horses."

NYPD horses hold a special place in the hearts of New Yorkers. They usually lead all the big parades and have been fixtures for decades at major events like opening day at Yankee Stadium and Times Square on New Year's Eve. The NYPD spends around $4,000 for each gelding. For every four horses purchased, usually just one will be cut out for police work. The ones that don't make the grade get returned to the seller.

The NYPD trains its horses in Pelham Bay Park in the Bronx. Because horses are prey animals, they are naturally skittish, and it takes upward of six months to prepare them for law enforcement work.

"You've got to train them diligently so that everything becomes a habit," Stefanie says. "When the shit hits the fan, the horse will remember the habit, but that takes a lot of yielding and ring work in addition to getting them used to the streets. When a horse is in Times Square and has to squeeze by a forty-foot crane, whoever is in the saddle has to be in charge. Otherwise the horse might balk. He might not go through. Even worse, he might run."

Day after day, police horses in training face an onslaught of smoke bombs, clanging metal pots, hissing flares, and blanks fired close by. With their riders, they spend weeks moving over tarps and marching against would-be demonstrators. All of this nuisance training pays off. Law enforcement agencies know there is nothing like a ten-foot cop, atop a thousand-pound animal to convince the mischief-minded the error of their ways.

"The NYPD Mounted Unit is the oldest and largest in the United States," Stefanie says. "There is a huge historical significance there. Even more important is that a good cop on a horse is worth ten on the ground."

* * *

Stefanie is blunt when it comes to the things she found frustrating about her life as a police officer. "We are all frustrated with the media," she says. "When we have to take a life to protect our own or someone else's, why do reporters always bring up race? A comprehensive study found that white officers respond in the same way as minority officers when confronted with a situation where lethal force is called for. But nobody working for a television station or a newspaper seems to have read it. Any time there is an incident with a white police officer and a black suspect, the media accuses us of acting out racial prejudice rather than dealing with the situation at hand. Police officers are trying to stop problems, and we are a very diverse group, yet the media portrays us like we're all a gang of white cops preying on innocent minorities.

"When I worked in the 2-5 in Harlem, we had the number one angel dust building in the city. When the white boys from New Jersey drove in to buy their fix, they did not get treated well by the police. If they were white and they were from New Jersey, we assumed they were there for one reason. We racially profiled them. Did anyone scream about that?

"Angel dust has a strange smell and causes bizarre behavior. If we saw someone trying to swim in the middle of the street in winter with no clothes on and generally acting out of his mind, we knew it was PCP. If these druggies saw us coming, they would dump the packet of PCP in the car, where it disappeared in the carpeting. If we couldn't catch them with the drugs, often we wrote them up them up for a moving violation. We'd write 'drug-prone location' on the side of the summons, hoping their parents would see it and realize their kids were coming into New York City to buy narcotics."

Stefanie is also offended by the endless stories about corrupt cops. "I understand that tales about rogue cops sell newspapers, but the media has us under a microscope, and most of these stories are blown way out of proportion. I remember one situation. We started calling it Ice Cream Gate. A cop orders an ice cream, and the girl behind the counter gives her two scoops but only charges her for one. Standing behind her is someone who works for the District Attorney's office. This person calls the Department and reports they witnessed an officer getting free ice cream. Some reporter gets the story, and now the NYPD starts an investigation. A Chief, who will be forever known as Chief Two Scoops, begins his inquiry. Even though it was winter, they watched the ice cream shop for six months."

Another frustration for Stefanie is liberal judges, the ones who set criminals free so they can rape, pillage, or kill again. "When I was working in Harlem, we had one case that still bothers me," she said. "Two adults and one juvenile were driving around in a stolen car, shooting out the window. We arrested all three of them. When we went before the judge, we begged him to put the younger one into the system as well. It was obvious that the kid had no adult supervision of value and no conscience.

"We pleaded with the judge. 'Take the boy. Put him in the system even if it's just for a few months.' We thought it would teach him a lesson. The judge refused. A few months later we saw his face on a wanted poster. He had killed someone for a leather jacket. When you see something like that, it's hard not to be angry.

"Most people don't remember the victims, but the cops do. We are there to see firsthand the heartbreaking aftermath, the terrible toll that violent crime takes on victims. I like to say, instead of *Dancing with the Stars*, if they did a reality show where you showed what happened to these crime victims, what these predators did to them, even people who think they're against the death penalty would be lining up to pull the trigger. They would be clamoring for justice for the victim."

Stefanie Hirschhorn has been a longtime proponent of the death penalty, but she believes the policy has been a failure because of the way it's carried out. "First, you need proof positive the person did the crime," she said. "Executing someone you later discover is innocent is not acceptable. If the death penalty is deemed warranted, it has to be carried out only when there is no doubt about the person's guilt. And it has to be done in a timely manner. It can't be twenty-five years later. By then the victims have been forgotten. Just look at the Daniel Faulkner case in Philadelphia. That poor family has gone through hell since 1981, when Danny was killed. Meanwhile, Mumia Abu-Jamal, the man who killed him, is a celebrity. It makes me sick."

* * *

What Stefanie liked most about being a cop is obvious. "The camaraderie," she says, "and the joy of working with people you love and those rare occasions when you make a positive difference in someone's life." Her affection for cops began when she was a waitress at Phoebe's. "It just grew from there," she said. "The police world is an amazing thing, and I feel blessed I'm a part of it. You make friends, you don't see them for twenty years, then you run into them, and it's like no time has gone by."

The close relationships make line-of-duty deaths particularly traumatic. "When it's in your own command, it's losing someone in your own family," she says.

Stefanie was in Street Crime when one of her coworkers was killed. Years have gone by, but she says she is sure everyone who knew and worked with Kevin Gillespie remembers exactly where they were and what they were doing when they heard the news that he had been shot.

It was around nine in the evening on March 14, 1996. Kevin and his partner that night, John McGreal, were patrolling in the Bronx when they pulled over a BMW that had been carjacked. When the officers got out of their car, several men in the BMW jumped out of theirs. They all were armed. Angel Diaz began firing a 9 mm handgun at the cops. One bullet hit Kevin in the shoulder, just above his vest. The autopsy revealed that the round went straight down his body.

John chased the suspects down the Grand Concourse, all the while exchanging gunfire. Two off-duty officers on their way to work rushed to help, and one of them was shot in the neck. A forty-year-old woman and two fourteen-year-old boys were also wounded. A search of the area by NYPD bloodhounds and scores of Emergency Service officers continued into the morning until the suspects were all in custody.

The men who took Kevin's life were members of a violent street gang known as the Park Avenue Boys. Even though they did not fire the gun that killed Kevin Gillespie, Ricardo Morales and Jesus Mendez were convicted of multiple counts of racketeering and two murders. They are serving life sentences without possibility of parole. The man who shot Kevin Gillespie, Angel Diaz, was charged with capital murder. He hanged himself in his prison cell on September 5, 1996.

"Kevin had just turned thirty-four, and his sons were young," Stefanie said. "The feelings are hard to explain to someone who's not a cop, but the grief and sadness are always with you. Kevin's dying didn't make me afraid to do my job, but it changed me forever. Over and over you keep asking yourself, Why weren't you there to help? Why didn't he wait for us to get there? Why didn't the bullet hit his vest? Why? Why? Why?

"What it does to the families is indescribable. They are the brave ones who have to go on. They get no privacy to mourn, which from my perspective is a double-edged sword."

Stefanie remembers Kevin's funeral. "There was a moment I will never forget," she said. "I was with Kevin's family in a limousine, driving to the church for the funeral. We had the windows in the back seat of the limousine rolled down. One of his two young sons pointed out the window at all the officers lined up along the street. 'Look at all the polie-cops who love my daddy,' he said. I will never forget that he couldn't pronounce the word 'police.' He started counting them as we passed. It was heartbreaking. Out of the blue, that four-year-old boy asked our PBA delegate, 'Were you there when my daddy got killed?' Did my daddy get shot right here?' He was pointing at his heart.

"When someone close to you dies, you are forced to confront the tenuous nature of life," Stefanie continued. "The reality that death can happen at any time makes you realize that if there's something you want to do, you better do it. This experience makes people who know they should be getting divorced, get divorced. People who are stagnant in their lives stop being stagnant. You learn the lesson that life is short and that you'd better get going and live it. And if you don't, shame on you."

* * *

On the morning of September 11, 2001, Stefanie was home in bed up in Westchester County. She had a 103° temperature. Her doctor had prescribed antibiotics, and she was drifting in and out of sleep when her phone rang. It was a cop from her precinct. She told Stefanie a plane had crashed into the World Trade Center. "I thought it was a bad joke, and I expressed my displeasure. Then I turned on the television."

She sat there dumbfounded as she looked at the rapidly transpiring events on her television screen. She tried to call her brother in California to tell him she was okay. Then she called her doctor and told him she was going to work. Despite his protestations, she got her pills and drove into the city.

"I was coming down the Thruway in Yonkers, and I saw the cloud," she said. "That will always be a frozen moment for me."

What transpired during the days following the attacks is confused in her mind, and Stefanie is not quite sure when she learned that fellow officer and close friend, Steve Driscoll, was missing. It might have been September 11, it might have been a couple days after. She was in the 44th Precinct up on the second floor when someone called with the news. She remembers her whole body shaking. She cried out, "No. It cannot be. We'll find him. He found a little air pocket to crawl into. I know Steve. I know we are going to find him. I know he'll be safe." She slid down the wall in the hall, laid her head down on her knees, and sobbed.

* * *

When you ask Stefanie if she felt uncomfortable being a female in the alpha-male world of law enforcement, she says no but does admit there were tough moments. "Everyone has prejudices," she said. "But as one sergeant used to say, when cops come to work, they'd better leave those biases in their lockers."

"I never wanted to be recognized as a good female cop. Being remembered as a good cop is enough for me. I steadfastly refused to join the Police

Women's Endowment Association. I've never believed in that kind of thing."

The most dramatic demonstration of tension between the sexes that she remembers erupted in her command after a police officer was killed serving a warrant in Brooklyn. His partner was a woman. Despite the fact that the slain officer's partner had an outstanding reputation and was known by everyone as a great cop, the *New York Post* ran an editorial conjecturing that the officer might still be alive if his partner had been a man.

"When that editorial appeared, everyone went berserk," Stefanie said. "The union came out and lambasted the paper. The Department did as well. But that didn't stop some idiot in our unit from making copies and putting them up all over the command. The word spread pretty fast. It was a supervisor who did it. The good news is they didn't stay up for long. Someone ripped them all down, tore them up, and dumped them into his locker.

"The next day, he accused me of tearing them down. Another female officer was standing there watching. Years earlier she had been forced to shoot someone to protect herself and her partner. Before she killed the suspect, he broke her breastbone. She walked the walk, as they say. When she heard this man accuse me of tearing down the articles, she walked over. He was a higher rank, but she didn't care. 'I fucking tore them down and stuffed them in your locker,' she told him. 'You have anything to say?' He looked scared, and now I got fired up. I got right in his face. I said, 'Let me tell you something. You don't sign my paycheck, and you don't ride in a car with me, so I don't give a flying fuck what you think. But let me tell you, no cop has ever gotten hurt physically working with me, and no cop has ever gotten hurt jobwise working with me. So stick it up your ass.' It was rare for me to act like that."

"If people have prejudices, whether they are racist or sexist, you are not going to change their opinions by screaming and hollering. You cannot go stomping your feet and banging your head hoping to force people not to be prejudiced. That is a sure way to fail if you are trying to change behavior. But if you work side by side, maybe you'll end up saving their life. For cops who believe women can't do police work, that's the only thing that will change their mind. Other than that, I say ignoring them is the best option."

* * *

When Stefanie retired after twenty-one years with the NYPD, a big crowd showed up at Frankie and Johnny's Pine Tavern in the Bronx to celebrate. The speeches went on for over an hour. One by one her colleagues and bosses took the microphone and talked about what a privilege it had been to work with her.

"I was in tears," she said. "I remember feeling that if I died right then, I would die rich surrounded by the greatest people on this Earth. We all have to ask ourselves, as human beings, what is our legacy? Your legacy is your family, your work, and your reputation. It's everything you did and, more importantly, how you did it. I knew that night, listening to my friends talk, that I had a legacy.

"When it was my turn to speak, I talked about what I felt my job was as a sergeant. I believed in protecting the officers under me. That sergeants are the ones who stand between the cops and harm's way. I spoke about the importance of not forgetting your roots, that even with all the great jobs I'd had, I truly believe patrol is the heart and soul of a police department. They are everything to the organization, and that is the job that's the hardest to master."

Stefanie has been retired for only two years, but there is a lot she misses. "I miss the horses and the riding," she says. "I miss my friends, and I miss my cops. I just hope I was able to pass on the fabulous lessons I learned from all the great cops I met along the way."

Sergeant Hirschhorn, 2006. "The police world is an amazing thing," she says, "and I feel blessed I'm a part of it. You make friends, you don't see them for twenty years, then you run into each other and it's like no time has gone by. The close relationships make line of duty deaths particularly traumatic. When it's in your own command, it's like losing someone in your own family."

Above, Stefanie (third from right) with other members of the NYPD Mounted Unit. When Stefanie realized she was going to get paid to ride a horse for the New York City Police Department, she thought she had died and gone to heaven. At right, Steffanie Hirschhorn at Yankee Stadium.

Stefanie was born in New York City. By the time she was ten she was living with her Mom in Tehran. That was when she went to school for the first time and rekindled her interest in horses. Below, riding on the beach in Ireland.

Stefanie's roots in New York City go way back. This photo of Stefanie's grandmother, Selma (left), was taken in 1918 at the tennis courts in Harlem on 148th St. and St. Nicholas Avenue.

At right, December 1971, Stef and her Mom, Joyce, in New Mexico. Below, Joyce and stepfather Tom Hard, on the day Stefanie was promoted to detective in 1999.

Stefanie with her son, Steven on police horse, Dizzie.

• • • •

"We have to ask ourselves, as human beings, what is our legacy? Your legacy is your family, your work, and your reputation. It's everything you did and more importantly how you did it. I knew that night, listening to my friends talk, that I had a legacy. Later, I spoke about my job as a sergeant – that I believed in protecting the officers under me, that sergeants are the ones who stand between the cops and harm's way. Even with all the great jobs I had, I truly believe patrol is the heart and soul of a police department. They are everything to the organization and that is the job that's the hardest to master."

– Stefanie Hirschhorn

Chapter Thirteen

JOE HERBERT: Supersleuth

"Love cannot be attained ... without true humility, courage, faith, and discipline. In a culture in which these qualities are rare, the attainment of the capacity to love must remain a rare achievement." —Erich Fromm

On November 17, 1989, a handwritten letter arrived at the NYPD's 75th Precinct. It was addressed to the 75 Anti-Crime Unit and contained a large circle with lines divided into sections representing the signs of the Zodiac. Scribbled over the sign of Taurus were the words, "The first sign is dead."

Underneath the sign, the note read:

This is the Zodiac.
The First Sign is dead.
The Zodiac will Kill the twelve signs in the
Belt when the Zodiacal light is seen

The Zodiac will spread fear
I have seen a lot of police in Jamaica Ave and Elden Lane
but you are no good and will not get the Zodiac.
Orion is the one that can stop Zodiac and the Seven Sister

Detectives in the busy precinct checked open cases to see if there was a connection, but nothing came up. Hundreds of letters are sent to the NYPD every day. Most of them come from harmless crackpots. There was no way for the police to know this letter wasn't written by one of them.

The first victim was shot at three in the morning on March 9, 1990, four months after the letter arrived at the police station in Brooklyn. Mario Orozco, a forty-nine-year old man, was on his way home, using his wooden cane for balance, after finishing up at a local restaurant where he worked as a dishwasher. The shooter emerged from the shadows of the cemetery clutching a 9 mm zip gun under his coat. He came up on Orozco from behind, pressed the gun into his back, and fired a single shot. Orozco survived, but surgeons were unable to remove the bullet that lodged near his spine.

Twenty-one days later, Jermaine Montenesedro was staggering down the street after a night of heavy drinking. As he was trying to decide whether to go up to the Bronx and stay with his girlfriend or walk over to his father's nearby apartment, a single round tore into his lower back and ripped through his liver. He collapsed on the street. It was six blocks away from the Orozco shooting.

Like Mario Orozco, Jermaine Montenesedro recovered from his wounds, but the Zodiac was getting better at his work. The next victim did not fare as well.

On May 31, 1990, Joseph Proce, an elderly World War II combat veteran in the early stages of dementia, was taking his usual walk in the Woodhaven section of Queens. It was a little after midnight when a man came out of the shadows. As the round tore into his back and kidney, Joe Proce dropped like a stone. Before the gunman fled into the inky night, he left a note under some rocks near the old man's body. A hastily drawn cross was put on top of a star. "Zodiac. Time to die." Joe Proce died three weeks later.

There was no reason for the police to suspect that the Orozco, Montenesedro, and Proce attacks were connected. Orozco and Montenesedro were shot within blocks of each other, but in 1990, the 75th Precinct in East Brooklyn had one of the highest rates of violent crime in the city. Murders and armed assaults were common in the neighborhood some called "the killing fields." It was impossible to know that this was the beginning of New York City's most terrifying crime spree since Son of Sam killed six and wounded seven in the mid-1970s.

On June 6, one week after Joseph Proce was shot, identical handwritten letters were mailed to the *New York Post* and the CBS news program *60 Minutes*. "This is the Zodiac. No more games pigs. The 12 signs will die when the belts in the heaven are seen. The first sign is dead on March 8. The second sign is dead on March 29. The third sign is dead on May 31."

Each letter was signed with a cross, a circle, and three pie-shaped wedges marked with Gemini, Taurus, and Scorpio symbols, three of the twelve signs of the Zodiac.

"Riddle of the Zodiac Shooter" blared in huge headline type on page one. The story caught on like a wildfire. Reporters began to wonder if the California Zodiac, a serial killer who claimed to have killed thirty-seven people over several decades, had moved to New York City. It seemed every time New Yorkers turned on the television, another expert on astrology was the guest. Fear rippled through the city like a bad strain of the flu.

Once detectives with the 75th Precinct Detective Squad realized the letters to *60 Minutes* and the *Post* were eerily similar to the note left by the body of Joseph Proce, they pored through the records searching for people who were murdered on the dates of March 8, March 29, and May 31. Proce came up on May 31, but there were no homicides on March 8 or March 29. When they broadened the search to include people who were shot on those dates but survived, they learned a man named Mario Orozco was wounded on March 8 and Jermaine Montenesdro on March 29. The detectives knew they were on to something when they discovered that Orozco and Montenesdro, like Proce, were all shot from the rear without warning. When they checked the victims' birth dates, excitement must have given way to panic as they realized Orozco was a Gemini, Montenesdro a Taurus, and Proce a Scorpio. With three down, there were nine to go.

New York City had a serial killer on the loose.

The Department assigned fifty of their top investigators to find the killer. Dubbed Operation Watchdog, it was the largest NYPD task force since the hunt for Son of Sam beginning in July 1976 until his arrest in August 1977. The fifty detectives did nothing else for the next nine months but work on this case.

One of the first things the detectives did was contact the San Francisco Police Department to learn more about the Bay Area Zodiac. Soon they were knee-deep in thousands of documents collected over decades by their colleagues on the West Coast. To this day no one is sure how many people the California Zodiac killed. The case has never been solved. Over 2,500 suspects were questioned. At several points police were confident they had identified the killer, but the evidence was not conclusive enough to convince the court to issue a warrant.

NYPD investigators read and reread everything they could find on the Orozco, Montenesdro, and Proce shootings. They studied the research on serial killers, got a crash course on the occult, and searched for a pattern.

The pattern indicated the Zodiac would strike again on Thursday morning, June 21, twenty-one days after the Joe Proce shooting. On June 20, the NYPD flooded East New York with cops, but the Zodiac was not in Brooklyn. He was uptown in Central Park.

As darkness settled on Frederick Law Olmstead's magnificent 843-acre park in the heart of Manhattan, a homeless man named Larry Parham found a bench, arranged some blankets, and tucked his wallet inside his sneaker. He never noticed the man staring from a nearby bench.

When the killer was sure Parham was asleep, he walked over and looked through his wallet before putting it back in the sneaker. He never touched the $49 in cash. Before disappearing into the night, he turned, aimed, and fired a single shot at Larry Parham's chest. The bullet barely missed his aorta on its way through his right armpit.

A note, weighted down with stones, was left near the bench. In the fourth section of a pie, the author had drawn a circle with a sketch of a crab—the sign of Cancer—in the center. Responding officers used extreme care not to touch the letter when they removed it from the scene. That enabled detectives to lift a partial eight-point fingerprint from the document, evidence that later identified the killer.

Larry Parham was the Zodiac's fourth victim. He was a Cancer. He survived.

The next morning another letter was delivered to the *New York Post*. Along with the same ramblings, the writer was trying his best to convince his readers he was the California Zodiac.

The following day the *Post* ran the story. People were terrified, and the Police Department was under enormous pressure. No matter how bizarre or outlandish, detectives followed up every lead.

Then the attacks stopped. When four months passed with nothing from the Zodiac, Operation Watchdog ceased operations and the detectives returned to their precincts.

* * *

On August 10, 1992, after a two-year hiatus, he struck again.

The Zodiac found Patricia Fonti in Highland Park, a weed-infested open space with a body of water the city once used as a city reservoir. He shot her once with his zip gun, but when she fought back, he used a knife. Her body was found several hours later propped up against a fence that bordered a bridge.

Patricia Fonti was stabbed more than one hundred times. She was a Leo.

On June 4, 1993, almost one year after Patricia Fonti was shot and stabbed, Jim Weber, a forty-year-old unemployed construction worker, walked by Highland Park on his way home. A man clad in a dark sweatshirt and pants with a bandana placed partially over his face moved in quickly from behind. He aimed and fired one shot.

Jim Weber, a Libra, survived.

Over the next four months, the Zodiac shot two more people. On June 20, a forty-year-old mental patient named Joseph Diacone was shot in the neck at point-blank range just outside of Highland Park. Mortally wounded, he died before the ambulance could get him to the hospital.

Joseph Diacone was a Virgo.

On October 2, 1993, Diane Ballard was sitting on a bench in Highland Park when a man approached her from behind. He shot her once in the neck. The bullet, which surgeons were unable to remove, missed her major arteries on its path toward her spine. She survived but never recovered from the painful nerve damage in her back and neck.

Diane Ballard was a Taurus.

* * *

In the early 1990s, New York City, home to eight million people, was averaging five homicides a day. Without some evidence that these shootings fit a pattern, it was only natural for the police to assume they were random acts of violence.

The first four Zodiac shootings in 1990 all occurred on Thursdays, but Fonti, Weber, Diacone, and Ballard were shot on other days of the week. And after Larry Parham was wounded, no notes were found by the victims or sent to television programs or newspapers. But the police were well aware the killer might be trying to throw them off the scent by changing the pattern.

On August 4, 1994, a letter was delivered to the *New York Post*. It started out with the ominous message: "I'm back. Sleep my little dead how we lothe them."

The sender had drawn a strange totem pole code. There was a list of dates, each of which was followed by a short description. "Female white shoot and stab in Highland Park. Male white shot 1 times in back in Highland Park. Female black, shot 1 time in neck Highland Park." It was signed, "The Zodiac."

The *Post* ran the story on page one. Once again, the city was gripped with fear.

The NYPD quickly assembled its second Zodiac Task Force, calling in thirty of their most experienced investigators, including Sergeant Joe Herbert, a soft-spoken, highly regarded detective.

Joe said the situation was pure angst for the Police Department. "We had a killer on the loose. He's sending these letters to the *New York Post*. He's taunting us. He's announcing he's going to kill one person for each of the twelve signs of the Zodiac. In every letter he wrote, 'No one can catch me. Only Orion can catch me. Six, six, six.' Every time he did anything, it was headlines for days."

The fact the killer used the word "Zodiac" added to the confusion. "These kinds of cases take on a life of their own," Joe continued. "People all over the world study the stars. Unfortunately for us, we heard from a lot of them. We got bombarded with calls and tips from Belgium, India, and Russia, to name just a few. But every one of them turned out to be bogus. With a case like this, you have to stay focused and follow the evidence, not the signs of the Zodiac or some astrologer's far-fetched theories about the belts of heaven."

The first three shootings occurred in the same neighborhood. Most times, that indicates the assailant lives close and is choosing to work on his home turf.

Joe and his team mapped out a square-mile area around the location of each of the first three shootings. They went house by house making a list of every person in each dwelling. They cross-checked those names with arrest records going back ten years. The project took months. When they tallied the list of everyone who had been arrested, they had 4,500 names. Now the work got harder.

"We compared the Zodiac's fingerprints to the prints of every one of those people who had been arrested," Joe explained. "Fifteen latent print experts worked on the project. In those days we did it manually. It took months."

Joe waited for his beeper to go off, hoping someone from the Latent Print Unit would call to say they found a match. When they finally did get a call, the Latent Print crew reported they had exhausted the list. No match. Nothing. It appeared that months of tedious work had been in vain.

Joe was about to hang up when Detective Ronald Alongis, one of the top people in the Unit, told him that out of the 4,500 people on the list, 1,500 had no prints on file. Either they were found not guilty, the case was dismissed, or the judge ordered the records sealed. Whatever the reason, the evidence collected for that particular crime, including the defendant's fingerprints, had been purged from the system.

* * *

Then it happened again. After Diane Ballard was shot, the Zodiac vanished. Two years later, in early 1995, the department disbanded the second Zodiac Task Force.

Joe's next assignment was the 75th Precinct Detective Squad in East Brooklyn, where he worked homicides, robberies, and shootings.

"In those days, the 75th Precinct had over one hundred murders a year," Joe said. "It was total mayhem." Despite his heavy caseload, Joe Herbert would not forget about Mario Orozco, Jermaine Montenesdro, Joseph Proce, Larry Parham, Patricia Fonti, Jim Weber, Joseph Diacone, and Diane Ballard.

On his own time, he became an expert on serial murderers. He found behavioral scientist John Douglas's work especially informative. He read and reread the Zodiac's notes and letters. He studied the diagrams and handwriting. He devoured everything published about the Bay Area Zodiac. On the nights his wife, Barbara, worked late at the hospital, often she would come home to find her husband asleep on the couch with handwriting samples, police reports, and books on serial killers scattered all around him.

Three years later, on the morning of June 18, 1996, Joe had moved to the Brooklyn North Homicide Squad. He was at his desk reviewing a report of a recent murder when a lieutenant called to tell him a young woman had been shot and her boyfriend was being held hostage on Pitkin Avenue. Herbert had taken a hostage negotiations course, and the lieutenant wanted him to get over there fast.

When the "shots fired" call came in, seven police cars sped to the location. As the cops got out of their cars and prepared to enter the house, gunfire came at them from a fourth-floor window. Within minutes, close to one hundred officers were on the scene. One witness said it took only seconds after the sound of gunfire before chaos erupted on the streets. Dozens of people screamed and ran up Pitkin Avenue while others took cover inside the Euclid Avenue subway station. Leonida Roja, a thirty-year-old man walking down the street, was struck in the neck with pieces of brick that had been shattered by a bullet. Four officers were rushed to the hospital where they were treated for trauma, cuts, and bruises. Emergency Service officers cordoned off an area of eighteen square blocks surrounding the gunman's apartment while other officers evacuated hundreds of residents to safer ground.

When Joe arrived, he ran over to the bulletproof barrier ESU cops had erected in front of the building. Huddled behind the portable cement fortress, the Emergency Service officers briefed the sergeant on what they knew. The gunman's sister, who had just turned seventeen, managed to escape to the safety of a neighbor's apartment after her brother shot her in the back. As the cops arrived, the gunman began firing wildly at the police and people walking down the street. The shooter's name was Heriberto Seda. His nickname was ·Eddie, and he was holding his sister's boyfriend hostage in their fourth-floor apartment.

Joe Herbert positioned himself behind the barrier. Cupping his hands around his mouth, he yelled up to the fourth-floor window. "Eddie. Eddie." He could see the hostage standing at the window, but the gunman was nowhere to be seen. Joe decided he had no choice but to go into the building and try to talk to Seda outside his apartment door.

"They evacuated the building," Joe recalled. "I would have been in his line of fire if I went in through the front door, so I climbed through a first-floor window. Kenny Bowen and some other ESU officers were armed with shotguns and other heavy weapons and were already in position in the hallway. It was over 100°. Because it was an active shooting scene, we were all wearing heavy ceramic vests and helmets. Sweat was pouring down my face, and I was having a hard time seeing."

Joe talked to Eddie through the closed door for close to an hour, but there was no response. "I think the Emergency Service cops were going crazy, listening to me talk all that time," Joe said. "Everyone must have been relieved when a few minutes into the second hour, Seda started to talk.

"He asked me how his sister was doing. I told her she was going to be a little uncomfortable, but she would be all right."

Joe knew he was making progress when Seda asked him to promise he would not be sent to Rikers. "That was pretty easy to do," Joe said. "People only go to Rikers for one year at the most. This guy engaged police officers in a gun battle and wounded his sister. He was going away for a lot longer than one year."

Most people in and outside of law enforcement are nervous in high-stress situations with lots of variables. Even seasoned street cops can be overcome by adrenaline when there is an armed suspect who has shot a family member, taken a hostage, and may have more weapons.

It takes a special constitution and skill set to remain calm in those scenarios, especially if you are the one trying to talk a crazed gunman into surrender. Joe Herbert is one of those rare people. After a two-hour standoff in the street and one hour of negotiations in the hallway, Eddie Seda told Sergeant Herbert he would give up his guns and come out.

Before the eight-man team of Emergency Service officers entered the apartment, Eddie was instructed to drop his guns—one at a time—into the bucket that officers on the roof would lower down to the window. When the cops hoisted the bucket up for the third and last time, Seda had relinquished a total of thirteen homemade zip guns.

The police were still not sure all the weapons were out of the apartment. Yelling through the door, officers with the ESU entry team told Seda to turn around and put his hands up high against the wall. "Hold it," Eddie responded as they were about to make the entry. "You have my guns, but you didn't tell me what to do with the bombs."

"It was unreal," Joe said. "We called in the Bomb Squad, and the Emergency Service cops regrouped back behind the bulletproof barrier."

Standing to the side of the door, Joe told Seda not to touch the bombs—the cops would get them out later. Later that day when officers with the Bomb Squad searched Heriberto Seda's apartment, they found two fully assembled pipe bombs and enough pipe and other material to make at least nine more.

Four hours after Eddie Seda shot his sister and fired on scores of New York City police officers who rushed to the scene to help her, his wrists were cuffed and fastened behind his back. Once he posed no threat, the Emergency Service cops turned him over to Joe, who put him in the backseat of a police car. Seda was booked for shooting his sister and firing on the police and innocent people walking down the street.

If anything, the day seemed to be getting warmer. After spending two hours under a blazing sun followed by an hour in a cramped hallway on the fourth floor of a hot apartment building, Joe Herbert looked like he had been swimming, fully dressed.

* * *

Back at the station, Joe handed Seda over to Detective Danny Powers, the lead investigator on the case. It was Danny's job to get Eddie's signed confession, his admission in writing that he had shot his sister.

While Danny questioned Seda, Joe went back to the apartment building to pick up the unmarked car he'd left there earlier. He was in the street talking to officers from the Bomb Squad when he saw Danny Powers and another detective, Tommy Maher, walking toward him. Danny was holding a piece of paper.

"It's Seda's confession," Danny told Joe. "He put it all in writing—that he shot at our guys and wounded his sister."

When Joe glanced at the confession, what he saw took his breath away. "As sure as I am standing here," Joe told Danny and Tommy, "this is the handwriting of the Zodiac."

Joe Herbert had been studying the odd scrawl for years. "It was the T's, the S's, the M's," Joe said. "It was the way he underlined certain letters. There was no doubt in my mind. Heriberto Seda was the Zodiac."

Joe asked to see the Commanding Officer of the Brooklyn North Detectives. "I told him, 'Look, I am not an alarmist or conspiracy person, but I am positive we have the Zodiac killer sitting in a cell at the police station.'"

Tommy took Heriberto Seda's prints—both fingers and palms—and rushed them down to One Police Plaza where Detective Ron Alongis was on standby.

When Ron compared Seda's fingerprints to the partial print recovered from the letter left near the bench Larry Parham was sleeping on, it was a perfect match. Seda's fingerprints matched the partial prints left by the Zodiac in Central Park. Alongis and Maher were euphoric when they called Joe Herbert and told him his suspicions were confirmed. Seda's prints matched the Zodiac's.

"That was a very exciting moment for me," Joe said.

Joe vouchered the zip guns retrieved from Seda's residence and sent them to the Ballistics Laboratory. After a meticulous examination, detectives handed Joe his second piece of evidence. The rounds were the same as the ones recovered at the Zodiac shootings in East Brooklyn and Central Park, and they had been fired from the same kind of homemade zip gun the police had removed from Seda's apartment.

When a round goes through a regular firearm, it leaves lands and grooves on the bullet. It is akin to the fingerprint of the gun. When homemade zip guns are fired, the bullets cannot be traced by the lands and grooves. In several of the letters the Zodiac sent to the police, he wrote, "No lands, no grooves." But identifiable tool marks are left on the bullets as they travel through the barrel of a zip gun. It was these tool marks that provided the ballistic evidence linking the Zodiac's guns to Heriberto Seda.

Joe felt an incredible sense of calm; a confidence that comes when you know you have it right. "I'm an evidence guy," he says. "That's what detectives do. We chase evidence. We knew the handwriting was a match, and we had the prints. When Ballistics ran their tests, they were sure the guns we took out in those buckets were the same type the Zodiac used."

Oddly enough, one of the people whose records had been deleted in the fingerprint search Joe had worked on in 1993 was a man the cops had picked up for carrying a zip gun. When the Ballistics Lab could not get the gun to operate, the case was dismissed, and the fingerprints were purged from the records. That man was Heriberto Seda.

Then they got more good news. The DNA found on two letters sent to the *New York Post* was identical to the DNA of Heriberto Seda.

Now came the hard part—getting his confession.

Lou Savarese, a veteran of the Zodiac Task Force, was called in to assist with the interrogation. Lou, like Joe, was obsessed with apprehending the Zodiac killer.

"Lou and I had gone to a seminar on serial killers," Joe said. "We'd learned that if you put pictures of their victims up on the wall, they can't resist looking at them. It's an ego thing. They like to admire their work."

They retrieved crime scene photos of Patricia Fonti and Joseph Diacone and tacked them up on the wall of the interview room.

"We knew he'd see them as he came in," Joe recalled. "Our plan was to seat him with his back to the wall. We hoped he would not be able to resist looking backward over his shoulder."

When Herbert and Savarese entered the interrogation room, Seda was already seated. There was a table, a few chairs, and a one-way window for observers on the outside. From the moment Joe and Lou took their seats, Seda tried to twist around in his seat and look at the pictures. When Joe asked him if he recognized his work, he shrugged.

For the first eight hours, the detectives got nothing. Except for brief breaks, Lou and Joe did all the talking. The goal was to wear him down.

"Finally he spoke," Joe said. "He asked for a King James Bible. Once he started talking, he went on nonstop about religion. He seemed to think it was his responsibility to clean up society."

The Zodiac had not been active for three years, but the fact that the crimes were never solved and the killer was still on the loose was always on Joe's mind.

"When a case goes cold, it takes perseverance and patience to stick with it," he explained. "You have to master the evidence so that if you are lucky and you make the arrest, the suspect knows that you know everything. All those nights I read and reread those files were about to pay off.

"At some point I asked him, 'Eddie, who is the Clown Killer?' He comes right back. 'John Wayne Gacy.' 'Who is the Night Stalker?' 'Richard Ramirez.' 'Who was the cannibal?' 'Jeffrey Dahmer.' When I asked him, 'Who is the Zodiac?' you could see he wanted to say 'me,' but he wasn't quite ready. 'Eddie Seda,' I told him. 'You hit the big time, just like your buddies.'"

After nine hours, Eddie Seda confessed. "He admitted to everything," Joe said.

* * *

Twenty-eight-year-old Heriberto Seda was arraigned in Criminal Court in Queens, where he was charged with attempted murder and possession of a weapon stemming for shooting his sister and firing on the police. In addition, Seda was facing three counts of second-degree murder, one count of attempted murder, and seven counts of weapons possession. The judge ordered him held without bail.

When the police searched Seda's home where he lived with his mother and half-sister—the girl he shot in the back—they found old issues of *Soldier of Fortune* magazine and books on serial killers piled high. It was clear Seda admired Ted Bundy, the man who had confessed to thirty murders between 1973 and 1978 but was a suspect in over a hundred more. Bundy bludgeoned and raped his victims before strangling them to death.

But Seda's number one hero was the Bay Area Zodiac. He had every book, magazine article, newspaper clipping, and picture ever published on the Zodiac, including a dog-eared copy of Robert Graysmith's *Zodiac*, a best-selling book that was made into a film starring Jake Gyllenhaal, Mark Ruffalo, and Robert Downey Jr.

Once the *New York Post* published his first letter, news stories on the New York Zodiac were prolific. Seda had kept a scrapbook of every article. They were clipped and pasted neatly inside.

Along with his odd home library and macabre scrapbook filled with stories about the people he had wounded and killed, the police also found a small arsenal of homemade weapons and bombs. Seda ordered ammunition from catalogs and made the zip guns himself. When the Bomb Squad did their search, they found two pipe bombs and a smoke grenade.

"When we questioned him, he confessed he tested a third pipe bomb, and it worked," Joe said. "This is a guy who got thrown out of high school for carrying a weapon. He never worked a day in his life. I guess his ambition in life was to move up from a serial killer to a serial bomber."

* * *

At his trial Heriberto Seda repeatedly shouted at the judge. First he demanded a new lawyer, then he screamed he did not want to be in court. "I feel like I'm invisible," he said when Judge Robert Hanophy ignored his outbursts. "Get me out of here," he screamed. "I'm losing my mind." When his lawyers tried to quiet him, he lashed out at them, too.

Robert Masters, the Assistant District Attorney, painstakingly detailed each of the Zodiac's crimes for the jury. He mapped out a time line of the shootings starting in March 1990 and lasting up through October 1993. Masters described Eddie Seda as a cowardly killer who stalked the weak, the elderly, the homeless, and people with drug and alcohol problems.

The jury found Heriberto Seda guilty on all counts. The judge sentenced him to serve a sentence of 236 years at the Attica Correctional Facility.

At age thirty-six, Seda fell in love with inmate No. 97A0308—Synthia-China Blast—a preoperative male-to-female transsexual who has a large scorpion tattooed on her face. Blast was convicted in 1996 for a gang-related murder. When the Department of Corrections turned down Blast's request for a sex change so he and Seda could marry and moved him to another facility, the couple sued, claiming the prison was violating their civil rights.

Joe said when the word got back to the Detective Squad, they were incredulous. "Some people thought it couldn't be true," Joe said. "Not me. Who could possibly make this stuff up?"

The attention-starved Seda must have been pleased when his crimes made it into episodes of *Forensic Files* and *Psychic Detectives*, both aired on Court TV. But nothing would compare to the thrill of learning that his favorite author, Robert Graysmith—the man who wrote Zodiac—was out with a new book. *Zodiac Unmasked* was all about Heriberto Seda, the New York City Zodiac.

His victims were not as fortunate. Joe Proce, Patricia Fonti, and Joseph Diacone were dead. Mario Orozco, Jermaine Montenesdro, Larry Parham, Jim Weber, and Diane Ballard survived their shootings, but all suffered with serious lifelong physical and psychological problems after their unlucky encounters with Heriberto Seda.

* * *

Joe Herbert grew up in Brooklyn, the fifth child in a family of six boys and two girls. Joe's father, the late John Herbert, served with the New York City Fire Department for thirty-eight years. His mother, Veronica, stayed busy at home caring for her husband and eight children. It was a large, close-knit Irish family, and it was expected that every one of Veronica and John's children would devote their lives to public service. "My parents expected all of us to do something with our lives that would help others," Joe said.

He was especially close to his older brother John, a talented detective who spent the bulk of his career with the Brooklyn North Homicide Squad. Everyone knew when it came time to choose a career, the chances were good Joe would follow John into the NYPD.

"I spent a lot of time listening to my brother and his friends talk about their work," he said. "I learned that you have to take pride in your paperwork, that you have to be very careful when you write your reports. He taught me that if you do it the right way at the ground level, your work can lead to an arrest and conviction but that it takes time and experience to develop those skills. There are no shortcuts. John always said that even one careless mistake in a police report or something as small as writing a phone number down wrong can mean a guilty person might go free."

Besides mastering the written work, people who excel as investigators must be communicators. Joe credits his family for helping him develop an ability to establish rapport through conversation—a skill that's both innate and learned.

"Along with John, another brother, James, had a tremendous influence on me," Joe said. "He was an extremely caring, tolerant person and a great listener. Watching James, I learned that those are the things that break down barriers and make people want to talk to you, even if you are the cop and they are the suspect. A lot of detective work is all about getting people to talk."

Joe Herbert began his career in the 71st Precinct in Brooklyn, a high-crime area located at the southern end of Crown Heights. "I still remember my first foot post," he recalled. "It was my second day on the street. My sergeant told me, 'Herbert, your area is Patrol Post 31, Nostrand Avenue between Linden and Empire Boulevards. Please be advised this is the last known address of Anthony LaBorde, a member of the Black Panther Party and the Black Liberation Army. LaBorde was convicted last year of the murder of Officer John Scarangella and the attempted murder of Scarangella's partner, Richard Rainey.' That was something to hear your second day on the job."

During those first few years Joe made an unusual number of felony arrests for a rookie cop. His good work was rewarded with a transfer to the Precinct's Anti-Crime Unit.

Joe and his partner, Dennis Schwab, made 129 gun arrests the first year they worked together. When one of their gun collars matched a weapon used in another crime, detectives working the case made a special effort to seek them out and explain that it was Joe and Dennis's work that had given them the evidence they needed to make the arrest.

Those visits reinforced everything Joe's brother John had taught him: You never know if the evidence you collect for one crime will be linked to others.

From 1983 to 1984, Joe and Dennis worked in plainclothes with the Anti-Crime Unit in Crown Heights. They had only been there two weeks and were still learning the nuances of working out of uniform when disaster struck.

Officer Angelo Brown worked the day shift at the 84th Precinct in Brooklyn. A couple of times a week he would stop at his favorite pool hall for an hour or so on his way home from work. On this particular evening, when the off-duty cop leaned over to take a shot, witnesses said they saw two men staring at the partially exposed gun Angelo had in his shoulder holster. They hung back until Angelo finished his game. When the young officer made his way to the front door, the men followed him. As Officer Brown walked to his car, they tackled him from behind, beat him, took his gun, and left him semi-conscious in the middle of the snowy, icy parking lot. Despite his injuries, the officer made a superhuman effort to get up. Somehow he managed to get himself in front of the car as the men were pulling out. When they didn't stop, Angelo Brown threw himself on the hood. That's when one of the men aimed the gun and fired the fatal shot.

Thirty days later the mood was grim. Despite an enormous manhunt, the two men were still unidentified and at large. Everyone took it personally that these cop killers were still on the loose.

On day thirty-one, Joe and Dennis were on a routine patrol when they observed a man wearing a three-quarter-length leather coat. He looked in their direction and quickened his gait. Joe made a fast U-turn. The man began to run. Both officers were sure he was frantically reaching for his weapon.

"Dennis chased him on foot, and I drove past him," Joe said. "I cut back and blocked him with the car. I jumped out and ran after him. He disappeared into the lobby of a building, with both of us running close behind. We grabbed him just as he reached the elevator.

"During the foot chase, Dennis had seen the man toss a gun. When he went back and found it, it was a Smith & Wesson revolver with a two-inch barrel. Dennis wondered if it belonged to Angelo Brown."

When Joe and Dennis questioned the suspect back at the precinct, he told the detectives he was not the person who killed the cop, but he knew the officer was not killed with a small gun. He said the weapon that killed the officer had a longer barrel.

Joe and Dennis had no way to know if this was reliable information, but they wasted no time finding out. The 77th Precinct Detective Squad was handling the homicide investigation of Officer Brown, and they called them immediately. When Joe repeated the conversation he and Dennis had with their suspect, it only took a few minutes before a contingent of detectives arrived at the 71st Precinct.

Joe and Dennis continued the interrogation. Reluctantly, the suspect told the detectives he hung out at a certain spot in the neighborhood where he sold marijuana. On the night Angelo Brown was murdered, two men came by and tried to trade a gun for pot. But the weapon was warm, and he could smell gunpowder, so he refused the trade. But he knew who they were and where the police could find them. It broke the case wide open. That gun collar led to the arrest and conviction of the men who murdered Angelo Brown.

A week later, Lieutenant Timmy Burns, the 77th Precinct Detective Squad Commander, told Joe and Dennis he was recommending them both for an award. "He asked us if we wanted medals," Joe said. "We told him to forget the medals. We said what we really wanted was to be detectives."

Joe was twenty-seven years old and had only three years under his belt working as a New York City cop. Dennis had just few months more. But six months later the Brooklyn South Borough Commander made a telephone call to the precinct to report that Joe Herbert and Dennis Schwab were being transferred to the 71st Precinct Detective Squad. Twenty months later, in August 1986, the Police Commissioner pinned on their gold detective badges. It was an unheard-of feat for officers with such a short time on the job.

* * *

The mid-1980s were a tough time to be a cop in New York City. It was the beginning of the crack epidemic, which first surfaced in the 71st Precinct in Brooklyn.

"There was this six-story building on Crown Street," Joe said. "It was the first crack house any of us had seen. It was a predominantly black neighborhood, but there were people living there from all over the world. Every day people purchasing drugs waited patiently in this huge line. The drug traffic spawned all kinds of criminal activity, including robberies, assaults, and shootings. The whole place was like a scene out of that movie *New Jack*

City.

"We had only been there a couple of weeks when the Commanding Officer of the 71st Precinct ordered us to pay special attention to the 250 Crown Street address. We drove over there right after the meeting. It was only a few minutes later when we saw a Lincoln Continental pull up. The driver got out of the car and went inside to buy crack. When he returned to the car, we approached him. We noticed he had a .25 caliber automatic pistol on the front seat of his car. When we ran his prints through the computer, we got a match. It turned out this man was the Flatbush rapist. He had brutally raped eight women over a two-month period but had never been caught.

"When the women were coming home from work, he'd grab them from behind, pull them into an alley or behind a garbage bin, and then assault and rape them. During one of his attacks, he had unscrewed a light bulb. We figured he didn't want to break it, so he unscrewed it to kill the light. We were pretty happy when the prints from the .25 caliber automatic matched the prints on that light bulb. His name was Gregory Pought."

When detectives arrive at a crime scene, they are trained to pay close attention to everything they see and hear. Even reaching up to retrieve a light bulb is standard practice because investigators never know what will turn out to be a valuable piece of evidence.

Joe Herbert said he can't even begin to remember all the odd items he's retrieved. "I think people would be surprised what we look at. I've collected rainwater from puddles, been down on my hands and knees and felt my way through mud. You go through everything, and you look at everything, no matter how small or insignificant, because you never know if it will lead you to the person who did the crime. Because someone was careful enough to unscrew the lightbulb and bring it to the lab for fingerprint tests, we were able to determine that the man we arrested with the gun was the same person who had raped eight women."

In one year's time, two of Joe's gun arrests had led the police to the Flatbush rapist and the men who killed Angelo Brown—"career cases," as they are known in the business.

Joe credits his success to the older, more experienced people he worked with who were willing to share their expertise with him. "That's the only way you learn this business," he says.

"I will never forget this one old-timer. Richie Gordon was a First Grade

Detective. Inside his brain there was this huge wealth of knowledge. Every time I wrote up a report, he would read it, show me the mistakes, and then crush the paper into a ball. Those crumpled papers filled wastebasket after wastebasket. When my work finally met his high standards, he'd shrug and say, 'Okay. That's good.' That training was key to my whole career. Richie Gordon taught me how to make a case."

Stevie Litwin was another officer who influenced the young Joe Herbert. "Stevie," Joe said, "solved more murders and other crimes while he was sleeping than ten people all put together did when they were working. He treated people with such respect. He made the nicest person you ever knew look like a bad guy. People in the neighborhood loved him. They would call him in the middle of the night and tell him about a shooting. They'd say here's who got shot, and here's who did it. The case would be all wrapped up, and he'd still be in bed. He was kind to everyone, even people who didn't deserve it. Watching him, I learned that treating people with respect and dignity goes a long way, especially when you're trying to get them to give you information.

"I already knew from my brother John how important interrogations are and that you need a strategy for developing a rapport. Even if they did horrific things, I was always nice to them.

"In 1996 when I was assigned to the 7-9 Detective Squad, I received a phone call around three o'clock in the morning. It was a night watch detective telling me a young mother and her five-year-old son had been stabbed to death inside their apartment. The woman's boyfriend was being detained as a suspect. My wife woke up, and she could tell from listening to my part of the conversation that a small child had been killed. She started crying. She kept saying, 'How can they do this to children? How could anybody kill a child?'"

Joe drove to Bedford-Stuyvesant. After looking around the crime scene and jotting down some notes, he went directly to the 7-9 squad room, where the suspect was being questioned.

"When I got there, the interview was going nowhere," Joe said. "The man wasn't responding, and the detectives felt they had hit a wall. I asked them if I could have a crack at it."

Joe pulled a chair in close. "I told him, 'Listen, I know you're not a killer. This was only an argument that got out of control. You didn't mean to hurt them.' I think I even put my hand on his shoulder. Within minutes, he was crying. He admitted to everything. He told me he killed his girlfriend in the midst of a heated argument, and then he killed the boy because he was a witness. He said he hid the knife in the boy's book bag in an alleyway. We went to the alley, and the knife was right where he said it would be—in the boy's schoolbag. I still remember the smiling kangaroo on the back of that little bag.

"I am a firm believer that being compassionate is how you get to them," Joe continued. "I offer to get them cigarettes or a soda. You don't get anywhere by screaming and throwing them against the wall. You can be the most experienced interrogator and you will fail with those tactics. Look at those prisoners at Guantanamo. Some were waterboarded, and they still didn't talk. You have to accept that being brutal doesn't work.

"It's hard for younger officers to use this approach. It takes a lot of experience for a police officer to master the art of separating yourself from the crime and its victims. Younger officers tend to overreact. But as you gain experience, you learn to keep your distance and not be emotional when you question them."

* * *

While Joe Herbert has experienced success, he has also known failure. "There were cases we worked on for years that were never solved."

He remembers one homicide—a doctor in Brooklyn. "Dr. Pete was an extremely promiscuous man," Joe explained. "He had a lot of women and girlfriends. He was tied up, suffocated, and beaten to death. Whoever killed him dumped him on the street. Narrowing down the list of suspects was hard because he had had so many different partners. We interviewed everyone we knew about, which was a lot of people. But in the end we had nothing—no latent prints, no evidence of any kind that would help us. We worked hard on that case, and it was discouraging not to find the person who killed him."

At the 75th Precinct in Brooklyn, boxes of folders containing paperwork on unsolved homicide investigations are stacked against the back wall of the second floor where the detectives work. "We always had too many new cases to focus on the dead ends," Joe said. "But it stays on your conscience that you couldn't get those victims justice. Several times a year, I made it a point to call in a lieutenant from the Cold Case Squad to see if they would take some of these unsolved cases. Some of the detective units didn't want to turn cases over to them. I'm not sure why. Maybe they were ashamed they couldn't solve the case. But I never felt that way. I showed the lieutenant the wall and encouraged him to help us. Several times their work resulted in arrests, and that was a great feeling.

* * *

Ask Joe if there's a case that haunts him, and he thinks for a moment. "The honest answer, from my heart, is that they were all important. All of them stay with you in one way or another. But if I had to talk about one, I would tell the story of Kayesean Blackledge. He was a four-year-old boy who was strangled to death and dumped into a trash compactor in the back of a building. When we recovered his mangled body, he was still wearing his Mr. T pajamas.

"When you see something like that, it's hard to explain the emotions you feel. It turned out the man who killed him was the boyfriend of his legal guardian."

When Joe and his partner learned that the guardian had the man's ATM card number, they drove to the bank. Bank officials set up a computer notification system and promised the cops they would call them as soon as the suspect used the card.

"The first time he used the card was in Okaloosa County, Florida, three days after the murder," Joe said. "Four of us flew down on the first plane out the next morning. We staked out the bank hoping he would come back and take out more money. It was a very rural area. We'd been there about an hour when we see a dog chasing a chicken. The dog catches the chicken and soon there's feathers flying all over the place. As we sat there laughing about four New York City cops sitting in a deserted parking lot watching a chicken getting torn apart by a dog, the bank called to tell us he used the card. He was in Biloxi, Mississippi."

When the detectives got to Biloxi, the bank had video footage of the man and his car. "It was poor quality," Joe said. "We still needed the plate number, but at least we knew what kind of vehicle he was driving. The Biloxi cops advised us to take the video to the local casino. They had state-of-the-art photo labs, which meant we had a better chance of getting the plate number from a video that was grainy and out of focus."

The casino's equipment was top-notch. It was only minutes before Joe and the other detectives had a clear image of the car and the plate number. Within an hour information was broadcast to every law enforcement agency in the country. The next day an officer with the Texas Department of Public Safety on patrol in Conway, Texas, recognized the vehicle. He put on his lights and pulled him over.

"We flew to Dallas and interrogated him that night," Joe recalled. "He had been on the run for almost one week, and he was extremely tired. He gave it all up pretty fast. He told us after he had a fight with the boy's guardian, he took the youngster to Brooklyn and killed him. We only worked that case for a week, and it happened over eighteen years ago, but I still think about that little boy."

* * *

In 1983 Joe and Dennis were working in plainclothes with the Anti-Crime Unit. It was five minutes to one in the morning.

"We heard the sound of gunfire," Joe said. "It sounded like it came from Flatbush Avenue. We hit the gas and drove in that direction. Within seconds we saw a man running around the corner. He looked like he was clutching a large gun. Dennis jumped out of the car and chased the guy for half a block. When he got within touching distance, he grabbed him from the back. The man swung around and stabbed Dennis in the face with a large knife. They both went down like a ton of bricks. People say the face bleeds more than the rest of the body, and there was a lot of blood. It was everywhere. I was terrified that Dennis was dying. Now the guy gets up and starts running. I pull my gun, chase him, and jump on his back. I'm screaming, 'Drop the knife. Drop the knife,' but his knuckles are white, he's holding it so tight. All of a sudden he flips me over, and I see this big, sharp shiny blade coming right at my face." Joe fired one round, and the man crumpled to the ground.

Dennis recovered, but he suffered nerve damage to his face. Eventually he returned to work, but several years later he was seriously injured in an accident in his police car and was forced to retire from the Police Department. It's been two decades, but Joe says he still misses working with Dennis.

Despite the fact that the man tried to kill him and his partner, Joe still wrestled with the emotional repercussions of taking a life. It is not easy to cope after you kill someone, especially for a twenty-five-year-old who became a cop to help people, not hurt them. "I grew up in a religious family," he said. "I believe in the Ten Commandments, that it's wrong to take a life.

It's a very difficult thing to do and then live with."

The support he received from his colleagues was tremendous. "I talked to other guys involved in similar situations, and every one of them said they'd had a hard time, too. But I still needed to find something more to justify the fact that I had killed this man. On some level I knew I did the right thing—he tried to kill me and my partner. But I couldn't stop going over the details in my mind."

When the feelings of guilt did not subside, Joe went to the neighborhood where the man had lived. He spent a long time just watching his apartment building. He found some solace when he learned the man was out on parole after being convicted of raping two women after he'd broken into their homes. At least now no other woman would be his victim.

* * *

When Joe Herbert's alarm went off at six a.m. on the morning of September 11, 2001, he grabbed a quick shower and wolfed down his customary piece of fruit and carton of yogurt. His wife Barbara, a registered nurse, had left their home an hour earlier for her job in the rehabilitation center at a major medical center in Manhattan. That morning Joe decided to forgo his customary ritual of flipping on the television and watching the news as he got ready to head to his office at Police Headquarters in Lower Manhattan. He got the news when his next door neighbor called to tell him two planes had crashed into the North and South Towers of the World Trade Center.

As he made his way to Lower Manhattan via the Brooklyn Queens Expressway, Joe saw the horrific site—a gigantic dust plume rising high in the sky. When he saw the second tower start to give way, he tried to comprehend the loss of life. Would it be fifty thousand? A hundred thousand?

"That first day we worked until late at night," he said. "Everyone was doing whatever they could. There was so much chaos, so much uncertainty. It's hard to describe what it was like. We thought there would be hundreds of survivors to rescue, but the people who didn't make it out before the towers fell all died. Some of us worked on the bucket brigade. The air was putrid. It smelled like death."

It must have been early on the morning of September 12 when, bone tired and covered with dust, Joe found his car and drove home to get a couple of hours of rest.

The next morning, he returned to the smoldering site. "The World Trade Center complex had a Marriott Hotel about two blocks south of Ground Zero," he recalled. "I was walking west on Albany Street near the Marriott with another detective, Russell Dunn. Two volunteer firemen standing on the hotel's third-floor landing asked us to get some body bags. We walked to West Street, grabbed the bags, and went back up to the landing. There, scattered around on the small white stones that covered the area, were the remains of what appeared to be six or seven people. They were dismembered—innocent victims turned into human carnage. Then we saw the seats. They were shattered, but it was obvious they were from one of the planes. The momentum must have been so intense that some of the passengers, along with their seats, fell down to that landing after they were sucked out of the aircraft."

Russell and Joe filled the body bags with the remains and wrote out descriptions of the grim contents as best they could. "We even put the airplane parts and seats in the bags," Joe said. "We thought if there was a seat number, it might help someone identify their loved one. Other than that, it looked to us like it was going to have to be DNA."

The detectives carried the bags down the stairs and gently placed them into one of the trolley carts transporting the remains to the Medical Examiner's Office. It was an experience, Joe says, that will never leave him.

* * *

Within twenty-four hours of the attacks, officials at Headquarters began a search for their top investigators, people with research and language skills and proven track records for attention to detail. They needed a team that would find out quickly who did this and why and then begin the monumental task of making sure it did not happen again.

On September 25, 2001, the first group of NYPD investigators, including Lieutenant Joe Herbert, were transferred to the Joint Terrorist Task Force. They joined officials from other local and federal agencies at a secret location on the Upper West Side of Manhattan.

Joe was happy when he learned that Inspector Charlie Wells would command the Task Force and that he would be reporting directly to him. "Charlie was a legend in the New York City Police Department," Joe said. "He was a Medal of Honor winner, had been one of the most fearless members of the NYPD Bomb Squad, and was my Captain when I worked in the Brooklyn

North Detective Squad. He had a profound influence on me. The first time I saw him after the attacks, the bags under his eyes were down to his chin."

The newly formed Task Force began its work in a large, empty auto garage. The FBI had the lease on the building, but major adjustments were needed to get the space ready for what would eventually be a team of one thousand law enforcement officials from forty-six agencies, including the NYPD, the New York State Police, the FBI, ATF, DEA, IRS, Customs, and the Border Patrol.

"We jumped right into it," Joe said. "We all felt a passionate commitment. We wanted to wrap our arms around it and find out who aided and abetted the hijackers. There was this overwhelming urgency to find out who was involved and bring them to justice.

"The FBI had their top tech people come in and install everything," Joe continued. "They put in power lines, phones, faxes, computers, and hooked up Internet service. The minute a computer was up and running, someone was using it. It was a total madhouse."

Outside, heavily armed Emergency Service officers guarded the facility twenty-four hours a day, seven days a week, while cops with the NYPD Harbor Patrol and officers with the U.S. Coast Guard patrolled back and forth on the Hudson River.

Bobby Losada, a Detective Sergeant and veteran of the NYPD's Homicide Division, was also one of the first people assigned to the Joint Terrorist Task Force. "I walked into this enormous garage where the FBI had a temporary command center," Losada remembered. "Smoke was blowing up from Battery Park, and there was that horrible smell. There were folding tables and chairs everywhere. On the top of each table was a card listing a specific agency. You could see the FBI, Customs, Immigration, the New York State Police. It went on and on. The idea was if you needed specific information you could go to the agency in the best position to help you. There were hundreds of people milling around. It was very chaotic."

When Bobby saw Joe Herbert, Joe was standing at the front of the room gazing out at all those tables. His arms were folded, and he had one hand under his chin.

"I was so glad to see him," Bobby said. "You could see he was determined to come up with a plan even in the midst of all that chaos. There were so many details and bureaucratic issues that had to be worked out, but Joe figured out how to cut through the red tape. He organized the leads. He worked out a system with the FBI so that NYPD people got the necessary clearances to tap into FBI databases. The combination of his single-minded focus on getting the job done and an ability to know what's not working and switch gears fast has made him one of the most important players in the country's counterterrorism efforts during the immediate aftermath of the attacks."

Bobby says there is something else that's made Joe so successful. "Everyone loves him. He is a total gentleman. He's a typical Irish Catholic guy, but he can talk to anyone. He is humble, and he laughs at himself, and that is the kind of person no one minds taking orders from."

* * *

Right away callers with tips swamped the NYPD's phone lines. "At the beginning we had some serious, concrete leads," Joe said. "But then all these bogus tips started coming in. The most common call came from someone who was positive Osama was driving a cab down Fifth Avenue or working in a bodega in Queens. It was unreal. Whatever it was, we vetted it out, but in the end, almost every caller turned out to be someone who was irrationally suspicious of Muslims."

When it came to gathering information and analyzing it, things went better. Members of the Task Force questioned everyone who might have had a connection to the hijackers. They began tracking their communications and, more importantly, the money.

When Joe worked the Zodiac case, he had read every book and article he could find about people who kill multiple times. He used the same approach this time, devouring everything available on Al Qaeda and Islamic terrorists. "I went in there stone cold, and I think most Americans were just like me. We knew very little about militant Islamic culture."

Joe ran background checks on the hijackers. He studied Al Qaeda and spent a lot of time reading about Afghanistan and Pakistan. Nine years after the attacks, he estimates he has read over one hundred books on Muslim history and culture and Islamic terrorism. Piles of books, some rising twenty-five volumes high, are still stacked in the corners of his home.

Since 2001 Joe has run into a lot of people who believe Osama got lucky, that it was a one-shot deal. "Forget that," he says. "I have learned to pay close attention, take everything they say seriously, and be aware of emerging trends. A case in point is the Mumbai attacks of 2008. Ten heavily armed Pakistani men fanned out across the city and conducted highly coordinated shooting and bombing attacks in hotels, hospitals, movie theaters, and transportation facilities. A total of 173 people died, and 308 were badly wounded. This was a different approach. They changed their tactics."

The information gathered by investigators at the Joint Terrorist Task Force keeps the Police Commissioner, Ray Kelly, and his top people working in the Intelligence and Counterterrorism Bureaus informed about existing and developing threats everywhere in the world.

"The best way to stop these acts," Joe says, "is by having good intelligence. That's our job at the Joint Terrorist Task Force. We work hard to have our finger on everything. We discover the threats, then the Commissioner uses the resources of the New York City Police Department to address them."

When you ask Joe if subsequent attacks have been prevented by all this hard work, he pauses. "There have definitely been attacks prevented since 9/11," he says. "The threat has not diminished, so it's important we remain vigilant and aggressive."

* * *

Joe Herbert was destined to be a detective. "I love it and I embrace it," he said. "I have always tried to be the best that I can be."

He entered the Academy in January 1981 and could have retired eight years ago. "There's a lot of about law enforcement that's a young person's job," Joe says.

"Criminals don't work nine to five, so the work cannot be done on your schedule. Diet is another problem. I've worked in high-crime areas my whole life. We'd feel lucky if there was a diner open. Fast food was usually it. Years of that kind of eating takes its toll. I am fifty-two, and I know I can't do the stuff I used to do, but I still love this job."

For young people in law enforcement who want to become investigators, Joe has some advice. Number one on his list: Learn how to write a good police report. "Just the facts," he says. "Avoid embellishing. Any extra, superfluous information you give can be used against you in court. Keep it bare bones, just enough so the prosecutors can win the case. And when you're in court, just answer the question.

"You've got to learn to master the rules of evidence, and that takes time. Document everything. Talk to District Attorneys, and do what they tell you to do. You learn a lot interacting with prosecutors. They are the ones in charge, so if you want to get a conviction, get them what they need and do what they say. You have to learn to be 100 percent consistent. Remember, the arrest is only the beginning. In most cases, it will be a year later before you are called to testify. You have to write everything down. Then read it over and over before you go into court."

Joe says follow-through is another key to success. "If you promise you are going to do something, do it. That builds your credibility. When the DA sees you come in the door, they trust you. They know you are bringing them a case they can prosecute and win."

So unless something happens beyond his control, Joe says he will keep his job with the NYPD until he turns sixty-three, the mandatory retirement age.

"When it comes to work, there's just no way there's anything better than this," he says. "The greatest detectives in the world work for the New York City Police Department, and I love being associated with them. And every one of us is very lucky. We have the most interesting jobs in the world."

Joe Herbert with his daughter Kristin and wife Barbara. Despite the long hours and periods of time away from home – especially since September 11, 2001 – Joe loves his work. Today he holds the rank of Inspector and is the section chief of Operations and Analysis at the NYPD's Intelligence Division.

Joe, left, with his older brother John, a skilled homicide detective who spent the bulk of his career in Brooklyn North. "I already knew from my brother John how important interrogations are," Joe said. "You need a strategy for developing a rapport. Even if they did horrific things, I am always nice to them."

Joe Herbert, far left, escorts Herberito Seda to a waiting police car after he shot at responding police officers and people on the street, wounded his sister and took her boyfriend hostage. When Joe saw Seda's signed confession, he recognized the handwriting. It was the unmistakable scrawl of New York City's second serial murderer – The Zodiac.

A few seconds after this photo was taken (Joe is second from left) Heriberto Seda was driven back to the station for questioning. At his trial, the assistant district attorney described Eddie Seda as a serial killer who stalked the weak, the elderly, the homeless and people with drug and alcohol problems. The evidence was overwhelming – fingerprints, ballistics, handwriting, DNA, and a signed confession. The jury found Heriberto Seda guilty on all counts.

A proud Sergeant Herbert was invited to speak at a press conference announcing to a relieved city that the Zodiac killer was in custody. "The situation was pure angst for the police department," Joe said. "We had a killer on the loose. He's taunting us. He's announcing he's going to kill one person for each of the twelve signs of the Zodiac. In every letter he wrote, 'No one can catch me.'"

Detectives Tommy Maher (right) and Danny Powers got Seda's signed confession after he shot his sister. When Joe glanced at the paper he was stunned. "There was no doubt in my mind," Joe said, "that Heriberto Seda was the Zodiac." Detective Lou Savarese (left) and Joe questioned Seda for nine hours before he admitted he had killed three people and wounded five.

Ground Zero, September 12 at 3:30 p.m. Left to right, Detective Rich Ockovic, Lieutenant Joe Herbert and Detective Russ Dunn survey the damage. ""There was so much chaos, so much uncertainty," Joe said. "We thought there would be hundreds of survivors to rescue, but the people who didn't make it out before the towers fell all died."

"My brother, James, had a tremendous influence on me," Joe said. "He was a caring, tolerant person and a great listener. I learned that those are the things that break down barriers and make people want to talk to you. A lot of detective work is all about getting people to talk."

Joe has some advice for those who want to become investigators. First thing, learn to write a good police report.	"Just the facts," he says. "Avoid embellishing. Keep it bare bones. Just enough so the prosecutor can win the case."	"Learn the rules of evidence. Talk to the district attorneys and do what they say. If you promise to do something, do it."

Left to right, Inspector Charlie Wells, Lieutenant Joe Herbert, and Detective-Sergeant Bobby Losada were in the first group of NYPD officials assigned to the Joint Terrorist Task Force just weeks after September 11. When Joe learned he would be reporting to Inspector Charlie Wells, the new commander of the JTTF, he was ecstatic. "Charlie was a legend on this job," Joe said. "He commanded enormous respect. The first time I saw him after September 11, the bags under his eyes were down to his chin."

Joe says his wife Barbara has always supported his career which took him away from his family more often than he would have liked. "She has always been there for me and my daughter," he says. "And that has made all the difference."

Joe (standing second from left) with his parents and brothers and sisters. it was expected that every one of Veronica and John's children would devote their lives to public service.

Chapter Fourteen

Alvin Rountree: He Gets the Guns

"A coward turns away, but a brave man's choice is danger." — *Euripides (c. 484 BC–406 BC)*

The investigation began after a confidential informant placed a call to Detective Alvin Rountree. Two Brooklyn men in their twenties were selling heavy weapons, and Rountree was alarmed as the informant rattled off the inventory—Tech-9s, Calicos, .454 Casulls, and Desert Eagles—profitable and powerful guns.

An experienced undercover with the NYPD's Firearms Investigation Unit, Alvin had developed an extraordinary list of confidential informants—people whom the Department can count on to tip them off when firearms are being sold illegally. Some CIs were more reliable than others, and this call had come in from one of the best.

After meeting with his sergeant and lieutenant—both agreed Alvin should follow up—the detective went to work. "We decided the informant would introduce me over the phone," he said. "I'd do my standard Jamaican gun dealer bit. 'Yo, mahn! Wassup, mahn? We gonna meet, mahn?'"

But Alvin was nervous. Every seasoned undercover knows how much rides on the first encounter, even if it's over the phone. There is a lot of pressure during this first interaction to put your subject at ease and remove any suspicion that you might be a cop or want to rob them.

The informant made the call to the dealer. He told the man with the guns he had a guy from Brooklyn ready to buy. The CI called Alvin back and told him the dealer would take his call.

Alvin said at first, the conversation seemed to be going well. "I was talking in my regular voice with a heavy Brooklyn accent. Everything seemed okay, but then he got quiet and hung up. He called the informant back and told him he didn't like the way I was talking. He said I sounded too aggressive, and the sound of my voice made him nervous. There was no way he was going to meet with me."

Alvin was devastated. Getting through the first encounter is one of the most important tasks for an undercover. He felt he'd failed. He wasn't sure what had gone wrong but decided he was not giving up. He called the CI back. "I told him to get the guy with the guns back on the phone and tell him if he didn't like the first guy, it was no big deal. He had another cash-paying customer—a Jamaican—lined up to buy."

The informant didn't like the plan. He told Alvin to forget it. He said it was his life on the line, and he wasn't taking chances. But the CI had several outstanding warrants, and that gave Alvin leverage. After some back-and-forth about the warrants, the informant reluctantly agreed to call the suspect back. "Forget that other guy," the CI told the man selling the guns. "I've got someone else, a Jamaican guy. I think you'll like him better."

Good undercovers need a diverse set of skills. Several, like being an accomplished actor, are not typically associated with law enforcement work. Depending on the situation, along with his Brooklyn and Jamaican personas, Alvin had several other people he morphed into. It was a skill he was going to need to convince the suspect he was a different person. Learning to play these different parts requires a lot of practice. Good undercovers will spend hundreds of hours developing accents and mannerisms. Alvin became so adept at posing as a Jamaican that some of the cops he worked with had a hard time believing he was born and brought up in New York City.

A few minutes later the informant called back. He told Alvin he was good to go. Alvin called the suspect back, but this time he used a different name, lowered his voice, and spoke with a finely honed Jamaican accent. After a short conversation, the man with the guns agreed to meet Detective Rountree.

Alvin had done it hundreds of times, but he was always nervous before the first face-to-face meeting. His first task was to set up it up somewhere other than Brooklyn. "You have to get these guys out of their environment," he explains. "If you meet them on their own turf where they're comfortable, there's a greater chance they will kill you."

Alvin had an array of excuses so that he could pick the time and place without arousing suspicion. "Sometimes I say I live upstate, and it's too far to drive all the way into the city. I like to avoid meeting on the weekends, so I make up a story about having to visit my wife's sick father on Saturday and Sunday."

The Brooklyn man agreed to meet Alvin at a McDonald's in Manhattan. Alvin got into the suspect's car, a large silver Mercedes, with a pocket full of cash.

"We knew he was working with another guy," Alvin said. "But he showed up alone. You could tell he had no clue I was a cop. We talked for a little over an hour, with me playing my Jamaican gun dealer role. He sold me three guns, two Tech-9s and a Calico."

This type of police work requires tremendous mental discipline, and good undercovers have to stay focused. Some will slip into their character for several hours before they meet the suspect. Drifting in and out of character is not an option if you want to stay alive.

"One time I screwed up," Alvin said. "It was my day off. I was in my own car carrying both my personal cell and the one I use for job-related calls. I was working six different cases at the time, but none of these people had ever called me on my work phone, so when it rang, I answered it in my normal voice. I figured it was someone I work with."

The caller turned out to be a man Alvin had been investigating for months. The detective knew immediately he had blown his Jamaican cover just by uttering a simple hello. He worried that months of hard work by a lot of people might be for nothing. He could tell the man on the other end of the line was panicked, and he switched gears. "I made some noises like someone else was in the car and I was wrestling him for the phone. This guy knew me as a Jamaican, and I got right into it. I told the caller, 'Easy, boss. Me bredren pick up me phone. Everyting cool.' Then I yelled over to my imaginary friend, 'Hey! Wass you doin' answerin' me phone, mahn? That's no good, mahn.'"

The charade worked. Alvin convinced his target that someone else in the car had answered his cell phone.

* * *

The investigation of the two Brooklyn men trafficking illegal firearms lasted seven months. During that time Alvin bought 107 guns, many of them .50 caliber weapons. "We bought Tech-9s, machine guns, and bulletproof vests," he said. "One night one of the men pulled out a .454 Casull handgun out of the waist of his pants. At the time that weapon was the most powerful handgun on the market, and they sold it to me for $1,200. They were even selling Desert Eagles, which are very powerful pistols. Rounds fired from that gun rip right through the body armor cops wear, so we are happy when we get them off the street."

As the evidence from wiretaps, surveillance tapes, and eyewitness accounts began to mount, the police learned that the men were involved with other criminal activities, including a massive credit card scam. The FBI and Customs were called in.

It was at this time that the Department decided to take the case down. Everyone agreed that they were not going to get to anyone higher in the organization, and once that happens, whatever evidence has been collected is presented to the District Attorney. If the DA signs off, the warrants are approved, and the police move in and make the arrests. The Brooklyn men, only twenty-six and twenty-seven years old at the time, were convicted of a number of crimes, including criminal possession of weapons, criminal sale of weapons, illegal transporting of weapons, and fraud. They were both sentenced to seven years in prison.

* * *

Alvin worked undercover at the NYPD's Firearms Investigation Unit for seven years. During that time the detective removed serious firepower and their dealers from the streets of New York City. "These were heavily armed bad guys," he said. "Along with trafficking in illegal weapons, they were committing other crimes including extortion, kidnappings, armed robberies, and murder. My heart was always pounding when I had to go up against them."

During the years when he was posing as a gun dealer trafficking in the sale of illegal firearms, Alvin took over 2,500 guns off the streets of New York City. It was a phenomenal record. The weapons ran the gamut, everything from small .25 caliber handguns to Uzis with silencers to Street Sweepers to Calicos, a particularly lethal weapon that holds fifty rounds and costs over $1,000. One year his team—fourteen undercovers assigned to the NYPD's citywide Gun Task Force—broke several records when, over one twelve-month period, they seized over nine hundred illegal firearms and sent many of the people selling them to prison.

* * *

There is wide agreement throughout the law enforcement profession that working undercover is the most dangerous work in the business. The most important criteria for undercover officers making gun buys is the rock-solid ability to remain calm, no matter how scared they are. As one longtime NYPD sergeant noted, "To go out there and do what Alvin Rountree does, you have to have balls of steel."

For undercover officers, it is not an easy feat to convince someone selling illegal guns that you are one of them. "You've got to be a good actor," Alvin explains. "There are times when you are terrified, but you can never show it. You focus on the details."

Alvin admits that when he got his first undercover assignment at the Firearms Investigation Unit, he had a hard time pretending to be someone he wasn't. But he learned the ropes fast. A high-ranking officer in the unit said it was obvious to everyone early on that Alvin had the potential to be a great undercover.

"After I was introduced to a subject, I would talk and try to get a rapport going," he explains. "I got the routine down pretty well. Without giving away too much, let's just say I looked the part. I talked the talk and drove a flashy car. I got pretty good at making them believe I was who I said I was."

One of the challenges of the work is figuring out ways to avoid spending time with the people you are trying to arrest. Alvin made it a point to interact as much as possible with his suspects over the telephone. "Once you get to be friends, they'll call you up to meet them at a bar or party. If they are doing drugs, they get suspicious if you don't join in. Socializing with these people only leads to trouble. I always tried to come up with an excuse why I couldn't go to their parties or meet them at a club."

When he was working as an undercover with the Firearms Unit, Alvin worked six or seven investigations at a time. Each case required hundreds of phone calls and scores of face-to-face meetings. Alvin would bring the money and buy the guns. But every once in a while, something would alarm the suspects, and the detective could tell there was a chance they might have found out he was a cop. "Those were the times I was scared," he said. "You knew that if they knew, you were going to be dead."

He's not sure where he came up with the idea, but this one always got him out of a jam if he sensed the suspects were on to him. "I had a stack of porno magazines under the seat," he said. "If they were in my car and starting to act nervous like they knew something was up, I'd pull them out and show them pictures and make lewd remarks. So far I never had a time it didn't work. Instead of worrying about me, their attention was on those pictures."

* * *

There are two categories of gun cases, inner-city gun cases and interstate trafficking cases. "Criminals engaged in interstate trafficking go south, buy the guns legally, and bring them back to New York," Alvin explains. "Inner-city cases involve people selling guns they buy locally. These guns are more expensive for us to purchase, but I always get a lot satisfaction from inner-city cases. You know you are cleaning up the neighborhood and making it safer for the people who live there. That is very rewarding work."

A typical day at work for an undercover working on a Gun Task Force might mean a visit to an apartment to buy $6,000 worth of guns.

"No matter how many times I did it, my heart was always racing," Alvin said. "With these low-level firearms dealers who are out to make a fast buck, you never know if they will sell you the guns; steal your money; or kill you, steal your money, and keep the guns. It's stressful work."

People outside the business are surprised when Alvin tells them one of his biggest fears is getting into a situation with young adults or kids. "When you are up against a young kid or even an eighteen-year-old, it's scary," he says. "They have no concept of death or that there are consequences to their actions. The idea they could die is not a reality for kids this age. That means they could kill you without even thinking about what that might mean for them."

Alvin is proud of his work with the Firearms Unit but admits there are some things about undercover gun buys that are frustrating. "Some of the cases don't get finished up," he says. "People get arrested, but they don't go to jail, and that can be aggravating to a law enforcement officer. If we think it will help us get other gun traffickers off the street, we work hard to get them to flip and become confidential informants. We're always looking to get to the next level, the people who are higher up. Often the guy we just arrested is the key to doing that."

* * *

Alvin Rountree is passionate about training and not just for undercover work. "I'm very inquisitive," he says. "They never had to force me to do training. When I worked undercover, I always signed up for all the training seminars. I saw it as the best way to keep myself safe. Even as a rookie cop, I was curious about everyone's job. I wanted to understand what everybody's different responsibilities were and what they were doing out on the street."

There were many times when the extra training enabled Alvin to react quickly. "One time I was on a car chase," he said. "At some point the situation deteriorated, and I had to come out of my undercover role. No one who does this work wants to be exposed as a police officer. It's extremely dangerous, and sometimes it means you can never go back and work undercover again. But there are times when you have no choice. Something happens, and you are forced to take police action."

That night Alvin's assignment was to ghost—an undercover who is responsible for the safety of other undercover officers. It's the ghost's responsibility to call in the troops if anything goes wrong. Alvin was watching over two detectives who were following a man they were about to arrest for selling illegal firearms. Along with the detectives and Alvin, there was a sergeant supervising the scene. The plan was to trap the dealer between the two police cars when he pulled into a gas station. The sergeant would pull in behind the suspect's car. The unmarked car with the two detectives would pull in front. Once the suspect was trapped, the detectives would move in and make the arrest.

But things did not go according to plan. As the sergeant pulled in from behind, the suspect put his car in reverse, his foot to the gas, and rammed the sergeant's car. Then he put the car in forward and slammed into the unmarked car in front of him. Both cars were now pushed slightly to the side, which gave him enough room to drive his car out of the gas station parking lot.

"We chased him," Alvin remembered. "With me in my car, the sergeant in his, and the car with the two detectives, there were three police cars in pursuit. The suspect flew around a corner and hit a car parked on the side of the road. Thank God, it was one in the morning and there weren't that many people out on the street. He drove between two parked cars and knocked them out of the way. He pulled up onto the sidewalk and floored it. Now he's driving down the sidewalk, knocking down parking meters and hitting parked cars."

The chase came to an end when the man's car flipped over after he crashed into another parked car. "At that point there were lots of red lights flashing and cops on the scene," Alvin added. "We all jumped out of our cars, including me. We pulled our guns and ran over to the overturned car."

The adrenaline was flowing. Alvin was totally focused on stopping the man who had endangered so many lives. He is not sure of the exact moment he realized he was in his undercover garb, and there was no way for the other officers to know he was one of them. Looking back, he thinks it was when he was running over to the suspect's car that it dawned on him. He looked just like a bad guy with a gun. The week before, Alvin had attended a training session on how to avoid a "friendly fire" incident—shooting one of your own because you mistake him for a bad guy. He remembered the special code—what he had to say and do so his colleagues would know he was a cop. To this day, Alvin believes that training saved his life.

* * *

Most undercover work is deadly serious, but every once in a while, something comes up that has everyone laughing.

"I had this one investigation," Alvin recalled. "We were approaching the first-year mark and still had not identified our suspect, who was dealing some pretty heavy weapons. All we had was a nickname. He kept bragging he was going to be on a reality television program. It was like, 'Yeah! Right!' We tried everything to identify him, but so far we had nothing.

"One day I'm driving into work to go to a training. It was five thirty in the morning. I had the radio on, sort of half-listening, and I hear someone say his nickname. I turned up the volume. He started talking, and I recognized his voice. I was having a hard time believing it. They were interviewing him because he was on the reality show. I pulled over to the side of the road and called my team. 'Oh my God,' I said. 'We got him. Turn to 97.1.' When I got to the office, I went to the radio station's Web site. There he was. Just like that. It was such a fluke. I am still curious why a guy who's winning lots of money on TV would be selling weapons on the street. He had all kinds of guns—good ones like Glocks and Rugers and high-powered weapons like Desert Eagles. He even had crap guns like High-Points."

* * *

Alvin has never cared that much about medals or awards. The satisfaction he gets from getting thousands of guns out of the hands of criminals is enough reward for him. But there have been times when a big case goes down and the newspaper reporters and television news crews arrive en masse, but undercovers, whose risks and hard work led to the arrests, are not acknowledged. That bugs him.

"I understand that undercovers cannot be seen on television or in the newspapers," Alvin says with a hint of frustration in his voice. "But I do think more of an effort could be made to acknowledge our work. Maybe before the press conference with the Mayor, the Commissioner, the District Attorney, and all the bosses, someone could bring us into a Chief's office and thank us for the job we did. Maybe they could give us a pen or something. When I see a table of guns I purchased all laid out and other people standing there, smiling and taking the credit, it doesn't make me feel great."

Over his years with the NYPD, Alvin has become acutely aware how important it is for supervisors to give the people under them a pat on the back. "We need positive reinforcement," he says. "When I was on the Gun Task Force, every time I saw Chief Izzo, he would go out of his way. He'd say, 'Hey, what's up, Al? I'm watching you.' It meant a lot that he called me by my first name and treated me like a human being. It's an easy way to show your people respect. Anthony Izzo heads up the Organized Crime Control Bureau. He's in charge of six thousand people, so when he knew who I was and said hello, it was very motivating. It made me want to do a better job."

When Alvin got his one thousandth gun off the street, his Sergeant, Bob

Delaney, took everyone out for a drink. Alvin said it was a great night. "We don't do enough of this in law enforcement. A simple thing like a sergeant taking the team out for a beer to celebrate some good police work is a good way to boost morale. It's hard to understand why it doesn't happen more often."

* * *

Anybody who was paying attention knew that Alvin Rountree was destined for big things in the New York City Police Department. He became a police cadet in the early 1990s, an intern program open to New York City residents who were enrolled in college and completed forty-five or more credits. As a cadet, he had already taken several of the courses required at the Police Academy. Looking back, Alvin said because of his cadet experience, the Academy seemed too easy. "I felt like I was in the thirteenth grade of high school and going backward. People would tell you to be quiet in the hallway, and there was always some jerk in the class who would ask four million questions and never give the instructor time to answer."

He found some of the recruits annoying. "I'd hear them talking about going to clubs, how much they drank, who had the best weed. I never used drugs, and I was shocked that some of these kids thought it was okay to get high even though they were training to be law enforcement officers. I will never forget the time we had a pop drug test. One of the guys in my class failed and was fired that same day. I couldn't believe anyone could be that stupid. It may sound naive, but I felt like he betrayed the whole Police Department. I still feel that way about cops who do illegal things."

* * *

During his first two years on the street, Alvin Rountree made 197 arrests, most of which were felonies. But he was still a rookie, and he had a lot to learn.

Alvin says he was very lucky, early in his career, to have had a mentor who taught him why police cannot react emotionally to something that happens on the street. "I had been on the job only three months," he recalled. "I was out on patrol with Sergeant Ronnie Pastiglione. We got a call that someone was being assaulted. When we arrived at the location, a woman opened the door and began screaming that her husband had just raped their fourteen-year-old daughter.

"I felt a lot of conflicting emotions, but mostly I remember being extremely angry that someone could do something like that to their own child. I asked the sergeant if we were going to lock the guy up. I remember feeling this urge to hurt the man who raped his daughter."

The sergeant grabbed Alvin's arm. "He told me to calm down. He said the police are not judge, jury, and executioner; we were there to write down the facts and hand them off to the detectives who would investigate the case. He reminded me that we had no idea who was telling the truth. Once I calmed down, I could see my emotions had gotten the better of me. I have always been grateful to Sergeant Pastiglione for setting me straight."

After that first year on the job, his impressive number of felony arrests prompted his Lieutenant to recommend him for a thirty-day stint with the Manhattan Robbery Squad. Alvin was ecstatic to get the assignment, but he was ill prepared for what awaited him when he reported to the elite unit.

"When they found out I had only a little over a year on the job, the Lieutenant gave me a desk job, where I spent most of my time filing reports and reading the *Patrol Guide*. It's not easy to complain if you're a cop in the New York City Police Department, but I was miserable, and I finally got up my nerve and went to speak to the Sergeant. I asked him why they were having me work a desk job. He told me he would look into it. It seemed to work because after that meeting, they did give me a few more things to do."

While Alvin was busier, he was still bored. He may be the only person in the history of the Department to read the *Patrol Guide*—a sixteen-hundred-page manual outlining everything police officers of every rank and every unit are required to know—not once, but twice. On his second time through, the section on vice enforcement got his attention.

"I remember it like it was yesterday," he said. "When I read about the Vice Unit, I said to myself, 'Wow! Is that what they do?' It sounded so cool."

He called and was surprised when the person answering the phone gave him a serious sales pitch. "I don't know who he was, but he was very enthused about his assignment. He started telling me about all the stuff they do. It sounded pretty exciting, especially compared with filing reports and reading the *Patrol Guide*. He told me they were looking for undercovers."

That was all Alvin needed to hear. He asked for an interview. As soon as Officer Rountree walked in the room, a Lieutenant jumped up from his desk. "He asked me where I worked," Alvin recalled. "We chatted for a bit. Then he shook my hand and told me he'd have me transferred there within the month."

Four weeks later, Alvin was transferred to Vice. During his year and a half with the unit, he worked on several prostitution stings, a crime, he says, some people believe has no victim.

"Prostitution promotes all kinds of bad things," Alvin says, "including divorce. Think about it. Instead of trying to find sexual satisfaction in your marriage, you go to hookers. Prostitution fuels the crime of human trafficking, and it nurtures a culture where women have no self-esteem. They get diseases, and then they have no one to take care of them. On the street, some little kids look up to them. Can you imagine having a prostitute as a role model? It's a bad business all the way around."

Alvin says there was one particular raid he still can't get out of his mind. "There were charts on the wall, and next to each girl's name were these little stick-on bubbles. Each bubble indicated a different customer for that particular day. Some of these girls were seventeen years old. They had twenty-five bubbles next to their name. One girl I arrested told me she was just trying to feed her family. She said they were hungry. That day she accumulated twenty-three bubbles. That was for four hours of work. She got $10 per customer, and the house got thirty-five. That seemed like a hard way for a young woman to make $230. That night I went home, and I looked at my kids sleeping. I tried to imagine them growing up and having that kind of life. It seemed so sad."

Sometimes Alvin and the other cops would talk to the girls they arrested and try to give them advice. "We wanted to help them," Alvin said. "But at the same time, you couldn't get too close. If you get too friendly, there's always a chance they'll come back and make allegations against you. Anyone can make an accusation, whether it's true or not, and all of us in law enforcement understand you have to be very careful not to give someone that opportunity."

Prostitution was just one crime for vice cops. "We made arrests for drugs, murder for hire, after-hours clubs, illegal cigarette sales, and Internet stalking," Alvin said. "You name it, we did it. Whatever illegal activities we got our hands on, we'd go after.

"We'd go into restaurants and bodegas. If they had Jokai poker machines—they're illegal—we arrested the person behind the counter. That really bothered me. We would go in on a late tour, and most of the time the person you were putting the cuffs on wasn't the owner or even the manager, just some poor person trying to make a living. After doing that for a while, I decided it was time to look around for another assignment."

From Vice, Alvin was transferred to the Narcotics Unit. "For undercover work in Narcotics, you dress down," he explains. "I got carbon paper and rubbed it all over my hands and neck so I looked like a drug addict who never showered. If you live on the street and have no place to wash, the grime collects on the skin. I even rubbed the carbon paper on my pants so they looked really dirty. Some guys really got into it. They would buy stage make-up and put scars on their face. One cop went to his dentist and had him loosen his caps so he could pop them in and out. I never got into it to that extent, but a lot of undercovers did. They got really creative to look the part."

While Alvin was working undercover in Narcotics, a prisoner at Rikers Island decided he wanted a woman killed. "We call that a murder for hire case," he explains. "This guy reached out to a friend on the outside to do the job. The guy at Rikers didn't know it, but the man had been working with the police as a confidential informant, and he called me with the information. I called the guy at Rikers. He offered me a half a kilo of drugs to kill this woman. He told me once he had proof she was dead, someone would give me the drugs. If that man had called someone other than our informant, the woman would probably be dead right now. You have to ask yourself, for what? Some drugs? Is that worth killing someone?" The man at Rikers was rearrested and charged with kidnapping, attempted murder, and conspiracy.

When Alvin worked Narcotics, he did his homework. "I studied my targets," he said. "I hung out on the corner. I watched their mannerisms, how they passed the money, how they signaled each other. I learned that drug addicts always had cash in their hand. Then I'd go home, stand in front of a mirror, and practice."

Alvin has arrested a lot of criminals over the course of his career. Most of the details are long forgotten, but there are some people whose memories stick with you, no matter how many arrests you've made or how much time has gone by.

"One time when I was out on the sidewalk, I noticed this little kid," Alvin said. "He couldn't have been more than thirteen. He was small, and he had a runny nose. I'm standing there looking around when he walks over and says, 'Hey! What you lookin' for?' He asks me if I'm looking for 'nicks.' That's slang for a $5 bag of crack. Then he pulls a bag of drugs out of his crotch. He was just a child, and I had to arrest him. The whole time I was wondering if arresting young kids is why I became a cop.'"

At first Alvin thought working Narcotics was a dream come true. But then he would see the same people he arrested back on the street in no time.

"I had no problem putting my life on the line," he said, "but I wanted to make a difference. After a while I could not see how these drug arrests were making an impact. You'd arrest the same dealers on the same corners over and over again. I began to realize these people really wanted to use drugs, and we were never going to stop it. It was just going to go on and on whether we were there or not. We could make it harder or suppress it on one corner, but it just popped up somewhere else. I decided it was time to move on."

Alvin began to ask around. Another undercover told him the Firearms Investigation Unit was looking for people, and he called for an interview.

When the young Narcotics cop walked in the door, the Sergeant jumped out of his chair and ran across the room to greet him. "Where do you work?" he asked. "Do you really want to come here?"

"He called me every week," Alvin recalled. "He kept telling me as soon as the Commissioner signed off on the paperwork, I'd be there."

Two weeks later, Alvin was the new guy at the Firearms Investigations Unit. He would spend the next seven years there, doing one of the most dangerous jobs in law enforcement. "I was pretty scared the whole time," he says. "Everyone I dealt with had at least one gun and most had several. You never forgot that they were armed, and they would kill you.

"Some people say undercovers aren't real detectives because we don't solve crimes. But I never bought into that. We go out and get information on how things work on the street and figure out who the players are. Then we start collecting the evidence that builds the case against them."

* * *

Three of Alvin Rountree's close friends have been killed working undercover. Despite the fact that eleven years have passed, he still has trouble coping with the death of his close friend, Sean Carrington. Sean was gunned down on a buy-bust operation in the Bronx on January 19, 1998.

The assailant was Leon Smith, a career criminal who had been out on parole for nine days after serving eight years on a manslaughter charge. After

Detective Carrington and his partner made a successful narcotics purchase in the lobby of a Bronx apartment building, Leon Smith and his accomplice, Maurice Bolling, opened fire on the officers with their semiautomatic weapons. Carrington, who was not wearing a vest because he was undercover, was shot through the heart. He died thirty minutes later. His partner was also shot, but the round hit his radio, and he recovered from his wounds. The detectives' backup team were able to return fire, and Leon Smith died at the scene. Bolling was apprehended a short time later by Emergency Service officers. A jury found Bolling guilty of second-degree murder, and he was sentenced to twenty years in prison.

Alvin had met Sean when they were in the Academy. After graduating, they both patrolled in the same housing project in Harlem. Later, when Alvin went to Vice, Sean moved to Narcotics. They were in separate commands but stayed good friends.

"The night he died, Sean was making a drug buy," Alvin said. "Maybe they thought he was a rival gang member set to steal their drugs or money, or maybe they knew he was a cop. Who knows? What we do know is that Leon Smith pulled out a gun and killed him."

A few weeks before, Alvin and Sean had spent New Year's Eve together. "We were at a club, hanging out waiting for the ball to drop. We made a New Year's resolution that even though we had different assignments, we wanted our kids to get to know each other. We made a promise to spend more time together."

Sean Carrington's death devastated Alvin. Eleven years later he still has a hard time talking about it. "After Sean died, I got really scared," he said. "I thought it was going to happen to me next. I started to worry that I was going to die like him. In my heart, I knew it was okay to be scared. If you're not scared, you get complacent. But I was angry, too. I thought about my own kids, about who would take them to games or go to their graduations and weddings if I got killed. I started second-guessing my decision to become a police officer. I didn't know if my job was worth having my kids grow up without a father."

Even now Alvin still has to fight back tears when he talks about the death of Sean Carrington. "My heart goes out to his partner that night who survived," he says. "He is not the same person. All you have to do is look at him to understand that he has had a very hard time coping. He used to be a big guy, but since Sean was killed, he's lost so much weight it's hard to recognize him."

On the eleventh anniversary of Sean's death, his mother agreed to bring her daughter and meet her son's partner and Alvin at the gravesite. "It was so emotional," Alvin said, "even eleven years later. Everyone was crying. I felt like it had just happened yesterday. We went out to a restaurant afterward and sat there and talked. As we got up to go our separate ways, Sean's partner wrote down his phone number and gave it to Mrs. Carrington. He asked her to call him if she ever needed anything."

* * *

In 2003 Alvin had another devastating loss when James Nemorin and Jay Andrews, fellow undercovers in the Firearms Investigation Unit, were shot in the back of their heads during an undercover gun buy in Staten Island. After he shot and killed the officers, the gunman tossed the detectives' bodies into the street.

At the trial of Ronell Wilson, who was convicted of first-degree murder and sentenced to death for the murders of Detectives James Nemorin and Rodney "Jay" Andrews, the prosecutor told the jurors that after seeing his partner executed, James Nemorin had begged for his life. "He begged to live," Morris Fodeman told jurors in a packed federal courtroom in Brooklyn. "Pleading for his life, begging to live, knowing he would never see his family again, knowing that this was the end. That, ladies and gentlemen, is how James Nemorin spent his last moments on this Earth."

"I was close to them both," Alvin said. "They were on my sister team on the Firearms Investigation Unit. The day before Jay died, we'd all attended one of our regular citywide meetings where the Commander tells us what his goals are, what the Police Commissioner wants, how he will reward us if we meet the objectives. The day before that, James ghosted for me while I was out on the street making a gun buy."

* * *

Alvin Rountree grew up in a housing project in Manhattan. He was the second oldest in a family of two boys and two girls. It makes him sad that a lot of the kids he grew up with are still in the projects. "They have this mentality that the system sucks," he says. "They feel everything is against them. I never bought into that. They're sitting on the same benches, doing the same things.

They made the choice not to do anything with their lives. It didn't have to be that way."

Growing up in the projects meant there was no way to avoid seeing people getting beat up and shot. "The cops were there all the time," he said.

Those early experiences with the police instilled a sense of admiration into the young Alvin Rountree. "I always looked up to them. Unlike a lot of my friends, I thought they were good people.

"I had one friend who was always in trouble. I will never forget this one Sunday morning. I was in tenth grade, on my way home from church, when I heard shots. I ran up the block and saw my friend lying in the street. He had had an argument with someone the day before, and he had set his dog on the guy. The next day that person came back with a gun and shot and killed him. I looked at his face. He was just lying there. I was only sixteen years old, but from that day on, I made a vow that I was not going to be a part of the problem, only the solution. That was the day I decided to become a cop."

Alvin's father, Ernest, worked at Jacobi Hospital for thirty-seven years, most of that time as a pulmonary technician in the Burn Unit. Alvin's mother, Blanche, worked in the post office until she had her first child. "My father wanted her to stay at home and raise their kids," Alvin said. "To this day I have never met anyone who is a better person than my mother. She was always there for us." Alvin's older sister is an engineer, his brother works for the Sanitation Department, and his younger sister is a director of a community center.

Alvin is married and the proud father of three children. It's clear he loves and admires his wife, Lani, but does admit there is some stress over who comes first—family or the NYPD.

"We battle about this," he says. "She tells me the NYPD is more important to me than her. I try to explain how intense it is. When I get out of a car to do my work, I literally have to count on the people who are with me to save my life. That seems to make her feel worse. She thinks I'm closer to the guys on the job than I am to her."

Alvin understands her frustration. "A while back my son was in a play. I'd arranged to leave work early so I could be there, but just as I was headed out the door, we got a call for a possible buy. If we were successful, we had the chance to get eight heavy weapons off the street, but it meant I would miss the play. I hated to call and tell her. I knew they were going to be disappointed. I told her, 'Babe, I understand you are upset, but if these eight guns end up on the street, they'll be used to kill people.' Disappointing your family like this is a serious downside of law enforcement work."

He was working as an undercover when he met Lani at a traffic light. They were both driving down Third Avenue. Alvin was on his motorcycle, and she had her windows down when they pulled up next to each other. They exchanged phone numbers before the light turned green. They've been together for thirteen years, and Alvin is looking forward to many more, but he is aware they have to work hard to avoid the fate of so many police marriages.

Alvin says that when he first came on the job, people told him it wasn't a good idea to tell your wife about things that happen when you're working. "At the time I wasn't sure that was good advice," he says. "But now, I have to admit there is some truth to it. My wife is supportive of my work, but I can tell she is frightened when she hears me on the phone playing one of my roles. If I start swearing and talking with my Jamaican accent, she always leaves the room."

* * *

Along with the deaths of Sean Carrington, James Nemorin, and Jay Andrews, Alvin Rountree has faced hard times during his career in the New York City Police Department. One low point occurred when someone he was ghosting got shot. Another time he was on a gun buy, and federal agents mistook him for a bad guy.

"There are code words you are supposed to yell out," Rountree explains. "But it's hard. In New York City there are so many different agencies working on various task forces. Everyone has different protocols and paperwork. Unless you can whip out your shield or have an ID number that's immediately recognizable, people from other agencies or even your own guys can believe you are a bad guy. If they have reasonable cause to believe their lives are in danger, you can be killed.

"I was in the process of buying guns when the agents moved in," he continued. "They didn't know I was an undercover. The two men I was doing a deal with pointed at me. They told the agents that the crazy Jamaican guy with the dreadlocks was with them. Within seconds, the situation for me turned very dangerous."

What happened next turned out to be one of the most frightening experiences of Alvin's life. "The feds ordered me out of the car and told me to get down on the ground. Usually I have three guns when I'm undercover buying guns. I have one in the door of the car, a gun between my legs, and a gun on my ankle. But my instincts told me something was wrong, and I decided to take the gun from the door of the car and tuck it into my pants. If I hadn't done that, when the agents told me to open the door and get out, they might have seen the gun. They could have shot me right then. I still thank God I got that gun out of the door."

When Alvin's field team saw the agents ordering him out of the car and down on the ground, they moved in. Now anything could happen, and Alvin was terrified. He knew his chances of getting killed by what's called "reflective fire"—a situation where rounds are fired, no one knows where they are coming from, and everyone starts shooting—were high. He laid motionless on the street while the NYPD cops explained who he was to the federal law enforcement officers.

Alvin accepts the reality that people are going to stereotype. One of the reasons he's good at what he does is that he looks the part. "Officers from other agencies who don't know I'm a cop, look at me, the way I dress, the fact that I'm black, and they come to the conclusion that I'm a bad guy."

After the deaths of his three friends, the newspapers ran several commentaries accusing the Department of discriminating against black officers because so many undercovers, like Alvin Rountree, are black. They posed the question: Why doesn't the NYPD have more white officers doing this dangerous work? It's an argument that Alvin does not buy. "You have to volunteer for undercover work," he says. "No one forces you to do it."

But there have been times he feels he's been a victim of racial profiling. "If you don't know who I am and you see me walking by with dreadlocks down to my waist and all the gold, it's easy to believe I'm a criminal because I'm dressed up to look like one, and I'm black. The real story is I am a police officer. But there are some people who look at me and will never perceive me for the person I really am."

Alvin tries not to let this stereotyping bother him, but it is a fact of life that sometimes undercover officers feel separated, even ostracized, by other officers on the force.

"It's rough," Alvin says. "And it's not just a social problem where you get your feelings hurt. This kind of racial profiling—stereotyping people because of the way they look—is what could get me killed by one of my own guys. I believe you have to tell yourself you are working in a professional atmosphere. If one of your fellow officers can't see you for who you really are, I feel I have an obligation to take responsibility and reach out to them and begin breaking down those barriers."

* * *

Alvin's proudest moment so far working for the New York City Police Department was the day he was promoted to detective. "There are only three things I ever wanted in life," he says. "I wanted to get married, I wanted to work undercover, and I wanted to get promoted to detective. The day I got my detective shield—that was my proudest moment as a cop. When the Police Commissioner gave me my gold shield, I felt like my life was a total success. I still believe nothing better will ever happen to me.

"But it's a tough job," he adds. "There are so many emotions and conflicts you feel doing this work, and nobody understands more than police officers how complicated life can be.

"I think people would be surprised how many cops worry about the people we have to arrest. When I see someone go off to jail for killing someone, I think, there go the lives of two human beings, the person who died and the person who committed the crime.

"The years I worked undercover, there were times I had to be in the suspect's home. If they had little kids, I would look at them and realize that in a couple of weeks, a month, or maybe a year, these children won't have a daddy because I am going to arrest him. You think about your own family, you look at your kids, and you feel their love for you. Then you realize that the little boy whose father you are about to send to jail loves his dad the same way your kids love you. You ask yourself, who is really being hurt? Sometimes you can't avoid the answer. It's the kids who suffer. A lot of people don't dig that deep when they think about police work. If they did, I think they would understand and appreciate us more than they do."

A proud Mom and Dad. Alvin, Lani and Alvin, Jr. on their son's graduation day.

Alvin and Johnny Walker. Johnny and Alvin worked together at the NYPD's Firearms Inspection Unit during the years Alvin was undercover. Johnny was an investigator in the Unit.

PROMOTION DAY. Police Commissioner Ray Kelly promotes Alvin to the rank of second grade detective. That day, Alvin says, was a very proud moment. "I only wanted three things in life," he said. "I wanted to get married, I wanted to work undercover and I wanted to be a detective. I guess dreams do come true."

Alvin and Lani enjoy taking their kids into the city. "I avoid the events with lots of crowds like the ball dropping on New Year's Eve or the Christmas tree lighting at Rockefeller Center," Alvin says. "I feel too responsible. But just to walk around the city, go shopping, go to a play, it's fantastic. As an undercover I got to see some of the greatest places in New York City and I love showing my kids those spots."

ACKNOWLEDGMENTS

Writing a book is often a lonely exercise in which the author spends weeks, months, even years, alone, struggling to craft a tale. The writing of *Brave Hearts,* like law enforcement work itself, was a team effort. Every person profiled in these pages spent countless hours correcting and editing his or her story. For all that hard work and the close friendships that developed, I am truly grateful.

A profound thank you to my husband, *Jim Brown,* who enthusiastically supported this project from day one despite the substantial inconvenience it caused to his life. On those occasions when the project seemed a bit overwhelming, it was Jim who told me, "You've got to finish. The world needs to hear these stories."

Immense gratitude to *Rich Miller,* a veteran NYPD officer who is also the subject of one of the chapters. I met Rich several months after the attacks of September 11 when I was doing a story for *American Police Beat* about the first flag raising at Ground Zero. After that story appeared, he was relentless in encouraging me to write a feature piece for *American Police Beat* about the NYPD's Emergency Service Unit. While doing research for that story, I became aware of the breathtaking acts of bravery and courage that are routine for ESU cops. Despite our friendship, I was unaware of Rich's own history of heroic acts. It was only when his colleagues pulled me aside and told me about some of the things he had done that I knew he had to have his own place in this book, something he never expected or asked for.

Heartfelt appreciation to *Police Commissioner Ray Kelly,* who encouraged me to write this book. His confidence that I could do justice to the stories of these remarkable people will always be one of the greatest compliments of my life.

I would also like to thank the following people whose efforts I will always treasure: *Mark Nichols*, the editor of *American Police Beat*. His editing expertise added immeasurably to the final outcome of the book. *Margaret Weitz*, author of *Sisters in the Resistance: How Women Fought to Free France, 1940–1945*, who spent countless hours editing the final manuscript. *Joseph Wambaugh*, who read the manuscript, gave me the idea to use photographs, and encouraged me to keep going. *Karin Henderson*, who designed the cover. *Marty Linsky*, who believed in the project from the beginning and introduced me to my agents, *Larry Kirschbaum* and *Lisa Leshne* of LJK Literary. Larry and Lisa's enthusiastic response to the stories and people in this book was more important to the final outcome than they will ever know. *Nan Wilson*, for the great ideas she gave me throughout. *Joe and Jane Hanauer*, for their input on how to make the book better. *Joe Mancini*, from the PBA of New York City, who was incredibly generous with his time and expertise. *Dave Fitzpatrick*, a retired detective with the NYPD who took several of the pictures in the book. More of Dave's extraordinary photographs can be seen in *Above Hallowed Ground,* the definitive photographic history of the attacks of September 11. *Sarah Vallee*, the production manager at *American Police Beat*, for her great work producing the photo sections and getting the entire manuscript ready for publication. *Carolann Barrett*, who did a terrific job on the final editing and proofreading and gave me a newfound appreciation for these highly skilled, complex tasks.

From the NYPD's Office of Public Information: *Sergeant Joe Gallagher*, *Assistant Commissioner John McCarthy*, and *Deputy Commissioner Paul Browne*. Their guidance and support was crucial.

I would be remiss if I didn't acknowledge the fabulous cops I worked with in the police station in Boston so many years ago: *John Sacco; Mickey McDonald; Jim MacDonald; Bill Bratton*, who went on to become Chief in Boston, New York City, and Los Angeles; and so many others. No one had a more fun or interesting job than I did during those three wonderful years.

Finally, I would like to thank all the men and women of U.S. law enforcement. For twenty years they have trusted me to tell their stories in the pages of *American Police Beat* and now in *Brave Hearts*.

This has been the greatest honor anyone could have.